MznLnx

Missing Links Exam Preps

Exam Prep for

Environmental Geology

Keller, 8th Edition

The MznLnx Exam Prep is your link from the texbook and lecture to your exams.
The MznLnx Exam Preps are unauthorized and comprehensive reviews of your textbooks.

All material provided by MznLnx and Rico Publications (c) 2010
Textbook publishers and textbook authors do not particpate in or contribute to these reviews.

MznLnx

Rico
Publications

Exam Prep for Environmental Geology
8th Edition
Keller

Publisher: Raymond Houge	*Product Manager:* Dave Mason
Assistant Editor: Michael Rouger	*Editorial Assitant:* Rachel Guzmanji
Text and Cover Designer: Lisa Buckner	*Pedagogy:* Debra Long
Marketing Manager: Sara Swagger	*Cover Image:* Jim Reed/Getty Images
Project Manager, Editorial Production: Jerry Emerson	*Text and Cover Printer:* City Printing, Inc.
Art Director: Vernon Lowerui	*Compositor:* Media Mix, Inc.

(c) 2010 Rico Publications
ALL RIGHTS RESERVED. No part of this work covered by the copyright may be reproduced or used in any form or by an means--graphic, electronic, or mechanical, including photocopying, recording, taping, Web distribution, information storage, and retrieval systems, or in any other manner--without the written permission of the publisher.

For more information about our products, contact us at:
Dave.Mason@RicoPublications.com

For permission to use material from this text or product, submit a request online to:
Dave.Mason@RicoPublications.com

Printed in the United States
ISBN:

Contents

CHAPTER 1
Philosophy and Fundamental Concepts — 1

CHAPTER 2
Earth Materials and Processes — 16

CHAPTER 3
Soils and Environment — 33

CHAPTER 4
Natural Hazards: An Overview — 42

CHAPTER 5
Rivers and Flooding — 47

CHAPTER 6
Landslides and Related Phenomena — 54

CHAPTER 7
Earthquakes and Related Phenomena — 61

CHAPTER 8
Volcanic Activity — 71

CHAPTER 9
Coastal Hazards — 79

CHAPTER 10
Water: Process, Supply, and Use — 88

CHAPTER 11
Water Pollution and Treatment — 97

CHAPTER 12
Waste Management — 108

CHAPTER 13
The Geologic Aspects of Environmental Health — 114

CHAPTER 14
Mineral Resources and Environment — 126

CHAPTER 15
Energy and Environment — 136

CHAPTER 16
Global Change and Earth System Science — 148

CHAPTER 17
Air Pollution — 157

CHAPTER 18
Landscape Evaluation and Land Use — 164

ANSWER KEY — 172

TO THE STUDENT

COMPREHENSIVE

The *MznLnx* Exam Prep series is designed to help you pass your exams. Editors at MznLnx review your textbooks and then prepare these practice exams to help you master the textbook material. Unlike study guides, workbooks, and practice tests provided by the texbook publisher and textbook authors, *MznLnx* gives you **all** of the material in each chapter in exam form, not just samples, so you can be sure to nail your exam.

MECHANICAL

The MznLnx Exam Prep series creates exams that will help you learn the subject matter as well as test you on your understanding. Each question is designed to help you master the concept. Just working through the exams, you gain an understanding of the subject--its a simple mechanical process that produces success.

INTEGRATED STUDY GUIDE AND REVIEW

MznLnx is not just a set of exams designed to test you, its also a comprehensive review of the subject content. Each exam question is also a review of the concept, making sure that you will get the answer correct without having to go to other sources of material. You learn as you go! Its the easiest way to pass an exam.

HUMOR

Studying can be tedious and dry. MznLnx's instructional design includes moderate humor within the exam questions on occassion, to break the tedium and revitalize the brain

Chapter 1. Philosophy and Fundamental Concepts

1. _____ involves the study of the interaction of humans with the geologic environment including the biosphere, the lithosphere, the hydrosphere, and to some extent the atmosphere.
   a. Ubehebe Crater
   b. Isostasy
   c. Engineering geology
   d. Environmental geology

2. _____ is the science and study of the solid matter that constitute the Earth. Encompassing such things as rocks, soil, and gemstones, _____ studies the composition, structure, physical properties, history, and the processes that shape Earth's components.
   a. 1509 Istanbul earthquake
   b. 1703 Genroku earthquake
   c. 1700 Cascadia earthquake
   d. Geology

3. _____ is an island in the south Pacific Ocean belonging to Chile. The island is famous for its numerous moai, the stone statues located along the coastlines.
   a. AASHTO Soil Classification System
   b. Easter Island
   c. AL 333
   d. AL 129-1

4. An _____ is any piece of land that is completely surrounded by water, above high tide. There are two main types of islands: continental islands and oceanic islands. There are also artificial islands. A grouping of geographically and/or geologically related islands is called an archipelago.
   a. AL 333
   b. AL 129-1
   c. AASHTO Soil Classification System
   d. Island

5. '_____' is an inspirational prose poem about attaining happiness in life. It was first copyrighted in 1927 by Max Ehrmann.

   The poem begins: Go placidly amid the noise and the haste, and remember what peace there may be in silence.

   In the 1960s, it was widely circulated without attribution to Ehrmann, sometimes with the claim that it was found in Saint Paul's Church, Baltimore, Maryland, and that it had been written in 1692 (the year of the founding of Saint Paul's.)

   a. 1703 Genroku earthquake
   b. 1509 Istanbul earthquake
   c. 1700 Cascadia earthquake
   d. Desiderata

6. A _____ or geophysical hazards is a threat of an event that will have a negative effect on people or the environment. Many natural hazards are related, e.g. earthquakes can result in tsunamis, drought can lead directly to famine and disease. A concrete example of the division between hazard and disaster is that the 1906 San Francisco earthquake was a disaster, whereas earthquakes are a hazard.
   a. 1703 Genroku earthquake
   b. 1700 Cascadia earthquake
   c. 1509 Istanbul earthquake
   d. Natural hazard

7. The _____ is believed to be a gaseous cloud from which Earth's solar system formed. This was first proposed by Emanuel Swedenborg. Immanuel Kant, who was familiar with Swedenborg's work, developed the theory further. He argued that nebulae slowly rotate, gradually collapsing and flattening due to gravity and eventually forming stars and planets.
   a. 1509 Istanbul earthquake
   b. Solar nebula
   c. 1703 Genroku earthquake
   d. 1700 Cascadia earthquake

Chapter 1. Philosophy and Fundamental Concepts

8. A _____ is an interstellar cloud of dust, hydrogen gas and plasma. It is the first stage of a star's cycle.
   a. Nebula
   b. 1700 Cascadia earthquake
   c. 1703 Genroku earthquake
   d. 1509 Istanbul earthquake

9. _____ generally refers to patterns of human activity and the symbolic structures that give such activities significance and importance. Cultures can be 'understood as systems of symbols and meanings that even their creators contest, that lack fixed boundaries, that are constantly in flux, and that interact and compete with one another'.

   _____ can be defined as all the ways of life including arts, beliefs and institutions of a population that are passed down from generation to generation.

   a. 1700 Cascadia earthquake
   b. 1509 Istanbul earthquake
   c. Nationality
   d. Culture

10. _____ is a general term that includes rocks and materials that are not by definition rocks but are commonly regarded as rocks.
    a. AASHTO Soil Classification System
    b. AL 129-1
    c. AL 333
    d. Earth materials

11. An _____ is an assessment of the likely influence a project may have on the environment. The purpose of the assessment is to ensure that decision-makers consider environmental impacts before deciding whether to proceed with new projects.
    a. Environmental impact
    b. AL 129-1
    c. AASHTO Soil Classification System
    d. AL 333

12. An _____ is an assessment of the likely influence a project may have on the environment. It is the process of identifying, predicting, evaluating and mitigating the biophysical, social, and other relevant effects of development proposals prior to major decisions being taken and commitments made, to ensure that decision-makers consider environmental impacts before deciding whether to proceed with new projects.
    a. AL 129-1
    b. AASHTO Soil Classification System
    c. AL 333
    d. Environmental Impact Report

13. A _____ is a term used by naturalists for the scientific study of free-living wild animals in which the subjects are observed in their natural habitat, without changing, harming, or materially altering the setting or behavior of the animals under study.
    a. 1703 Genroku earthquake
    b. 1700 Cascadia earthquake
    c. 1509 Istanbul earthquake
    d. Field study

14. The _____ is part of the Neogene and Quaternary periods. Human civilization dates entirely within the _____. The _____ was preceded by the Younger Dryas cold period, the final part of the Pleistocene epoch. The _____ starts late in the retreat of the Pleistocene glaciers. It can be considered an interglacial in the current ice age.
    a. Holocene
    b. 1509 Istanbul earthquake
    c. 1703 Genroku earthquake
    d. 1700 Cascadia earthquake

Chapter 1. Philosophy and Fundamental Concepts

15. A hypothesis consists either of a suggested explanation for a phenomenon or of a reasoned proposal suggesting a possible correlation between multiple phenomena. The scientific method requires that one can test a scientific hypothesis. Scientists generally base such _____ on previous observations or on extensions of scientific theories. Even though the words "hypothesis" and "theory" are often used synonymously in common and informal usage, a scientific hypothesis is not the same as a scientific theory.
    a. 1700 Cascadia earthquake
    b. 1509 Istanbul earthquake
    c. Hypotheses
    d. 1703 Genroku earthquake

16. A _____ comprises the visible features of an area of land, including physical elements such as landforms, living elements of flora and fauna, abstract elements such as lighting and weather conditions, and human elements, for instance human activity or the built environment.
    a. 1703 Genroku earthquake
    b. 1700 Cascadia earthquake
    c. 1509 Istanbul earthquake
    d. Landscape

17. The _____ on the geologic timescale had been intended to cover the world's recent period of repeated glaciations. The _____ follows the Pliocene and is followed by the Holocene. The _____ is the third epoch of the Neogene period or 6th epoch of the Cenozoic era. The end of the _____ corresponds with the end of the Paleolithic age used in archaeology. The _____ is divided into the Early _____, Middle _____ and Late _____, and numerous faunal stages.
    a. 1509 Istanbul earthquake
    b. 1700 Cascadia earthquake
    c. 1703 Genroku earthquake
    d. Pleistocene

18. _____ is a body of techniques for investigating phenomena and acquiring new knowledge, as well as for correcting and integrating previous knowledge. It is based on gathering observable, empirical and measurable evidence subject to specific principles of reasoning,
    a. 1509 Istanbul earthquake
    b. 1700 Cascadia earthquake
    c. 1703 Genroku earthquake
    d. Scientific method

19. There are two distinct views on the meaning of _____. One view is that _____ is part of the fundamental structure of the universe, a dimension in which events occur in sequence, and _____ itself is something that can be measured. A contrasting view is that _____ is part of the fundamental intellectual structure in which _____, rather than being an objective thing to be measured, is part of the mental measuring system.
    a. 1703 Genroku earthquake
    b. Time
    c. 1700 Cascadia earthquake
    d. 1509 Istanbul earthquake

20. _____ is the process of breaking a complex topic or substance into smaller parts to gain a better understanding of it. The technique has been applied in the study of mathematics and logic since before Aristotle, though _____ as a formal concept is a relatively recent development.

As a formal concept, the method has variously been ascribed by Ibn al-Haytham, Descartes (Discourse on the Method), Galileo, and Isaac Newton, as a practical method of physical discovery.

    a. AL 333
    b. Analysis
    c. AASHTO Soil Classification System
    d. AL 129-1

Chapter 1. Philosophy and Fundamental Concepts

21. _____ is the part of environmental philosophy which considers the ethical relationship between human beings and the natural environment.
    a. AL 333
    b. AL 129-1
    c. AASHTO Soil Classification System
    d. Environmental ethics

22. The _____ is a perspective on environmental ethics first championed by Aldo Leopold in his book A Sand County Almanac. In it he wrote that there was a need for a 'new ethic', an 'ethic dealing with man's relation to land and to the animals and plants which grow upon it'.

    The prevailing ethos for the US Forest Service in his day, from the founder of the USFS, Gifford Pinchot, was economic and utilitarian, while Leopold argued for an ecological approach, one of the earliest popularizers of this term created by Henry Chandler Cowles of the University of Chicago during his early 1900's research at the Indiana Dunes.

    a. 1703 Genroku earthquake
    b. 1509 Istanbul earthquake
    c. 1700 Cascadia earthquake
    d. Land ethic

23. _____ is a layer of gases surrounding the planet Earth and retained by the Earth's gravity, protecting life on Earth by absorbing ultraviolet solar radiation and reducing temperature extremes between day and night.
    a. AL 333
    b. AL 129-1
    c. AASHTO Soil Classification System
    d. Earths atmosphere

24. _____ is a chemical, physical, or biological agent that modifies the natural characteristics of the atmosphere. The atmosphere is a complex, dynamic natural gaseous system that is essential to support life on planet Earth. Stratospheric ozone depletion due to _____ has long been recognized as a threat to human health as well as to the Earth's ecosystems. Worldwide _____ is responsible for large numbers of deaths and cases of respiratory disease.
    a. AL 129-1
    b. AASHTO Soil Classification System
    c. AL 333
    d. Air pollution

25. _____ is the conversion of forested areas to non-forest land use such as arable land, pasture, urban use, logged area or wasteland. _____ results from removal of trees without sufficient reforestation and results in declines in: habitat and biodiversity, wood for fuel and industrial use and decline in quality of life.
    a. 1700 Cascadia earthquake
    b. 1703 Genroku earthquake
    c. 1509 Istanbul earthquake
    d. Deforestation

26. _____ is the extraction of valuable minerals or other geological materials from the earth, usually from an ore body, vein, or seam. Any material that cannot be grown from agricultural processes, or created artificially in a laboratory or factory, is usually extracted from the earth by this method.
    a. 1700 Cascadia earthquake
    b. 1703 Genroku earthquake
    c. 1509 Istanbul earthquake
    d. Mining

27. _____ (March 2, 1829 - May 14, 1906) was a German revolutionary, American statesman and reformer, and Union Army General in the American Civil War. He was also an accomplished journalist, newspaper editor and noted orator, who in 1869 became the first German-born American elected to the United States Senate.

Chapter 1. Philosophy and Fundamental Concepts

His wife, Margarethe Schurz, and her sister, Berthe von Ronge, were instrumental in establishing the kindergarten system in the United States.

a. Milutin Milankovi䇠b. Marie SkÅ‚odowska Curie
c. Hafez Al-Assad
d. Carl Schurz

28. For morphological image processing operations, see Erosion (morphology)For use of in dermatopathology, see Erosion (dermatopathology) Severe _____ in a wheat field near Washington State University, USA.

Erosion is the removal of solids (sediment, soil, rock and other particles) in the natural environment. It usually occurs due to transport by wind, water, or ice; by down-slope creep of soil and other material under the force of gravity; or by living organisms, such as burrowing animals, in the case of bioerosion.

Erosion is distinguished from weathering, which is the process of chemical or physical breakdown of the minerals in the rocks, although the two processes may occur concurrently.

a. 1509 Istanbul earthquake
b. 1703 Genroku earthquake
c. 1700 Cascadia earthquake
d. Soil erosion

29. _____ is a large set of adverse effects upon water bodies such as lakes, rivers, oceans, and groundwater caused by human activities. Although natural phenomena such as volcanoes, algae blooms, storms, and earthquakes also cause major changes in water quality and the ecological status of water, these are not deemed to be pollution. _____ has many causes and characteristics.

a. 1509 Istanbul earthquake
b. Water pollution
c. 1703 Genroku earthquake
d. 1700 Cascadia earthquake

30. _____ is displacement of solids by the agents of ocean currents, wind, water, or ice by downward or down-slope movement in response to gravity or by living organisms.

a. AASHTO Soil Classification System
b. AL 333
c. AL 129-1
d. Erosion

31. In agriculture, _____ is the process of gathering mature crops from the fields. Reaping is the _____ of grain crops. The harvest marks the end of the growing season, or the growing cycle for a particular crop. _____ in general usage includes an immediate post-harvest handling, all of the actions taken immediately after removing the crop—cooling, sorting, cleaning, packing—up to the point of further on-farm processing, or shipping to the wholesale or consumer market.

a. 1703 Genroku earthquake
b. Harvesting
c. 1509 Istanbul earthquake
d. 1700 Cascadia earthquake

32. A _____ is a naturally occurring substance formed through geological processes that has a characteristic chemical composition, a highly ordered atomic structure and specific physical properties. A rock, by comparison, is an aggregate of minerals and need not have a specific chemical composition. Minerals range in composition from pure elements and simple salts to very complex silicates with thousands of known forms.

a. Mineral
b. 1703 Genroku earthquake
c. 1700 Cascadia earthquake
d. 1509 Istanbul earthquake

Chapter 1. Philosophy and Fundamental Concepts

33. _____ is the introduction of substances or energy into the environment, resulting in deleterious effects of such a nature as to endanger human health, harm living resources and ecosystems, and impair or interfere with amenities and other legitimate uses of the environment.
   a. 1700 Cascadia earthquake
   b. 1703 Genroku earthquake
   c. 1509 Istanbul earthquake
   d. Pollution

34. _____ is the study of physical or virtual environment of objects; and in Nature, it is the study of interactions among physical, chemical, and biological components of the environment.
   a. AASHTO Soil Classification System
   b. AL 333
   c. Environmental science
   d. AL 129-1

35. _____ (April 21, 1915 - September 14, 2003) was a leading and controversial ecologist from Dallas, Texas, who was most known for his 1968 paper, The Tragedy of the Commons. He is also known for Hardin's First Law of Ecology, which states 'You cannot do only one thing', and used the familiar phrase 'Nice guys finish last' to sum up the 'selfish gene' concept of life and evolution.

Hardin received a B.S. in zoology from the University of Chicago in 1936 and a PhD in microbiology from Stanford University in 1941.

   a. Carl Schurz
   b. Cecil John Rhodes
   c. Luna Bergere Leopold
   d. Garrett James Hardin

36. _____, officially the Republic of _____, is a country in Central Europe. _____ is bordered by Germany to the west; the Czech Republic and Slovakia to the south; Ukraine, Belarus and Lithuania to the east; and the Baltic Sea and Kaliningrad Oblast, a Russian exclave, to the north. The total area of _____ is 312,679 square kilometres, making it the 69th largest country in the world and 9th in Europe.
   a. 1700 Cascadia earthquake
   b. 1703 Genroku earthquake
   c. 1509 Istanbul earthquake
   d. Poland

37. In biology a _____ is the collection of inter-breeding organisms of a particular species; in sociology, a collection of human beings. A _____ shares a particular characteristic of interest, most often that of living in a given geographic area. In taxonomy _____ is a low-level taxonomic rank.
   a. Metapopulation
   b. 1509 Istanbul earthquake
   c. 1700 Cascadia earthquake
   d. Population

38. _____ is the change in population over time, and can be quantified as the change in the number of individuals in a population per unit time. The term _____ can technically refer to any species, but almost always refers to humans, and it is often used informally for the more specific demographic term _____ rate, and is often used to refer specifically to the growth of the population of the world.
   a. 1509 Istanbul earthquake
   b. 1700 Cascadia earthquake
   c. 1703 Genroku earthquake
   d. Population growth

39. The _____ is a landlocked endorheic sea in Central Asia; it lies between Kazakhstan in the north and Karakalpakstan, an autonomous region of Uzbekistan, in the south

a. AL 333
b. AL 129-1
c. AASHTO Soil Classification System
d. Aral Sea

40. _____, officially the Federal Democratic Republic of _____, is a landlocked country situated in the Horn of Africa. _____ is bordered by Eritrea to the north, Sudan to the west, Kenya to the south, Somalia to the east and Djibouti to the north-east.

_____ is one of the oldest countries in the world and Africa's second-most populous nation.

a. AL 333
b. AASHTO Soil Classification System
c. AL 129-1
d. Ethiopia

41. In mathematics, _____ occurs when the growth rate of a function is always proportional to the function's current size. Such growth is said to follow an exponential law; the simple-_____ model is known as the Malthusian growth model.
   a. Exponential growth
   b. AASHTO Soil Classification System
   c. AL 333
   d. AL 129-1

42. The _____ (1968) is a book written by Paul R. Ehrlich. A best-selling work, it predicted disaster for humanity due to overpopulation and the 'population explosion'. The book predicted that 'in the 1970s and 1980s hundreds of millions of people will starve to death', that nothing can be done to avoid mass famine greater than any in the history, and radical action is needed to limit the overpopulation.
   a. Amblypoda
   b. Ambulocetus
   c. Andrija Mohorović iÄ‡
   d. Population bomb

43. A _____ is a bipedal primate belonging to the mammalian species Homo sapiens in the family Hominidae. Compared to other living organisms on Earth, a _____ has a highly developed brain capable of abstract reasoning, language, and introspection.
   a. 1703 Genroku earthquake
   b. 1700 Cascadia earthquake
   c. Human
   d. 1509 Istanbul earthquake

44. An interbasin _____ is a hydrological project undertaken to divert water from one drainage basin into another. This is usually to boost water levels for hydroelectricity, or to supply drinking water nearby.

- Campbell-Heber Diversion
- Coquitlam-Buntzen Diversion
- Kemano Diversion
- Vernon Irrigation District Diversion

- Churchill Diversion-Southern Indian Lake

- Saint John Water Supply

- Bay d'Espoir Diversions
- Deer Lake Diversion
- Smallwood Reservoir-Julian Diversion
- Smallwood Reservoir-Kanairiktok Diversion
- Smallwood Reservoir-Naskaupi Diversion

- Wellington Lake Hydro Project Diversion (with Saskatchewan)

- Ingram Diversion
- Jordan Diversion
- Wreck Cove Diversions

- Long Lake Diversion
- Ogoki Diversion
- Opasatika Diversion
- Root River Diversion

- Barrière Diversion
- Boyd-Sakami Diversion
- Lac de la Frégate Diversion
- Laforge Diversion
- Manouane Diversion
- Mégiscane Diversion
- Sault aux Cochons Diversion

- Cypress Lake Diversion (with Alberta)
- Pasquia Land Resettlement Diversion (with Manitoba)
- Swift Current Diversion

a. Water diversion
b. 1703 Genroku earthquake
c. 1509 Istanbul earthquake
d. 1700 Cascadia earthquake

Chapter 1. Philosophy and Fundamental Concepts

45. _____ is a characteristic of a process or state that can be maintained at a certain level indefinitely. The term, in its environmental usage, refers to the potential longevity of vital human ecological support systems.
   a. Sustainability
   b. 1703 Genroku earthquake
   c. 1509 Istanbul earthquake
   d. 1700 Cascadia earthquake

46. An _____ is the realized social system of production, exchange, distribution, and consumption of goods and services of a country or other area. A given _____ is the end result of a process that involves its technological evolution, civilization's history and social organization, as well as its geography, resource endowment, and ecology, among other factors. These factors give context, content, and set the conditions and parameters in which an _____ functions.
   a. AASHTO Soil Classification System
   b. AL 129-1
   c. Economic development
   d. Economy

47. The _____ of South America is the largest river in the world by volume, with greater total river flow than the next eight largest rivers combined, and with the largest drainage basin in the world. Because of its vast dimensions it is sometimes called The River Sea.
   a. AL 129-1
   b. AASHTO Soil Classification System
   c. Amazon River
   d. AL 333

48. An _____ is a layer of gases that may surround a material body of sufficient mass, by the gravity of the body, and are retained for a longer duration if gravity is high and the _____'s temperature is low. Some planets consist mainly of various gases, and therefore have very deep atmospheres

   The term stellar _____ describes the outer region of a star, and typically includes the portion starting from the opaque photosphere outwards.

   a. AASHTO Soil Classification System
   b. AL 129-1
   c. AL 333
   d. Atmosphere

49. The _____ is the broadest level of ecological study, the global sum of all ecosystems. From the broadest biophysiological point of view, the _____ is the global ecological system integrating all living beings and their relationships, including their interaction with the elements of the lithosphere, hydrosphere, and atmosphere. This _____ is postulated to have evolved, beginning through a process of biogenesis or biopoesis, at least some 3.5 billion years ago.
   a. 1509 Istanbul earthquake
   b. 1703 Genroku earthquake
   c. 1700 Cascadia earthquake
   d. Biosphere

50. In thermodynamics, a _____ can exchange heat and work, but not matter, with its surroundings.
   a. 1700 Cascadia earthquake
   b. 1509 Istanbul earthquake
   c. 1703 Genroku earthquake
   d. Closed system

51. _____ is any action taken by a government, beyond the basic regulation of fraud and enforcement of contracts, in an effort to affect its own economy. Economic intervention can be aimed at a variety of political or economic objectives, such as promoting economic growth, increasing employment, raising wages, raising or reducing prices, promoting equality, managing the money supply and interest rates, or addressing market failures. The intervention may to direct, or indirect as in the case of indicative planning.

10   Chapter 1. Philosophy and Fundamental Concepts

a. AASHTO Soil Classification System
b. Economic interventionism
c. AL 333
d. AL 129-1

52. In physics, _____ is a scalar physical quantity that describes the amount of work that can be performed by a force. _____ is an attribute of objects and systems that is subject to a conservation law. Several different forms of _____ exist to explain all known natural phenomena.
a. AL 333
b. AL 129-1
c. AASHTO Soil Classification System
d. Energy

53. A _____ in physical geography describes the combined mass of water found on, under, and over the surface of a planet.

A thick _____ is thought to exist around the Jovian moon Europa. The outer layer of this _____ is almost entirely frozen, but current models predict that there is an ocean up to 100 km in depth underneath the ice.

a. Hydrosphere
b. 1703 Genroku earthquake
c. 1509 Istanbul earthquake
d. 1700 Cascadia earthquake

54. The _____ is the rigid outermost shell of a rocky planet.

In the Earth, the _____ includes the crust and the uppermost mantle, which constitute the hard and rigid outer layer of the planet. The _____ is underlain by the asthenosphere, the weaker, hotter, and deeper part of the upper mantle.

a. 1509 Istanbul earthquake
b. 1700 Cascadia earthquake
c. 1703 Genroku earthquake
d. Lithosphere

55. _____ is a hard, metamorphic rock which was originally sandstone. Sandstone is converted into _____ through heating and pressure usually related to tectonic compression within orogenic belts.
a. 1703 Genroku earthquake
b. 1509 Istanbul earthquake
c. Quartzite
d. 1700 Cascadia earthquake

56. The _____ is the period of time required for a quantity to double in size or value. It is applied to population growth, inflation, resource extraction, consumption of goods, compound interest, the volume of malignant tumours, and many other things which tend to grow over time. When the relative growth rate (not the absolute growth rate) is constant, the quantity undergoes exponential growth (also known as geometric growth) and has a constant _____ or period which can be calculated directly from the growth rate.
a. 1700 Cascadia earthquake
b. 1509 Istanbul earthquake
c. 1703 Genroku earthquake
d. Doubling time

57. _____ is the signal that is looped back to control a system within itself. A control system usually has input and output to the system; when the output of the system is fed back into the system as part of its input, it is called the "_____."
a. 1703 Genroku earthquake
b. 1700 Cascadia earthquake
c. 1509 Istanbul earthquake
d. Feedback

Chapter 1. Philosophy and Fundamental Concepts

58. The _____ of economics uses a matrix representation of a nation's (or a region's) economy to predict the effect of changes in one industry on others and by consumers, government, and foreign suppliers on the economy. Wassily Leontief (1905-1999) is credited with the development of this analysis. Francois Quesnay developed a cruder version of this technique called Tableau économique.
   a. AL 129-1
   b. Input-output model
   c. AL 333
   d. AASHTO Soil Classification System

59. _____ feeds part of a system's output, inverted, into the system's input; generally with the result that fluctuations are attenuated. Many real-world systems have one or several points around which the system gravitates. In response to a perturbation, a _____ system with such point(s) will tend to re-establish equilibrium.
   a. 1509 Istanbul earthquake
   b. Negative feedback
   c. 1703 Genroku earthquake
   d. 1700 Cascadia earthquake

60. _____, sometimes referred to as 'cumulative causation', is a feedback loop system in which the system responds to perturbation in the same direction as the perturbation. In contrast, a system that responds to the perturbation in the opposite direction is called a negative feedback system. These concepts were first recognized as broadly applicable by Norbert Wiener in his 1948 work on cybernetics.
   a. Positive feedback
   b. 1703 Genroku earthquake
   c. 1509 Istanbul earthquake
   d. 1700 Cascadia earthquake

61. _____ refers to the state of equilibrium among the various living things and forces in the natural world.
   a. 1703 Genroku earthquake
   b. 1509 Istanbul earthquake
   c. 1700 Cascadia earthquake
   d. Balance of nature

62. _____: An environmental reaction to change that occurs at multiple levels to multiple objects, and can induce a chain reaction of responses to a single initial change.

The reaction to a change at multiple, and possibly unforeseen, levels. This could include a chain reaction of responses to a single initial change, resulting in a complex set of results, which in turn, could lead to more, and again possibly unforeseen, change.

   a. 1703 Genroku earthquake
   b. 1700 Cascadia earthquake
   c. Complex response
   d. 1509 Istanbul earthquake

63. _____ is a scientific field which studies the common properties of systems considered complex in nature, society and science. It is also called _____ theory, complexity science, study of _____, sciences of complexity, non-equilibrium physics, and historical physics. The key problems of such systems are difficulties with their formal modeling and simulation.
   a. 1700 Cascadia earthquake
   b. 1703 Genroku earthquake
   c. 1509 Istanbul earthquake
   d. Complex systems

64. In ecology, a _____ is a temporary change in average environmental conditions that causes a pronounced change in an ecosystem. Outside _____ forces often act quickly and with great effect, sometimes resulting in the removal of large amounts of biomass. Ecological disturbances include fires, flooding, windstorm, insect outbreaks, as well as anthropogenic disturbances such as forest clearing and the introduction of exotic species.

a. 1700 Cascadia earthquake
b. 1703 Genroku earthquake
c. Disturbance
d. 1509 Istanbul earthquake

65. _____ refers to the phenomena of the physical world, and also to life in general. _____ is also generally distinguished from the supernatural. It ranges in scale from the subatomic to the galactic.
a. 1703 Genroku earthquake
b. 1509 Istanbul earthquake
c. 1700 Cascadia earthquake
d. Nature

66. _____ is a broadly useful concept that expresses how fast something moves through a system in equilibrium. It is the average time a substance spends within a specified region of space, such as a reservoir.
a. 1509 Istanbul earthquake
b. 1700 Cascadia earthquake
c. Residence time
d. 1703 Genroku earthquake

67. An _____ is the result from the sudden release of stored energy in the Earth's crust that creates seismic waves. At the Earth's surface, earthquakes may manifest themselves by a shaking or displacement of the ground. An _____ is caused by tectonic plates getting stuck and putting a strain on the ground. The strain becomes so great that rocks give way by breaking and sliding along fault planes.
a. AL 333
b. AASHTO Soil Classification System
c. AL 129-1
d. Earthquake

68. A _____ is a geological phenomenon which includes a wide range of ground movement, such as rock falls, deep failure of slopes and shallow debris flows. Although gravity's action on an over-steepened slope is the primary reason for a _____, there are other contributing factors affecting the original slope stability.
a. 1700 Cascadia earthquake
b. 1703 Genroku earthquake
c. 1509 Istanbul earthquake
d. Landslide

69. _____ is any particulate matter that can be transported by fluid flow and which eventually is deposited as a layer of solid particles on the bed or bottom of a body of water or other liquid.
a. 1703 Genroku earthquake
b. 1700 Cascadia earthquake
c. 1509 Istanbul earthquake
d. Sediment

70. A _____ is an opening in a planet's surface or crust, which allows hot, molten rock, ash, and gases to escape from below the surface. Volcanic activity involving the extrusion of rock tends to form mountains or features like mountains over a period of time.

Volcanoes are generally found where tectonic plates are diverging or converging.

a. 1509 Istanbul earthquake
b. 1703 Genroku earthquake
c. 1700 Cascadia earthquake
d. Volcano

71. A popular way of classifying magmatic volcanoes goes by their frequency of eruption, or _____, with those that erupt regularly called active, those that have erupted in historical times but are now quiet called dormant, and those that have not erupted in historical times called extinct.
a. 1700 Cascadia earthquake
b. 1509 Istanbul earthquake
c. Volcanic activity
d. 1703 Genroku earthquake

Chapter 1. Philosophy and Fundamental Concepts

72. The _____ is the centerpiece of the Greater Yellowstone Ecosystem, the largest intact ecosystem in the Earth's northern temperate zone. Located mostly in the U.S. state of Wyoming, the park extends into Montana and Idaho. The park is known for its wildlife and geothermal features; Old Faithful Geyser is one of the most popular features in the park.
   a. 1700 Cascadia earthquake
   b. 1703 Genroku earthquake
   c. 1509 Istanbul earthquake
   d. Yellowstone National Park

73. _____ are compounds containing chlorine, fluorine and carbon only, that is they contain no hydrogen. They were formerly used widely in industry, for example as refrigerants, propellants, and cleaning solvents. Their use has been regularly prohibited by the Montreal Protocol, because of effects on the ozone layer.
   a. 1509 Istanbul earthquake
   b. 1700 Cascadia earthquake
   c. 1703 Genroku earthquake
   d. Chlorofluorocarbons CFCs

74. _____ is the reprocessing of materials into new products. It prevents useful material resources being wasted, reduces the consumption of raw materials and reduces energy usage, and hence greenhouse gas emissions, compared to virgin production.
   a. Recycling
   b. 1509 Istanbul earthquake
   c. 1703 Genroku earthquake
   d. 1700 Cascadia earthquake

75. The term _____ refers to a gas or gasses which make up less than 1% of the earth's atmosphere.
   a. Trace gas
   b. 1509 Istanbul earthquake
   c. 1700 Cascadia earthquake
   d. 1703 Genroku earthquake

76. The _____ is an ecological hypothesis that proposes that living and nonliving parts of the earth are viewed as a complex interacting system that can be thought of as a single organism.
   a. 1703 Genroku earthquake
   b. 1700 Cascadia earthquake
   c. 1509 Istanbul earthquake
   d. Gaia hypothesis

77. _____ is the study of Earth's surface features or those of other planets, moons, and asteroids
   a. 1700 Cascadia earthquake
   b. 1703 Genroku earthquake
   c. 1509 Istanbul earthquake
   d. Topography

78. _____ refers to the principle that the same processes that shape the universe occurred in the past as they do now, and that the same laws of physics apply in all parts of the knowable universe.
   a. AASHTO Soil Classification System
   b. AL 129-1
   c. AL 333
   d. Uniformitarianism

79. A _____ consists either of a suggested explanation for a phenomenon or of a reasoned proposal suggesting a possible correlation between multiple phenomena.
   a. 1700 Cascadia earthquake
   b. Hypothesis
   c. 1703 Genroku earthquake
   d. 1509 Istanbul earthquake

80. In meteorology, an _____ is a deviation from the normal change of an atmospheric property with altitude. It almost always refers to temperature.
   a. AL 129-1
   b. AL 333
   c. Inversion
   d. AASHTO Soil Classification System

81. _____ is the production of food, feed, fiber, fuel and other goods by the systematic raizing of plants and animals.
   a. AL 129-1
   b. AASHTO Soil Classification System
   c. Agriculture
   d. AL 333

82. _____ is concerned with earth materials that can be utilized for economic and/or industrial purposes. These materials include precious and base metals, nonmetallic minerals, construction-grade stone, petroleum minerals, coal, and water. The term commonly refers to metallic mineral deposits and mineral resources. The techniques employed by other earth science disciplines might all be used to understand, describe, and exploit an ore deposit.
   a. Isostasy
   b. Ubehebe Crater
   c. Environmental geology
   d. Economic geology

83. _____ is the application of the geologic sciences to engineering practice for the purpose of assuring that the geologic factors affecting the location, design, construction, operation and maintenance of engineering works are recognized and adequately provided for.
   a. Engineering geology
   b. Ubehebe Crater
   c. Isostasy
   d. Environmental geology

84. _____ is the study of landforms, including their origin and evolution, and the processes that shape them.
   a. 1703 Genroku earthquake
   b. Geomorphology
   c. 1509 Istanbul earthquake
   d. 1700 Cascadia earthquake

85. _____ is the part of hydrology that deals with the distribution and movement of groundwater in the soil and rocks of the Earth's crust.
   a. 1703 Genroku earthquake
   b. 1700 Cascadia earthquake
   c. 1509 Istanbul earthquake
   d. Hydrogeology

86. _____ is the human modification of natural environment or wilderness into built environment such as fields, pastures, and settlements. The major effect of _____ on land cover since 1750 has been deforestation of temperate regions. More recent significant effects of _____ include urban sprawl, soil erosion, soil degradation, salinization, and desertification.
   a. 1700 Cascadia earthquake
   b. 1509 Istanbul earthquake
   c. 1703 Genroku earthquake
   d. Land use

87. _____ (October 8, 1915 in Albuquerque, New Mexico - February 23, 2006 in Berkeley, California) was a leading U.S. geomorphologist, and son of Aldo Leopold.

A famous U.S. hydrologist, he suggested that a new philosophy of water management is needed, one based on geologic, geographic, and climatic factors as well as traditional economic, social, and political factors. He argued that the management of water resources cannot be successful as long as it is naïvely perceived from an economic and political standpoint, as it is in the status quo.

   a. Roald Amundsen
   b. Hambali
   c. Hafez Al-Assad
   d. Luna Bergere Leopold

88. _____ is the study of soils in its natural environment. It is one of two main branches of soil science, the other being edaphology. _____ deals with pedogenesis, soil morphology, soil classification.

a. 1700 Cascadia earthquake
b. 1703 Genroku earthquake
c. Pedology
d. 1509 Istanbul earthquake

89. _____ is a field of geology which focuses on the study of rocks and the conditions by which they form. There are three branches of _____, corresponding to the three types of rocks: igneous, metamorphic, and sedimentary. _____ utilizes the classical fields of mineralogy, petrography, optical mineralogy, and chemical analyses to describe the composition and texture of rocks.
   a. 1703 Genroku earthquake
   b. Petrology
   c. 1509 Istanbul earthquake
   d. 1700 Cascadia earthquake

90. _____ encompasses the study of modern sediments and understanding the processes that deposit them. It also compares these observations to studies of ancient sedimentary rocks. Sedimentologists apply their understanding of modern processes to historically formed sedimentary rocks, allowing them to understand how they formed.
   a. 1700 Cascadia earthquake
   b. 1703 Genroku earthquake
   c. Sedimentology
   d. 1509 Istanbul earthquake

91. _____ is a field of study within geology concerned generally with the structures within the crust of the Earth, or other planets, and particularly with the forces and movements that have operated in a region to create these structures.
   a. 1700 Cascadia earthquake
   b. Tectonics
   c. 1703 Genroku earthquake
   d. 1509 Istanbul earthquake

92. _____ refers to a member of any human group whose adult males grow to less than 150 cm in average height or less than 155 cm. A member of a slightly taller group is termed pygmoid. The best known _____ are the Aka, Efe and Mbuti of central Africa.
   a. Pygmies
   b. 1703 Genroku earthquake
   c. 1509 Istanbul earthquake
   d. 1700 Cascadia earthquake

93. An _____ is a natural unit consisting of all plants, animals and micro organisms in an area functioning together with all the non living physical factors of the environment.
   a. AASHTO Soil Classification System
   b. Ecosystem
   c. AL 333
   d. AL 129-1

Chapter 2. Earth Materials and Processes

1. The _____ is the region of the Earth between 100-200 km below the surface that is the weak or "soft" zone in the upper mantle. It lies just below the lithosphere, which is involved in plate movements and isostatic adjustments. In spite of its heat, pressures keep it plastic, and it has a relatively low density. Seismic waves pass relatively slowly through the _____.
   a. AASHTO Soil Classification System
   b. AL 333
   c. AL 129-1
   d. Asthenosphere

2. In geology, a _____ is the outermost layer of a planet, part of its lithosphere. They are generally composed of a less dense material than its deeper layers. Earths' is composed mainly of basalt and granite. It is cooler and more rigid than the deeper layers of the mantle and core.
   a. 1509 Istanbul earthquake
   b. 1703 Genroku earthquake
   c. 1700 Cascadia earthquake
   d. Crust

3. _____ is the part of Earth's lithosphere that surfaces in the ocean basins. _____ is primarily composed of mafic rocks, or sima. It is thinner than continental crust, or sial, generally less than 10 kilometers thick, however it is more dense, having a mean density of about 3.3 grams per cubic centimeter.
   a. AL 129-1
   b. AASHTO Soil Classification System
   c. Oceanic crust
   d. AL 333

4. _____ refers to the movement of the Earth's continents relative to each other. _____ is a concept that said the shapes of continents on either side of the Atlantic Ocean seem to fit together and the similarity of southern continent fossil faunae could mean that all the continents had once been joined into a supercontinent. It was suggested that the continents had been pulled apart by the centrifugal pseudoforce of the Earth's rotation.
   a. Continental drift
   b. 1509 Istanbul earthquake
   c. 1703 Genroku earthquake
   d. 1700 Cascadia earthquake

5. _____ is a theory of geology that has been developed to explain the observed evidence for large scale motions of the Earth's lithosphere. The theory encompassed and superseded the older theory of continental drift.
   a. 1703 Genroku earthquake
   b. 1509 Istanbul earthquake
   c. 1700 Cascadia earthquake
   d. Plate tectonics

6. _____ is a field of study within geology concerned generally with the structures within the crust of the Earth, or other planets, and particularly with the forces and movements that have operated in a region to create these structures.
   a. 1703 Genroku earthquake
   b. 1700 Cascadia earthquake
   c. 1509 Istanbul earthquake
   d. Tectonics

7. The _____ the bottom of the ocean. At the bottom of the continental slope is the continental rise, which is caused by sediment cascading down the continental slope.
   a. 1509 Istanbul earthquake
   b. 1700 Cascadia earthquake
   c. 1703 Genroku earthquake
   d. Seafloor

8. _____ occurs at mid-ocean ridges, where new oceanic crust is formed through volcanic activity and then gradually moves away from the ridge. _____ helps explain continental drift in the theory of plate tectonics.
   a. 1703 Genroku earthquake
   b. 1700 Cascadia earthquake
   c. 1509 Istanbul earthquake
   d. Seafloor spreading

Chapter 2. Earth Materials and Processes 17

9. A _____ is a geological feature that is also known as a Rip in the earth causing magma to flow out and forming an undersea volcano, it also has geological features, a continuous elevational crest for some distance. Ridges are usually termed hills or mountains as well, depending on size.
   a. 1703 Genroku earthquake
   b. 1700 Cascadia earthquake
   c. 1509 Istanbul earthquake
   d. Ridge

10. _____ is a phenomenon of the plate tectonics of Earth. _____ is a variation on the fundamental process of subduction, whereby the subduction zone is destroyed, mountains produced, and two continents sutured together. _____ is known only from this planet and is an interesting example of how our different crusts, oceanic and continental, behave during subduction.
    a. 1703 Genroku earthquake
    b. Continental collision
    c. 1700 Cascadia earthquake
    d. 1509 Istanbul earthquake

11. _____ in the most general terms refers to the movement of currents within fluids. _____ is one of the major modes of Heat and mass transfer. In fluids, convective heat and mass transfer take place through both diffusion and by advection, in which matter or heat is transported by the larger-scale motion of currents in the fluid.
    a. 1700 Cascadia earthquake
    b. 1509 Istanbul earthquake
    c. 1703 Genroku earthquake
    d. Convection

12. In geology, a _____ zone is an area on Earth where two tectonic plates meet and move towards one another, with one sliding underneath the other and moving down into the mantle, at rates typically measured in centimeters per year. An oceanic plate ordinarily slides underneath a continental plate; this often creates an orogenic zone with many volcanoes and earthquakes.
    a. 1700 Cascadia earthquake
    b. 1703 Genroku earthquake
    c. 1509 Istanbul earthquake
    d. Subduction

13. A _____ is an area on Earth where two tectonic plates meet and move towards one another, with one sliding underneath the other and moving down into the mantle, at rates typically measured in centimeters per year. In a sense, subduction zones are the opposite of divergent boundaries, areas where material rises up from the mantle and plates are moving apart.
    a. 1703 Genroku earthquake
    b. 1700 Cascadia earthquake
    c. Subduction zone
    d. 1509 Istanbul earthquake

14. A _____ is a geological fault that is a special case of strike-slip faulting which terminates abruptly, at both ends, at a major transverse geological feature. Also known as a conservative plate boundary.
    a. Transform fault
    b. 1700 Cascadia earthquake
    c. 1509 Istanbul earthquake
    d. 1703 Genroku earthquake

15. Faults are planar rock fractures, which show evidence of relative movement. Large faults within the Earth's crust are the result of shear motion and active _____ zones are the causal locations of most earthquakes. Earthquakes are caused by energy release during rapid slippage along faults.
    a. 1703 Genroku earthquake
    b. 1700 Cascadia earthquake
    c. 1509 Istanbul earthquake
    d. Fault

Chapter 2. Earth Materials and Processes

16. A _____ is a planar rock fracture, which show evidence of relative movement. Large ones within the Earth's crust are the result of shear motion and active fault zones are the causal locations of most earthquakes. Earthquakes are caused by energy release during rapid slippage along a fault.
   a. 1509 Istanbul earthquake
   b. 1703 Genroku earthquake
   c. 1700 Cascadia earthquake
   d. Geologic fault

17. The _____ is a geological fault that runs a length of roughly 800 miles through western and southern California in the United States. The fault, a right-lateral strike-slip fault, marks a transform boundary between the Pacific Plate and the North American Plate.
   a. 1509 Istanbul earthquake
   b. 1700 Cascadia earthquake
   c. 1703 Genroku earthquake
   d. San Andreas fault

18. _____ is the process of formation of solid crystals from a uniform solution. It is also a chemical solid-liquid separation technique, in which mass transfer of a solute from the liquid solution to a pure solid crystalline phase occurs.
   a. 1509 Istanbul earthquake
   b. 1703 Genroku earthquake
   c. 1700 Cascadia earthquake
   d. Crystallization

19. _____ rocks form when molten rock, magma, cools and solidifies, with or without crystallization, either below the surface as intrusive, plutonic rocks or on the surface as extrusive, volcanic, rocks.
   a. Igneous
   b. AL 333
   c. AL 129-1
   d. AASHTO Soil Classification System

20. _____ forms when rock cools and solidifies either below the surface as intrusive rocks or on the surface as extrusive rocks. This magma can be derived from partial melts of pre-existing rocks in either the Earth's mantle or crust. Typically, the melting is caused by one or more of the following processes -- an increase in temperature, a decrease in pressure, or a change in composition.
   a. AL 129-1
   b. Igneous rock
   c. AL 333
   d. AASHTO Soil Classification System

21. _____ is the process in which sediments compact under pressure, expel connate fluids, and gradually become solid rock.
   a. 1703 Genroku earthquake
   b. 1509 Istanbul earthquake
   c. Lithification
   d. 1700 Cascadia earthquake

22. _____ is the result of the transformation of a pre-existing rock type, the protolith, in a process called metamorphism, which means "change in form". It makes up a large part of the Earth's crust and are classified by texture and by chemical and mineral assemblage. It is also formed when rock is heated up by the intrusion of hot molten rock called magma from the Earth's interior.
   a. 1700 Cascadia earthquake
   b. 1509 Istanbul earthquake
   c. Metamorphic rock
   d. 1703 Genroku earthquake

23. Metamorphic rock is the result of the transformation of a pre-existing rock type, the protolith, in a process called metamorphism. The protolith is subjected to heat and extreme pressure causing profound physical and/or chemical change. _____ make up a large part of the Earth's crust. They are formed deep beneath the Earth's surface by great stresses from rocks above and high pressures and temperatures.

Chapter 2. Earth Materials and Processes

a. Metamorphic rocks
b. 1509 Istanbul earthquake
c. 1703 Genroku earthquake
d. 1700 Cascadia earthquake

24. A _____ is a naturally occurring substance formed through geological processes that has a characteristic chemical composition, a highly ordered atomic structure and specific physical properties. A rock, by comparison, is an aggregate of minerals and need not have a specific chemical composition. Minerals range in composition from pure elements and simple salts to very complex silicates with thousands of known forms.
   a. 1700 Cascadia earthquake
   b. 1509 Istanbul earthquake
   c. 1703 Genroku earthquake
   d. Mineral

25. _____ is the supercontinent that existed during the Paleozoic and Mesozoic eras before each of the component continents were separated into their current configuration.
   a. Pangaea
   b. 1509 Istanbul earthquake
   c. 1700 Cascadia earthquake
   d. 1703 Genroku earthquake

26. In geology, _____ is a naturally occurring aggregate of minerals and/or mineraloids.

The Earth's outer solid layer, the lithosphere, is made of _____. In general rocks are of three types, namely, igneous, sedimentary, and metamorphic.

   a. 1509 Istanbul earthquake
   b. 1700 Cascadia earthquake
   c. 1703 Genroku earthquake
   d. Rock

27. The _____ is a fundamental concept in geology that describes the dynamic transitions through geologic time among the three main rock types: sedimentary, metamorphic, and igneous.
   a. 1703 Genroku earthquake
   b. 1700 Cascadia earthquake
   c. 1509 Istanbul earthquake
   d. Rock cycle

28. _____ rock is one of the three main rock groups. Rock formed from these covers 75% of the Earth's land area, and includes common types such as chalk, limestone, dolomite, sandstone, and shale.
   a. Sedimentary depositional environment
   b. Clasts
   c. Sedimentary basin
   d. Sedimentary

29. _____ is one of the three main rock groups. _____ covers 75% of the Earth's land area. Four basic processes are involved in the formation of a clastic _____: weathering caused mainly by friction of waves, transportation where the sediment is carried along by a current, deposition and compaction where the sediment is squashed together to form a rock of this kind.
   a. 1509 Istanbul earthquake
   b. 1703 Genroku earthquake
   c. Sedimentary rock
   d. 1700 Cascadia earthquake

30. _____ is the process of breaking down rocks, soils and their minerals through direct contact with the atmosphere. _____ occurs without movement. Two main classifications of _____ processes exist. Mechanical or physical _____ involves the breakdown of rocks and soils through direct contact with atmospheric conditions. The second classification, chemical _____, involves the direct effect of atmospheric chemicals in the breakdown of rocks, soils and minerals.

Chapter 2. Earth Materials and Processes

a. 1703 Genroku earthquake
b. Weathering
c. 1700 Cascadia earthquake
d. 1509 Istanbul earthquake

31. A _____ is one of several large landmasses on Earth. They are generally identified by convention rather than any strict criteria, but seven areas are commonly reckoned as continents – they are: Asia, Africa, North America, South America, Antarctica, Europe, and Australia.
   a. 1700 Cascadia earthquake
   b. 1703 Genroku earthquake
   c. 1509 Istanbul earthquake
   d. Continent

32. _____ involves the study of the interaction of humans with the geologic environment including the biosphere, the lithosphere, the hydrosphere, and to some extent the atmosphere.
   a. Ubehebe Crater
   b. Engineering geology
   c. Isostasy
   d. Environmental geology

33. _____ is the science and study of the solid matter that constitute the Earth. Encompassing such things as rocks, soil, and gemstones, _____ studies the composition, structure, physical properties, history, and the processes that shape Earth's components.
   a. Geology
   b. 1700 Cascadia earthquake
   c. 1703 Genroku earthquake
   d. 1509 Istanbul earthquake

34. _____ refers to the scientific study of the chemical, physical, geological, and biological processes and reactions that govern the composition of the natural environment and the cycles of matter and energy that transport the Earth's chemical components in time and space.
   a. 1509 Istanbul earthquake
   b. Biogeochemical
   c. 1700 Cascadia earthquake
   d. 1703 Genroku earthquake

35. In ecology and Earth science, a _____ is a circuit or pathway by which a chemical element or molecule moves through both biotic and abiotic compartments of an ecosystem. In effect, the element is recycled, although in some such cycles there may be places where the element is accumulated or held for a long period of time.
   a. 1703 Genroku earthquake
   b. 1700 Cascadia earthquake
   c. 1509 Istanbul earthquake
   d. Biogeochemical cycle

36. Fullerenes are a family of carbon allotropes, molecules composed entirely of carbon, in the form of a hollow sphere, ellipsoid, tube, or plane. Spherical fullerenes are also called buckyballs, and cylindrical ones are called carbon nanotubes or buckytubes. Graphene is an example of a planar _____ sheet.
   a. 1509 Istanbul earthquake
   b. 1700 Cascadia earthquake
   c. 1703 Genroku earthquake
   d. Fullerene

37. _____ is a chemical element in the periodic table that has the symbol C and atomic number 6. An abundant nonmetallic, tetravalent element, _____ has several allotropic forms.
   a. 1700 Cascadia earthquake
   b. 1509 Istanbul earthquake
   c. 1703 Genroku earthquake
   d. Carbon

38. The _____ is the biogeochemical cycle by which carbon is exchanged between the biosphere, geosphere, hydrosphere, and atmosphere of the Earth.

Chapter 2. Earth Materials and Processes   21

a. 1703 Genroku earthquake
b. 1700 Cascadia earthquake
c. Carbon cycle
d. 1509 Istanbul earthquake

39. _____ is a chemical compound, normally in a gaseous state, and is composed of one carbon and two oxygen atoms. It is often referred to by its formula CO2. It is present in the Earth's atmosphere at a concentration of approximately .000383 by volume and is an important greenhouse gas due to its ability to absorb many infrared wavelengths of sunlight, and due to the length of time it stays in the atmosphere.
a. 1703 Genroku earthquake
b. 1700 Cascadia earthquake
c. Carbon dioxide
d. 1509 Istanbul earthquake

40. _____ (ancient name acid of air or aerial acid) has the formula H_2CO_3. It is also a name sometimes given to solutions of carbon dioxide in water, which contain small amounts of H_2CO_3. The salts of carbonic acids are called bicarbonates (or hydrogen carbonates) and carbonates.
a. 1703 Genroku earthquake
b. 1509 Istanbul earthquake
c. 1700 Cascadia earthquake
d. Carbonic acid

41. _____ is an infection of the digestive system that results in severe diarrhea containing mucus and blood in the feces and is typically the result of unsanitary water containing micro-organisms which cause significant inflammation of the intestinal lining.
a. 1703 Genroku earthquake
b. Dysentery
c. 1509 Istanbul earthquake
d. 1700 Cascadia earthquake

42. The Earth's water is always in movement, and the _____, describes the continuous movement of water on, above, and below the surface of the Earth. Since the _____ is truly a "cycle," there is no beginning or end. Water can change states among liquid, vapor, and ice at various places in the _____, with these processes happening in the blink of an eye and over millions of years. Although the balance of water on Earth remains fairly constant over time, individual water molecules can come and go in a hurry.
a. 1509 Istanbul earthquake
b. 1703 Genroku earthquake
c. 1700 Cascadia earthquake
d. Hydrologic cycle

43. _____ is the chemical element in the periodic table that has the symbol P and atomic number 15. A multivalent nonmetal of the nitrogen group, _____ is commonly found in inorganic phosphate rocks.
a. 1509 Istanbul earthquake
b. 1700 Cascadia earthquake
c. 1703 Genroku earthquake
d. Phosphorus

44. The _____ is the biogeochemical cycle that describes the movement of phosphorus through the lithosphere, hydrosphere, and biosphere.
a. 1703 Genroku earthquake
b. 1700 Cascadia earthquake
c. 1509 Istanbul earthquake
d. Phosphorus cycle

45. An _____ is traditionally considered any chemical compound that, when dissolved in water, gives a solution with a hydrogen ion activity greater than in pure water, i.e. a pH less than 7.0. That approximates the modern definition of Johannes Nicolaus Brønsted and Martin Lowry, who independently defined an _____ as a compound which donates a hydrogen ion to another compound. Common examples include acetic _____ and sulfuric _____. _____/base systems are different from redox reactions in that there is no change in oxidation state.

Chapter 2. Earth Materials and Processes

a. AL 333
b. AL 129-1
c. Acid
d. AASHTO Soil Classification System

46. _____ is a layer of gases surrounding the planet Earth and retained by the Earth's gravity, protecting life on Earth by absorbing ultraviolet solar radiation and reducing temperature extremes between day and night.
a. AL 333
b. AL 129-1
c. AASHTO Soil Classification System
d. Earths atmosphere

47. _____ is the excrement (feces and urine) of seabirds, bats, and seals.

_____ manure is an effective fertilizer and gunpowder ingredient due to its high levels of phosphorus and nitrogen and also its lack of odor. Superphosphate made from _____ is used for aerial topdressing.

a. 1703 Genroku earthquake
b. Guano
c. 1509 Istanbul earthquake
d. 1700 Cascadia earthquake

48. _____ is an aluminium ore. It consists largely of the Al minerals gibbsite, boehmite and diaspore, together with the iron oxides goethite and hematite, the clay mineral kaolinite and small amounts of anatase.
a. 1509 Istanbul earthquake
b. 1700 Cascadia earthquake
c. 1703 Genroku earthquake
d. Bauxite

49. _____ is a common phyllosilicate mineral within the mica group. Primarily a solid-solution series between the iron-endmember annite, and the magnesium-endmember phlogopite; more aluminous endmembers include siderophyllite.
a. 1509 Istanbul earthquake
b. 1703 Genroku earthquake
c. 1700 Cascadia earthquake
d. Biotite

50. The carbonate mineral _____ is a chemical or biochemical calcium carbonate and is one of the most widely distributed minerals on the Earth's surface. It is a common constituent of sedimentary rocks, limestone in particular. It is also the primary mineral in metamorphic marble
a. 1509 Istanbul earthquake
b. 1700 Cascadia earthquake
c. 1703 Genroku earthquake
d. Calcite

51. In organic chemistry, a _____ is a salt of carbonic acid.
a. 1700 Cascadia earthquake
b. 1703 Genroku earthquake
c. 1509 Istanbul earthquake
d. Carbonate

52. _____ are those minerals containing the carbonate ion: CO_3^{2-}.
a. 1703 Genroku earthquake
b. Carbonate minerals
c. 1509 Istanbul earthquake
d. 1700 Cascadia earthquake

53. _____ is a term used to describe a group of hydrous aluminium phyllosilicate minerals, that are typically less than 2 micrometres in diameter. _____ consists of a variety of phyllosilicate minerals rich in silicon and aluminium oxides and hydroxides which include variable amounts of structural water. Clays are generally formed by the chemical weathering of silicate-bearing rocks by carbonic acid but some are formed by hydrothermal activity.

Chapter 2. Earth Materials and Processes

a. 1703 Genroku earthquake
b. 1700 Cascadia earthquake
c. 1509 Istanbul earthquake
d. Clay

54. _____ is a chemical element in the periodic table that has the symbol Cu and atomic number 29. It is a ductile metal with excellent electrical conductivity, and finds extensive use as a building material, as an electrical conductor, and as a component of various alloys.
   a. 1703 Genroku earthquake
   b. Copper
   c. 1700 Cascadia earthquake
   d. 1509 Istanbul earthquake

55. _____ is the name of a group of rock-forming minerals which make up as much as sixty percent of the Earth's crust. Feldspars crystallize from magma in both intrusive and extrusive rocks, and they can also occur as compact minerals, as veins, and are also present in many types of metamorphic rock.
   a. 1700 Cascadia earthquake
   b. Feldspar
   c. 1703 Genroku earthquake
   d. 1509 Istanbul earthquake

56. A _____ is one which contains both magnesium and iron.
   a. 1700 Cascadia earthquake
   b. 1703 Genroku earthquake
   c. 1509 Istanbul earthquake
   d. Ferromagnesian mineral

57. _____ is a chemical element in the periodic table that has the symbol Au and atomic number 79. A soft, shiny, yellow, dense, malleable, ductile (trivalent and univalent) transition metal, _____ does not react with most chemicals but is attacked by chlorine, fluorine and aqua regia.
   a. 1703 Genroku earthquake
   b. Gold
   c. 1509 Istanbul earthquake
   d. 1700 Cascadia earthquake

58. _____ is a common and widely occurring type of intrusive, felsic, igneous rock. Granites are usually medium to coarsely crystalline, occasionally with some individual crystals larger than the groundmass forming a rock known as porphyry. Granites can be pink to dark gray or even black, depending on their chemistry and mineralogy.
   a. Granite
   b. 1703 Genroku earthquake
   c. 1509 Istanbul earthquake
   d. 1700 Cascadia earthquake

59. _____ is a very common mineral, colored black to steel or silver-gray, brown to reddish brown, or red. It is mined as the main ore of iron. Varieties include kidney ore, martite iron rose and specularite. While the forms of it vary, they all have a rust-red streak. it is harder than pure iron, but much more brittle.
   a. 1703 Genroku earthquake
   b. 1700 Cascadia earthquake
   c. 1509 Istanbul earthquake
   d. Hematite

60. _____ is a ferrimagnetic mineral one of several iron oxides and a member of the spinel group. The chemical IUPAC name is iron oxide and the common chemical name ferrous-ferric oxide.
   a. 1700 Cascadia earthquake
   b. 1703 Genroku earthquake
   c. Magnetite
   d. 1509 Istanbul earthquake

61. An _____ is a volume of rock containing components or minerals in a mode of occurrence that renders it valuable for mining.

Chapter 2. Earth Materials and Processes

a. AL 129-1
b. AL 333
c. AASHTO Soil Classification System
d. Ore

62. An _____ is a chemical compound containing an oxygen atom and other elements. Most of the earth's crust consists of them. They result when elements are oxidized by air.
   a. AASHTO Soil Classification System
   b. AL 129-1
   c. AL 333
   d. Oxide

63. The mineral _____ is iron disulfide, FeS2. It has isometric crystals that usually appear as cubes. Its metallic luster and pale-to-normal, brass-yellow hue have earned it a nickname due to many miners mistaking it for the real thing.
   a. 1700 Cascadia earthquake
   b. 1703 Genroku earthquake
   c. 1509 Istanbul earthquake
   d. Pyrite

64. _____ is the second most common mineral in the Earth's continental crust. It is made up of a lattice of silica tetrahedra. _____ belongs to the rhombohedral crystal system. In nature _____ crystals are often twinned, distorted, or so intergrown with adjacent crystals of _____ or other minerals as to only show part of this shape, or to lack obvious crystal faces altogether and appear massive.
   a. Quartz
   b. 1703 Genroku earthquake
   c. 1509 Istanbul earthquake
   d. 1700 Cascadia earthquake

65. In geology and astronomy, the term _____ is used to denote types of rock that consist predominantly of _____ minerals. Such rocks include a wide range of igneous, metamorphic and sedimentary types. Most of the Earth's mantle and crust are made up of _____ rocks. The same is true of the Moon and the other rocky planets.
   a. Silicate
   b. 1509 Istanbul earthquake
   c. 1703 Genroku earthquake
   d. 1700 Cascadia earthquake

66. _____ is a chemical element with the symbol Ag and atomic number 47. A soft white lustrous transition metal, it has the highest electrical and thermal conductivity for a metal. It occurs as a free metal as well as various minerals such as argentite and chlorargyrite.
   a. 1703 Genroku earthquake
   b. 1509 Istanbul earthquake
   c. Silver
   d. 1700 Cascadia earthquake

67. The term _____ refers to several types of chemical compounds containing sulfur in its lowest oxidation number of −2.
   a. 1703 Genroku earthquake
   b. Sulfide
   c. 1700 Cascadia earthquake
   d. 1509 Istanbul earthquake

68. A _____ is a mineral containing sulfide as the major anion. Closely related and often included within the sulfide class are selenide and telluride minerals.
   a. 1703 Genroku earthquake
   b. 1509 Istanbul earthquake
   c. 1700 Cascadia earthquake
   d. Sulfide mineral

69. A _____ is any local separation or discontinuous plane in a geologic formation, such as joints or faults into two or more pieces under the action of stress.

Chapter 2. Earth Materials and Processes

a. 1509 Istanbul earthquake
b. 1703 Genroku earthquake
c. 1700 Cascadia earthquake
d. Rock fracture

70. _____ have the mechanical property of being capable of sustaining large plastic deformations due to tensile stress without fracture in metals, such as being drawn into a wire. It is characterized by the material flowing under shear stress. It is contrasted with brittleness.
a. 1700 Cascadia earthquake
b. 1703 Genroku earthquake
c. 1509 Istanbul earthquake
d. Ductile materials

71. _____ is reversible. Once the forces are no longer applied, the object returns to its original shape.
a. AL 333
b. AASHTO Soil Classification System
c. AL 129-1
d. Elastic deformation

72. _____ is an Earth Science focused around the chemistry, crystal structure, and physical properties of minerals. Specific studies within _____ include the processes of mineral origin and formation, classification of minerals, their geographical distribution, as well as their utilization.
a. 1509 Istanbul earthquake
b. Mineralogy
c. 1703 Genroku earthquake
d. 1700 Cascadia earthquake

73. In materials science, _____ is a change in the shape or size of an object due to an applied force. This can be a result of tensile (pulling) forces, compressive (pushing) forces, shear, bending or torsion (twisting.) _____ is often described as strain.
a. Deformation
b. 1509 Istanbul earthquake
c. 1700 Cascadia earthquake
d. 1703 Genroku earthquake

74. _____ in geology refers to the physical appearance or character of a rock, such as grain size, shape, and arrangement, at both the megascopic or microscopic surface feature level.
a. 1700 Cascadia earthquake
b. 1509 Istanbul earthquake
c. 1703 Genroku earthquake
d. Texture

75. _____ is the capacity of a material to withstand axially directed pushing forces.
a. Compressive strength
b. 1509 Istanbul earthquake
c. 1703 Genroku earthquake
d. 1700 Cascadia earthquake

76. _____ is molten rock located beneath the surface of the Earth, and which often collects in a _____ chamber. _____ is a complex high-temperature fluid substance. Most are silicate solutions. It is capable of intrusion into adjacent rocks or of extrusion onto the surface as lava or ejected explosively as tephra to form pyroclastic rock. Environments of _____ formation include subduction zones, continental rift zones, mid-oceanic ridges, and hotspots, some of which are interpreted as mantle plumes.
a. 1509 Istanbul earthquake
b. 1703 Genroku earthquake
c. Magma
d. 1700 Cascadia earthquake

77. _____ is a district in southwestern Los Angeles, California, in South Los Angeles. It is located on the central hills overlooking the Los Angeles Basin, and in the flats immediately to their north. _____ and other surrounding geography are named for the famous 19th century horse racing pioneer, Elias J. "Lucky" Baldwin. _____ Estates is also one of the wealthiest majority-African American areas in the United States.

Chapter 2. Earth Materials and Processes

   a. 1700 Cascadia earthquake
   b. 1703 Genroku earthquake
   c. 1509 Istanbul earthquake
   d. Baldwin Hills

78. _____ is an absorbent aluminium phyllosilicate generally impure clay consisting mostly of montmorillonite.
   a. Bentonite
   b. 1700 Cascadia earthquake
   c. 1509 Istanbul earthquake
   d. 1703 Genroku earthquake

79. _____ is a rock composed of angular fragments of rocks or minerals in a matrix, that is a cementing material, that may be similar or different in composition to the fragments.
   a. 1509 Istanbul earthquake
   b. 1703 Genroku earthquake
   c. Breccia
   d. 1700 Cascadia earthquake

80. _____ is when long fractures form vertically in rock as it cools and contracts.
   a. 1703 Genroku earthquake
   b. 1700 Cascadia earthquake
   c. 1509 Istanbul earthquake
   d. Columnar jointing

81. A _____ is a barrier across flowing water that obstructs, directs or slows down the flow, often creating a reservoir, lake or impoundment.
   a. 1700 Cascadia earthquake
   b. 1703 Genroku earthquake
   c. Dam
   d. 1509 Istanbul earthquake

82. _____ refers to the mode of igneous volcanic rock formation in which hot magma from inside the Earth flows out onto the surface as lava or explodes violently into the atmosphere to fall back as pyroclastics or tuff.
   a. AASHTO Soil Classification System
   b. AL 129-1
   c. Extrusive
   d. AL 333

83. A _____ is a landform that extends above the surrounding terrain, in a limited area. They often have a distinct summit, although in areas with scarp/dip topography a _____ may refer to a particular section of scarp slope without a well-defined summit.
   a. Hill
   b. 1509 Istanbul earthquake
   c. 1700 Cascadia earthquake
   d. 1703 Genroku earthquake

84. An _____ is a body of igneous rock that has crystallized from a molten magma below the surface of the Earth.
   a. AL 333
   b. AASHTO Soil Classification System
   c. AL 129-1
   d. Intrusion

85. _____ is molten rock expelled by a volcano during an eruption. When first extruded from a volcanic vent, it is a liquid at temperatures from 700 °C to 1,200 °C.
   a. Lava
   b. 1509 Istanbul earthquake
   c. 1703 Genroku earthquake
   d. 1700 Cascadia earthquake

86. _____ are clastic rocks composed solely or primarily of volcanic materials.
   a. 1703 Genroku earthquake
   b. Pyroclastics
   c. 1509 Istanbul earthquake
   d. 1700 Cascadia earthquake

87. _____ is air-fall material produced by a volcanic eruption regardless of composition or fragment size. It is typically rhyolitic in composition as most explosive volcanoes are the product of the more viscous felsic or high silica magmas.
   a. 1700 Cascadia earthquake
   b. 1509 Istanbul earthquake
   c. Tephra
   d. 1703 Genroku earthquake

88. _____ is a type of rock consisting of consolidated volcanic ash ejected from vents during a volcanic eruption.
   a. 1509 Istanbul earthquake
   b. 1700 Cascadia earthquake
   c. 1703 Genroku earthquake
   d. Tuff

89. A _____ is an opening in a planet's surface or crust, which allows hot, molten rock, ash, and gases to escape from below the surface. Volcanic activity involving the extrusion of rock tends to form mountains or features like mountains over a period of time.

Volcanoes are generally found where tectonic plates are diverging or converging.

   a. Volcano
   b. 1509 Istanbul earthquake
   c. 1703 Genroku earthquake
   d. 1700 Cascadia earthquake

90. _____ consists of very fine rock and mineral particles less than 2 mm in diameter that are ejected from a volcanic vent. The very fine particles may be carried for many miles, settling out as a dust-like layer across the landscape
   a. AL 333
   b. AASHTO Soil Classification System
   c. Ash fall
   d. AL 129-1

91. _____ refers to accumulations of large blocks of volcanic material often found around vents. They are defined as rocks containing at least 75% bombs. They typically consist of blocks of various igneous rocks, often mixed with material of rudimentary origin and embedded in a finer-grained matrix.
   a. Agglomerate
   b. AL 333
   c. AASHTO Soil Classification System
   d. AL 129-1

92. _____ are pyroclastic rocks formed by explosive eruption of lava and any rocks which are entrained within the eruptive column. This may include rocks plucked off the wall of the magma conduit, or physically picked up by the ensuing pyroclastic surge.
   a. 1703 Genroku earthquake
   b. 1700 Cascadia earthquake
   c. Volcanic breccia
   d. 1509 Istanbul earthquake

93. A _____ is a rock consisting of individual stones that have become cemented together. Conglomerates are sedimentary rocks consisting of rounded fragements and are thus differentiated from breccias, which consist of angular clasts. Both conglomerates and breccias are characterized by clasts larger than sand.
   a. Conglomerate
   b. 1700 Cascadia earthquake
   c. 1703 Genroku earthquake
   d. 1509 Istanbul earthquake

94. _____ is a common and widely distributed type of rock formed by high-grade regional metamorphic processes from preexisting formations that were originally either igneous or sedimentary rocks. Gneissic rocks are usually medium to coarse foliated and largely recrystallized but do not carry large quantities of micas, chlorite or other platy minerals.

Chapter 2. Earth Materials and Processes

   a. 1703 Genroku earthquake
   b. Gneiss
   c. 1509 Istanbul earthquake
   d. 1700 Cascadia earthquake

95. _____ is a sedimentary rock composed largely of the mineral calcite. _____ often contains variable amounts of silica in the form of chert or flint, as well as varying amounts of clay, silt and sand as disseminations, nodules, or layers within the rock. The primary source of the calcite in _____ is most commonly marine organisms. These organisms secrete shells that settle out of the water column and are deposited on ocean floors as pelagic ooze or alternatively is conglomerated in a coral reef.
   a. 1703 Genroku earthquake
   b. Limestone
   c. 1509 Istanbul earthquake
   d. 1700 Cascadia earthquake

96. _____ is a sedimentary rock composed mainly of sand-size mineral or rock grains. Most _____ is composed of quartz and/or feldspar because these are the most common minerals in the Earth's crust. Like sand, _____ may be any color, but the most common colors are tan, brown, yellow, red, gray and white.
   a. 1700 Cascadia earthquake
   b. 1703 Genroku earthquake
   c. Sandstone
   d. 1509 Istanbul earthquake

97. The _____ refers to a group of medium-grade metamorphic rocks, chiefly notable for the preponderance of lamellar minerals such as micas, chlorite, talc, hornblende, graphite, and others. Quartz often occurs in drawn-out grains to such an extent that a particular form called quartz _____ is produced.
   a. 1700 Cascadia earthquake
   b. 1703 Genroku earthquake
   c. Schist
   d. 1509 Istanbul earthquake

98. _____ is the process of a material being more closely packed together.
   a. 1703 Genroku earthquake
   b. 1509 Istanbul earthquake
   c. Compaction
   d. 1700 Cascadia earthquake

99. _____ is a geological term used to describe particles of rock derived from pre-existing rock through processes of weathering and erosion.
   a. 1703 Genroku earthquake
   b. 1700 Cascadia earthquake
   c. 1509 Istanbul earthquake
   d. Detrital

100. _____ is a fine-grained sedimentary rock whose original constituents were clays or muds. It is characterized by thin laminae breaking with an irregular curving fracture, often splintery and usually parallel to the often-indistinguishable bedding plane.
   a. 1703 Genroku earthquake
   b. 1700 Cascadia earthquake
   c. 1509 Istanbul earthquake
   d. Shale

101. The _____ was a federally built earthen dam on the Teton River in southeastern Idaho in the United States which when filling for the first time suffered a catastrophic failure on June 5, 1976. The collapse of the dam resulted in the deaths of 11 people and 13,000 head of cattle. The dam cost about USD $100 million to build, and the federal government paid over $300 million in claims related to the dam failure.
   a. 1509 Istanbul earthquake
   b. 1703 Genroku earthquake
   c. Teton Dam
   d. 1700 Cascadia earthquake

Chapter 2. Earth Materials and Processes

102. _____ are where one sedimetary deposit ends and another one begins. The rock is prone to breakage at these points because of the weakness between the layers.
   a. Bedding planes
   b. 1509 Istanbul earthquake
   c. 1703 Genroku earthquake
   d. 1700 Cascadia earthquake

103. A _____ substance is a material with a definite _____ composition. It is a concept that became firmly established in the late eighteenth century after work by the chemist Joseph Proust on the composition of some pure _____ compounds such as basic copper carbonate.
   a. Chemical
   b. 1700 Cascadia earthquake
   c. 1509 Istanbul earthquake
   d. 1703 Genroku earthquake

104. _____ has penetrative planar fabric present within it. It is common to rocks affected by regional metamorphic compression typical of orogenic belts.
   a. 1703 Genroku earthquake
   b. 1700 Cascadia earthquake
   c. 1509 Istanbul earthquake
   d. Foliated metamorphic rock

105. _____ is a fine-grained, homogeneous, metamorphic rock derived from an original shale-type sedimentary rock composed of clay or volcanic ash through low grade regional metamorphism. The result is a foliated rock in which the foliation may not correspond to the original sedimentary layering.
   a. 1509 Istanbul earthquake
   b. 1703 Genroku earthquake
   c. Slate
   d. 1700 Cascadia earthquake

106. _____ form at high latitudes where temperatures remain cold enough during the summer to keep the previous winter's snow from melting allowing snow and ice to accumulate. It is a glacier that spreads out from a central mass of ice.
   a. 1509 Istanbul earthquake
   b. Global warming controversy
   c. General circulation model
   d. Continental glacier

107. A glacier is a large, slow moving river of ice, formed from compacted layers of snow, that slowly deforms and flows in response to gravity. Glacier ice is the largest reservoir of fresh water on Earth, and second only to oceans as the largest reservoir of total water. _____ cover vast areas of polar regions but are restricted to the highest mountains in the tropics.
   a. 1700 Cascadia earthquake
   b. Glaciers
   c. 1509 Istanbul earthquake
   d. 1703 Genroku earthquake

108. An _____ is a mass of glacier ice that covers surrounding terrain and is greater than 19,305 mile². The only current ice sheets are in Antarctica and Greenland. Ice sheets are bigger than ice shelves or glaciers. Masses of ice covering less than 50,000 km² are termed an ice cap. An ice cap will typically feed a series of glaciers around its periphery. Although the surface is cold, the base of an _____ is generally warmer. This process produces fast-flowing channels in the _____.
   a. AL 129-1
   b. AL 333
   c. Ice sheet
   d. AASHTO Soil Classification System

109. _____ is a metamorphic rock resulting from the metamorphism of limestone, composed mostly of calcite. It is extensively used for sculpture, as a building material, and in many other applications. The word '_____' is colloquially used to refer to many other stones that are capable of taking a high polish.

a. Marble
b. 1509 Istanbul earthquake
c. 1700 Cascadia earthquake
d. 1703 Genroku earthquake

110. A _____ is a landform that extends above the surrounding terrain in a limited area. A _____ is generally steeper than a hill, but there is no universally accepted standard definition for the height of a _____ or a hill although a _____ usually has an identifiable summit.
   a. Mountain
   b. 1509 Istanbul earthquake
   c. 1703 Genroku earthquake
   d. 1700 Cascadia earthquake

111. _____ climate is the average weather for a region above the tree line. The climate becomes colder at high elevations—this characteristic is described by the lapse rate of air: air will tend to get colder as it rises, since it expands.
   a. AL 129-1
   b. AL 333
   c. AASHTO Soil Classification System
   d. Alpine

112. The _____ on the geologic timescale had been intended to cover the world's recent period of repeated glaciations. The _____ follows the Pliocene and is followed by the Holocene. The _____ is the third epoch of the Neogene period or 6th epoch of the Cenozoic era. The end of the _____ corresponds with the end of the Paleolithic age used in archaeology. The _____ is divided into the Early _____, Middle _____ and Late _____, and numerous faunal stages.
   a. 1703 Genroku earthquake
   b. 1509 Istanbul earthquake
   c. 1700 Cascadia earthquake
   d. Pleistocene

113. The _____ was a concrete gravity-arch dam, designed to create a reservoir as part of the Los Angeles Aqueduct. The dam was located 40 miles northwest of Los Angeles, California, near the city of Santa Clarita. It was built between 1924 and 1926 under the supervision of William Mulholland, chief engineer and general manager of the Los Angeles Department of Water and Power.
   a. 1700 Cascadia earthquake
   b. St. Francis Dam
   c. 1703 Genroku earthquake
   d. 1509 Istanbul earthquake

114. _____ is displacement of solids by the agents of ocean currents, wind, water, or ice by downward or down-slope movement in response to gravity or by living organisms.
   a. AL 333
   b. AL 129-1
   c. AASHTO Soil Classification System
   d. Erosion

115. Glacier ice is the largest reservoir of fresh water on Earth, and second only to oceans as the largest reservoir of total water. Glaciers cover vast areas of polar regions, are found in mountain ranges of every continent, and are restricted to the highest mountains in the tropics. The processes and landforms caused by glaciers and related to them are referred to as _____.
   a. 1509 Istanbul earthquake
   b. Global warming controversy
   c. General circulation model
   d. Glacial

116. _____ is a tidewater glacier in the U.S. state of Alaska and the Yukon Territory of Canada. From its source in the Yukon, the glacier stretches 122 km to the sea at Yakutat Bay and Disenchantment Bay. It is the longest tidewater glacier in Alaska, with an open calving face over ten kilometers wide.

Chapter 2. Earth Materials and Processes

a. 1700 Cascadia earthquake
b. 1509 Istanbul earthquake
c. 1703 Genroku earthquake
d. Hubbard Glacier

117. A sandur (plural sandar) is a glacial _____ plain formed of sediments deposited by meltwater at the terminus of a glacier.

Sandur are found in glaciated areas, such as Svalbard, Kerguelen, and Iceland. Glaciers and icecaps contain large amounts of silt and sediment, picked up as they erode the underlying rocks when they move slowly downhill, and at the snout of the glacier, meltwater can carry this sediment away from the glacier and deposit it on a broad plain.

a. AL 333
b. AASHTO Soil Classification System
c. AL 129-1
d. Outwash

118. A _____ is a section of a river of relatively steep gradient causing an increase in water flow and turbulence. A _____ is a hydrological feature between a run and a cascade. It is characterized by the river becoming shallower and having some rocks exposed above the flow surface.

a. 1700 Cascadia earthquake
b. 1703 Genroku earthquake
c. 1509 Istanbul earthquake
d. Rapid

119. The _____ is the line that separates earth from sky. More precisely, it is the line that divides all of the directions one can possibly look into two categories: those which intersect the Earth, and those which do not.

a. 1703 Genroku earthquake
b. 1509 Istanbul earthquake
c. 1700 Cascadia earthquake
d. Horizon

120. _____ refers to any glacially formed accumulation of unconsolidated debris which can occur in currently glaciated and formerly glaciated regions, such as those areas acted upon by a past ice age. This debris may have been plucked off the valley floor as a glacier advanced or fallen off the valley walls as a result of frost wedging. Moraines may be comprised of silt like glacial flour to large boulders. The debris is typically angular.

a. Medial moraines
b. 1509 Istanbul earthquake
c. 1700 Cascadia earthquake
d. Moraine

121. In geology, _____ is soil at or below the freezing point of water for two or more years. Ice is not always present, as may be in the case of nonporous bedrock, but it frequently occurs and it may be in amounts exceeding the potential hydraulic saturation of the ground material. Most _____ is located in high latitudes, but alpine _____ exists at high altitudes.

a. 1703 Genroku earthquake
b. Permafrost
c. 1509 Istanbul earthquake
d. 1700 Cascadia earthquake

122. In soil science, the sporadic permafrost zone is abbreviated SPZ and the extensive _____ zone _____ Z.

There are exceptions in un-glaciated Siberia and Alaska where the present depth of permafrost is a relic of climatic conditions during glacial ages where winters were up to 11 °C (20 °F) colder than those of today. At mean annual soil surface temperatures below −5 °C (23 °F) the influence of aspect can never be sufficient to thaw permafrost and a zone of continuous permafrost forms.

Chapter 2. Earth Materials and Processes

  a. 1700 Cascadia earthquake
  c. 1703 Genroku earthquake
  b. 1509 Istanbul earthquake
  d. Discontinuous permafrost

123. Among the classifications of soil types, _____, is a fine, silty, windblown type of unconsolidated deposit. It is derived from glacial deposits, where glacial activity has ground rocks very fine. After drying, these deposits are highly susceptible to wind erosion, and downwind deposits may become very deep. _____ deposits are geologically unstable by nature, and will erode even without being disturbed by humans.
  a. 1703 Genroku earthquake
  c. 1700 Cascadia earthquake
  b. Loess
  d. 1509 Istanbul earthquake

124. A _____ is a hill of sand built by eolian processes. Dunes are subject to different forms and sizes based on their interaction with the wind. Most kinds of _____ are longer on the windward side where the sand is pushed up the _____, and a shorter in the lee of the wind. The trough between dunes is called a slack. A "_____ field" is an area covered by extensive sand dunes. Large _____ fields are known as ergs.
  a. Dune
  c. 1509 Istanbul earthquake
  b. 1703 Genroku earthquake
  d. 1700 Cascadia earthquake

125. _____ is the flow of air. More generally, it is the flow of the gases which compose an atmosphere; since _____ is not only an Earth based phenomenon.
  a. Wind
  c. 1700 Cascadia earthquake
  b. 1509 Istanbul earthquake
  d. 1703 Genroku earthquake

126. _____ refers to directed, regular, or systematic movement of a group of objects, organisms, or people.
  a. 1703 Genroku earthquake
  c. 1700 Cascadia earthquake
  b. 1509 Istanbul earthquake
  d. Migration

127. A _____ is a meteorological phenomenon common in arid and semi-arid regions. Such a storm may result from the passage of a gust front or simply a substantial increase in wind velocity over a wider region. In all instances, the ground must be very dry and loosely consolidated.
  a. 1703 Genroku earthquake
  c. 1700 Cascadia earthquake
  b. 1509 Istanbul earthquake
  d. Dust storm

128. A _____ is any disturbed state of an astronomical body's atmosphere, especially affecting its surface, and strongly implying severe weather. It may be marked by strong wind, thunder and lightning, heavy precipitation, such as ice, or wind transporting some substance through the atmosphere.
  a. 1700 Cascadia earthquake
  c. 1509 Istanbul earthquake
  b. 1703 Genroku earthquake
  d. Storm

Chapter 3. Soils and Environment

1. _____ is unwanted or undesired material.
   a. Waste
   b. 1703 Genroku earthquake
   c. 1509 Istanbul earthquake
   d. 1700 Cascadia earthquake

2. _____ is the collection, transport, processing, recycling or disposal of waste materials, usually ones produced by human activity, in an effort to reduce their effect on human health or local aesthetics or amenity.
   a. Waste management
   b. 1509 Istanbul earthquake
   c. 1703 Genroku earthquake
   d. 1700 Cascadia earthquake

3. _____ consist of mineral layers which may contain concentrations of clay or minerals such as iron or aluminium, or organic material. In addition, they are defined by having a distinctly different structure or consistence to the A horizon above and the horizons below.
   a. B horizon
   b. 1700 Cascadia earthquake
   c. 1509 Istanbul earthquake
   d. 1703 Genroku earthquake

4. The _____ has been significantly leached of its mineral and/or organic content, leaving a pale layer largely composed of silicates.
   a. AASHTO Soil Classification System
   b. E horizon
   c. AL 333
   d. AL 129-1

5. The _____ is the line that separates earth from sky. More precisely, it is the line that divides all of the directions one can possibly look into two categories: those which intersect the Earth, and those which do not.
   a. 1509 Istanbul earthquake
   b. 1703 Genroku earthquake
   c. Horizon
   d. 1700 Cascadia earthquake

6. A _____ or geophysical hazards is a threat of an event that will have a negative effect on people or the environment. Many natural hazards are related, e.g. earthquakes can result in tsunamis, drought can lead directly to famine and disease. A concrete example of the division between hazard and disaster is that the 1906 San Francisco earthquake was a disaster, whereas earthquakes are a hazard.
   a. Natural hazard
   b. 1509 Istanbul earthquake
   c. 1703 Genroku earthquake
   d. 1700 Cascadia earthquake

7. The _____ is a soil layer being dominated by the presence of large amounts of organic material in varying stages of decomposition.
   a. O horizon
   b. AL 333
   c. AASHTO Soil Classification System
   d. AL 129-1

8. _____ farming is a form of agriculture that excludes the use of synthetic fertilizers and pesticides, plant growth regulators, livestock feed additives, and genetically modified organisms.
   a. AASHTO Soil Classification System
   b. AL 333
   c. AL 129-1
   d. Organic

9. _____, in soil science, means the underlying geological material in which soil horizons form. Soils typically get a great deal of structure and minerals from their _____.
   a. 1703 Genroku earthquake
   b. 1509 Istanbul earthquake
   c. 1700 Cascadia earthquake
   d. Parent material

10. A _____ is a specific layer in the soil which measures parallel to the soil surface and possesses physical characteristics which differ from the layers above and beneath. Horizon formation is a function of a range of geological, chemical, and biological processes and occurs over long time periods. Soils vary in the degree to which horizons are expressed.
   a. A horizon
   b. Soil horizon
   c. 1509 Istanbul earthquake
   d. 1700 Cascadia earthquake

11. _____ is the process of extracting a substance from a solid by dissolving it in a liquid.
   a. 1509 Istanbul earthquake
   b. Leaching
   c. 1703 Genroku earthquake
   d. 1700 Cascadia earthquake

12. In biology and ecology, an _____ is a living complex adaptive system of organs that influence each other in such a way that they function in some way as a stable whole.
   a. AL 333
   b. Organism
   c. AL 129-1
   d. AASHTO Soil Classification System

13. On a glacier, the _____ is the area above the firn line, where snowfall accumulates and exceeds the losses from ablation,. The annual Glacier equilibrium line separates the accumulation and ablation zone annually. The _____ is also defined as the part of a glacier's surface, usually at higher elevations, on which there is net accumulation of snow, which subsequently turns into firn and then glacier ice.
   a. Accumulation zone
   b. AASHTO Soil Classification System
   c. Accumulation zone
   d. AL 129-1

14. _____ is simply named so because they come 'after' A and B within the soil profile. These layers are little affected by soil forming processes, and their lack of pedological development is one of their defining attributes
   a. 1509 Istanbul earthquake
   b. 1703 Genroku earthquake
   c. 1700 Cascadia earthquake
   d. C horizon

15. _____ is a hardened deposit of calcium carbonate. This calcium carbonate cements together other materials, including gravel, sand, clay, and silt. It is found in aridisol and mollisol soil orders. _____ occurs worldwide, generally in arid or semi-arid regions.
   a. 1700 Cascadia earthquake
   b. 1703 Genroku earthquake
   c. 1509 Istanbul earthquake
   d. Caliche

16. The _____ basically denote the layer of partially-weathered bedrock at the base of the soil profile.
   a. 1700 Cascadia earthquake
   b. 1509 Istanbul earthquake
   c. 1703 Genroku earthquake
   d. R horizon

17. In geology, _____ are rock s with a grain size of usually no less than 256 mm diameter.
   a. 1703 Genroku earthquake
   b. 1700 Cascadia earthquake
   c. 1509 Istanbul earthquake
   d. Boulders

18. _____ is a term used to describe a group of hydrous aluminium phyllosilicate minerals, that are typically less than 2 micrometres in diameter. _____ consists of a variety of phyllosilicate minerals rich in silicon and aluminium oxides and hydroxides which include variable amounts of structural water. Clays are generally formed by the chemical weathering of silicate-bearing rocks by carbonic acid but some are formed by hydrothermal activity.

Chapter 3. Soils and Environment

a. 1700 Cascadia earthquake
b. 1703 Genroku earthquake
c. 1509 Istanbul earthquake
d. Clay

19. _____ are made up of the minerals hydrous aluminium phyllosilicates, sometimes with variable amounts of iron, magnesium, alkali metals, alkaline earths and other cations.
a. 1700 Cascadia earthquake
b. 1509 Istanbul earthquake
c. 1703 Genroku earthquake
d. Clay particles

20. Cobblestones are stones that were frequently used in the pavement of early streets. '_____' is derived from the very old English word 'cob', which had a wide range of meanings, one of which was 'rounded lump' with overtones of large size. 'Cobble', which appeared in the 15th century, simply added the diminutive suffix 'le' to 'cob', and meant a small stone rounded by the flow of water; essentially, a large pebble.
a. Cobblestone
b. 1703 Genroku earthquake
c. 1509 Istanbul earthquake
d. 1700 Cascadia earthquake

21. _____ is rock that is of a certain particle size range. In geology, _____ is any loose rock that is at least two millimeters in its largest dimension and no more than 75 millimeters.
a. 1703 Genroku earthquake
b. Gravel
c. 1509 Istanbul earthquake
d. 1700 Cascadia earthquake

22. _____ often indicates soil moisture status and is used for determining hydric soils. Often described by using general terms, such as dark brown, yellowish brown, etc., soil colors are also described more technically by using Munsell _____ charts, which separate color into components of hue (relation to red, yellow and blue), value (lightness or darkness) and chroma (paleness or strength.)

- 'The Color of Soil'. United States Department of Agriculture - Natural Resources Conservation Service. Retrieved on 2007-11-25.
- '_____ Contrast'. United States Department of Agriculture - Natural Resources Conservation Service. Retrieved on 2007-11-25.
- 'Why is the ground brown'. Retrieved on 2007-11-25.

a. 1703 Genroku earthquake
b. 1700 Cascadia earthquake
c. 1509 Istanbul earthquake
d. Soil color

23. The _____ is a geological fault that runs a length of roughly 800 miles through western and southern California in the United States. The fault, a right-lateral strike-slip fault, marks a transform boundary between the Pacific Plate and the North American Plate.
a. 1703 Genroku earthquake
b. 1509 Istanbul earthquake
c. 1700 Cascadia earthquake
d. San Andreas fault

24. Faults are planar rock fractures, which show evidence of relative movement. Large faults within the Earth's crust are the result of shear motion and active _____ zones are the causal locations of most earthquakes. Earthquakes are caused by energy release during rapid slippage along faults.

a. 1700 Cascadia earthquake
b. 1509 Istanbul earthquake
c. Fault
d. 1703 Genroku earthquake

25. _____ is the natural capability of giving life. As a measure, '_____ Rate' is the number of children born per couple, person or population. This is different from fecundity, which is defined as the potential for reproduction (influenced by gamete production, fertilisation and carrying a pregnancy to term.)
   a. Fertility
   b. 1700 Cascadia earthquake
   c. 1509 Istanbul earthquake
   d. 1703 Genroku earthquake

26. _____ generally refers to the presence of water, often in trace amounts.
   a. 1700 Cascadia earthquake
   b. 1703 Genroku earthquake
   c. 1509 Istanbul earthquake
   d. Moisture

27. _____ are soils formed in volcanic ash and defined as soils containing high proportions of glass and amorphous colloidal materials, including allophane, imogolite, and ferrihydrite. In the FAO soil classification, _____ are known as Andosols.
   a. AASHTO Soil Classification System
   b. AL 129-1
   c. AL 333
   d. Andisols

28. _____ are a soil order in USA soil taxonomy. They form in an arid or semi-arid climate. _____ dominate the deserts and xeric shrublands which occupy about one third of the Earth's land surface. They also have a very poor concentration of organic matter.
   a. AASHTO Soil Classification System
   b. AL 333
   c. AL 129-1
   d. Aridisols

29. Entisols are defined as soils that do not show any profile development. An _____ has no diagnostic horizons, and most are basically unaltered from their parent rock.
   a. AL 129-1
   b. AL 333
   c. AASHTO Soil Classification System
   d. Entisol

30. A _____ is a soil comprised primarily of organic materials. They are defined as containing at least 20 percent organic material to a depth of 40 centimetres. Most are acidic and many are very deficient in major plant nutrients which are washed away in the consistently moist soil.
   a. Histosol
   b. 1703 Genroku earthquake
   c. 1509 Istanbul earthquake
   d. 1700 Cascadia earthquake

31. _____ are a soil order in USDA soil taxonomy. They form quickly through alteration of parent material. They are older than entisols. They have no accumulation of clays, Fe, Al or organic matter.
   a. AASHTO Soil Classification System
   b. AL 333
   c. AL 129-1
   d. Inceptisols

32. _____ are a soil order in USA soil taxonomy. _____ form in semi-arid to semi-humid areas, typically under a grassland cover. Their parent material is generally limestone, loess, or wind-blown sand. The main processes that lead to the formation of grassland _____ are melanisation, decomposition, humification and pedoturbation.

a. 1509 Istanbul earthquake
b. Mollisols
c. 1703 Genroku earthquake
d. 1700 Cascadia earthquake

33. _____ are an order in USA soil taxonomy, best known for their occurrence in tropical rain forest, 15-25 degrees north and south of the Equator. They are defined as soils containing at all depths no more than 10 percent weatherable minerals, and less than 10 percent base saturation. _____ are always a red or yellowish color, due to the high concentration of iron III and aluminium oxides and hydroxides.
   a. AL 129-1
   b. AL 333
   c. Oxisols
   d. AASHTO Soil Classification System

34. _____ is the typical soil of coniferous, or Boreal forests. These soils are found in areas that are wet and cold and also in warm areas such as Florida where sandy soils have fluctuating water tables.
   a. Podzol
   b. 1509 Istanbul earthquake
   c. 1700 Cascadia earthquake
   d. 1703 Genroku earthquake

35. _____ is the practice and science of classification. Taxonomies, which are composed of taxonomic units known as taxa, are frequently hierarchical in structure, commonly displaying parent-child relationships.
   a. 1700 Cascadia earthquake
   b. 1703 Genroku earthquake
   c. 1509 Istanbul earthquake
   d. Taxonomy

36. _____ is a soil in which there is a high content of expansive clay known as montmorillonite that forms deep cracks in drier seasons or years. Alternate shrinking and swelling causes self-mulching, where the soil material consistently mixes itself.
   a. 1700 Cascadia earthquake
   b. 1509 Istanbul earthquake
   c. 1703 Genroku earthquake
   d. Vertisol

37. _____ in chemistry is the intermolecular attraction between like-molecules. It explains phenomena such as surface tension.
   a. 1509 Istanbul earthquake
   b. 1700 Cascadia earthquake
   c. 1703 Genroku earthquake
   d. Cohesion

38. The _____ (or _____) is a soil classification system used in engineering and geology disciplines to describe the texture and grain size of a soil. The classification system can be applied to most unconsolidated materials, and is represented by a two-letter symbol. Each letter is described below (with the exception of Pt):

   - AASHTO Soil Classification System
   - AASHTO
   - ASTM International

   a. AL 129-1
   b. AASHTO Soil Classification System
   c. AL 333
   d. Unified soil classification system

39. The _____ is the surface where the water pressure is equal to atmospheric pressure. A large amount of water within a body of sand or rock below the _____ is called an aquifer, and the ability of rocks to store such groundwater is dependent on their porosity and permeability.

Chapter 3. Soils and Environment

a. 1700 Cascadia earthquake
b. 1509 Istanbul earthquake
c. 1703 Genroku earthquake
d. Water table

40. _____ is a dynamic subject, from the structure of the system itself, to the definitions of classes, and finally in the application in the field. It can be approached from both the pespective of pedogenesis and from soil morphology.
a. Strip farming
b. Terrace
c. Vitrification
d. Soil classification

41. _____ is a discipline that applies principles of engineering mechanics, e.g. kinematics, dynamics, fluid mechanics, and mechanics of material, to predict the mechanical behavior of soils. Together with Rock mechanics, it is the basis for solving many engineering problems in civil engineering (geotechnical engineering), geophysical engineering and engineering geology. Some of the basic theories of _____ are the basic description and classification of soil, effective stress, shear strength, consolidation, lateral earth pressure, bearing capacity, slope stability, and permeability.
a. 1700 Cascadia earthquake
b. 1509 Istanbul earthquake
c. 1703 Genroku earthquake
d. Soil mechanics

42. _____ is the force that opposes the relative motion or tendency toward such motion of two surfaces in contact. It is not a fundamental force, as it is made up of electromagnetic forces between atoms.
a. 1700 Cascadia earthquake
b. 1703 Genroku earthquake
c. 1509 Istanbul earthquake
d. Friction

43. _____ can be a change from a gas to a liquid through condensation, usually by cooling, or a change from a solid to a liquid through melting, usually by heating or by grinding and blending with another liquid to induce dissolution.
a. Liquefaction
b. 1700 Cascadia earthquake
c. 1703 Genroku earthquake
d. 1509 Istanbul earthquake

44. Rock _____ is the controlled use of explosives to excavate or remove rock. It is a technique used most often in mining and civil engineering such as dam construction.

In 1990, 2.1 million tonnes (2.32 million short tons) of commercial explosives were consumed in the USA, representing an estimated expenditure of 3.5 to 4 billion 1993 dollars on _____.

a. 1700 Cascadia earthquake
b. Blasting
c. 1509 Istanbul earthquake
d. 1703 Genroku earthquake

45. _____ is deterioration of essential properties in a material due to reactions with its surroundings. In the most common use of the word, this means a loss of an electron of metals reacting with water or oxygen.
a. Corrosion
b. 1703 Genroku earthquake
c. 1700 Cascadia earthquake
d. 1509 Istanbul earthquake

46. _____ is the most commonly used technique within the science of archaeology. It is the exposure, processing and recording of archaeological remains.
a. Excavation
b. AASHTO Soil Classification System
c. AL 333
d. AL 129-1

Chapter 3. Soils and Environment

47. _____ is a very soft phyllosilicate mineral that typically forms in microscopic crystals, forming a clay. It is the main constituent of the volcanic ash weathering product, bentonite.

   a. Montmorillonite
   b. 1509 Istanbul earthquake
   c. 1703 Genroku earthquake
   d. 1700 Cascadia earthquake

48. In the earth sciences, _____ is a measure of the ability of a material to transmit fluids. It is of great importance in determining the flow characteristics of hydrocarbons in oil and gas reservoirs, and of groundwater in aquifers.

   a. Permeability
   b. 1703 Genroku earthquake
   c. 1509 Istanbul earthquake
   d. 1700 Cascadia earthquake

49. In geology, _____ is a naturally occurring aggregate of minerals and/or mineraloids.

The Earth's outer solid layer, the lithosphere, is made of _____. In general rocks are of three types, namely, igneous, sedimentary, and metamorphic.

   a. 1703 Genroku earthquake
   b. 1509 Istanbul earthquake
   c. Rock
   d. 1700 Cascadia earthquake

50. _____ refers to a member of any human group whose adult males grow to less than 150 cm in average height or less than 155 cm. A member of a slightly taller group is termed pygmoid. The best known _____ are the Aka, Efe and Mbuti of central Africa.

   a. 1700 Cascadia earthquake
   b. 1703 Genroku earthquake
   c. 1509 Istanbul earthquake
   d. Pygmies

51. Most often, a _____ refers to an artificial lake, used to store water for various uses. Reservoirs are created first by building a sturdy dam, usually out of cement, earth, rock, or a mixture. Once the dam is completed, a stream is allowed to flow behind it and eventually fill it to capacity.

   a. 1700 Cascadia earthquake
   b. 1703 Genroku earthquake
   c. 1509 Istanbul earthquake
   d. Reservoir

52. _____ is any particulate matter that can be transported by fluid flow and which eventually is deposited as a layer of solid particles on the bed or bottom of a body of water or other liquid.

   a. 1703 Genroku earthquake
   b. 1509 Istanbul earthquake
   c. 1700 Cascadia earthquake
   d. Sediment

53. Models of soil erosion play critical roles in soil and water resource conservation and nonpoint source pollution assessments, including: sediment load assessment and inventory, conservation planning and design for sediment control, and for the advancement of scientific understanding. The most widely used soil erosion model is the _____ or one of its derivatives.

The _____ was developed in the United States based on soil erosion data collected beginning in the 1930s by the USDA Soil Conservation Service (now the USDA Natural Resources Conservation Service).

   a. Universal Soil Loss Equation
   b. AASHTO Soil Classification System
   c. AL 333
   d. AL 129-1

Chapter 3. Soils and Environment

54. _____ is the introduction of substances or energy into the environment, resulting in deleterious effects of such a nature as to endanger human health, harm living resources and ecosystems, and impair or interfere with amenities and other legitimate uses of the environment.
   a. 1703 Genroku earthquake
   b. 1509 Istanbul earthquake
   c. 1700 Cascadia earthquake
   d. Pollution

55. _____ is matter that has come from a recently living organism; is capable of decay, or the product of decay; or is composed of organic compounds. The definition of _____ varies upon the subject it is being used for.
   a. AASHTO Soil Classification System
   b. AL 333
   c. Organic matter
   d. AL 129-1

56. _____ is soil or rock derived granular material of a specific grain size. _____ may occur as a soil or alternatively as suspended sediment in a water column of any surface water body. It may also exist as deposition soil at the bottom of a water body.
   a. Silt
   b. 1703 Genroku earthquake
   c. 1509 Istanbul earthquake
   d. 1700 Cascadia earthquake

57. _____ is the substance of which physical objects are composed. _____ can be solid, liquid, plasma or gas. It constitutes the observable universe.
   a. 1700 Cascadia earthquake
   b. 1509 Istanbul earthquake
   c. 1703 Genroku earthquake
   d. Matter

58. _____ is the human modification of natural environment or wilderness into built environment such as fields, pastures, and settlements. The major effect of _____ on land cover since 1750 has been deforestation of temperate regions. More recent significant effects of _____ include urban sprawl, soil erosion, soil degradation, salinization, and desertification.
   a. 1509 Istanbul earthquake
   b. 1703 Genroku earthquake
   c. 1700 Cascadia earthquake
   d. Land use

59. _____ is displacement of solids by the agents of ocean currents, wind, water, or ice by downward or down-slope movement in response to gravity or by living organisms.
   a. AASHTO Soil Classification System
   b. AL 129-1
   c. Erosion
   d. AL 333

60. For morphological image processing operations, see Erosion (morphology)For use of in dermatopathology, see Erosion (dermatopathology) Severe _____ in a wheat field near Washington State University, USA.

Erosion is the removal of solids (sediment, soil, rock and other particles) in the natural environment. It usually occurs due to transport by wind, water, or ice; by down-slope creep of soil and other material under the force of gravity; or by living organisms, such as burrowing animals, in the case of bioerosion.

Erosion is distinguished from weathering, which is the process of chemical or physical breakdown of the minerals in the rocks, although the two processes may occur concurrently.

Chapter 3. Soils and Environment

a. Soil erosion
b. 1700 Cascadia earthquake
c. 1703 Genroku earthquake
d. 1509 Istanbul earthquake

61. _____ can be defined as any process that uses microorganisms, fungi, green plants or their enzymes to return the environment altered by contaminants to its original condition.
a. 1509 Istanbul earthquake
b. 1700 Cascadia earthquake
c. 1703 Genroku earthquake
d. Bioremediation

62. _____ is the degradation of land in arid, semi arid and dry sub-humid areas resulting from various climatic variations, but primarily human activities. Current _____ is taking place much faster worldwide than historically and usually arises from the demands of increased populations that settle on the land in order to grow crops and graze animals.
a. 1703 Genroku earthquake
b. Desertification
c. 1700 Cascadia earthquake
d. 1509 Istanbul earthquake

63. _____ is the term used for a branch of public policy which encompasses various disciplines which seek to order and regulate the use of land in an efficient and ethical way.
a. Land use planning
b. 1700 Cascadia earthquake
c. 1509 Istanbul earthquake
d. 1703 Genroku earthquake

64. _____ refers to the area of the Central Valley of California that lies south of the Sacramento-San Joaquin Delta in Stockton. Although most of the valley is rural, it does contain major urban cities such as Stockton, Fresno, Modesto, Bakersfield, and Merced.
a. 1700 Cascadia earthquake
b. 1703 Genroku earthquake
c. 1509 Istanbul earthquake
d. San Joaquin Valley

65. In geology, a _____ is a depression with predominant extent in one direction. The terms U-shaped and V-shaped are descriptive terms of geography to characterize the form of valleys. Most valleys belong to one of these two main types or a mixture of them, at least with respect of the cross section of the slopes or hillsides.
a. 1700 Cascadia earthquake
b. Valley
c. 1703 Genroku earthquake
d. 1509 Istanbul earthquake

66. A _____ is a visual representation of an area--a symbolic depiction highlighting relationships between elements of that space such as objects, regions, and themes.

Many maps are static two-dimensional, geometrically accurate representations of three-dimensional space, while others are dynamic or interactive, even three-dimensional. Although most commonly used to depict geography, maps may represent any space, real or imagined, without regard to context or scale; e.g. Brain mapping, DNA mapping, and extraterrestrial mapping.

a. 1700 Cascadia earthquake
b. Cartography
c. 1509 Istanbul earthquake
d. Map

Chapter 4. Natural Hazards: An Overview

1. _____ (æ—¥æœ¬ Nihon or Nippon making it an archipelago. The largest islands are Honshū, Hokkaidō, Kyūshū and Shikoku, together accounting for 97% of _____'s land area. Most of the islands are mountainous, many volcanic; for example, _____'s highest peak, Mount Fuji, is a volcano.
   a. Kenya
   b. Java
   c. Kabul
   d. Japan

2. _____ (ç¥žæˆ¸å¸, Kō be-shi For most of its history the area was never a single political entity, even during the Tokugawa Period, when the port was controlled directly by the Tokugawa Shogunate. _____ did not exist in its current form until its founding in 1889. Its name comes from 'kanbe' Hyō go Port in the 19th century The Bund in _____ around 1890

   Stone artifacts and tools found in western _____ demonstrate that the area was populated at least from the Jō mon period.

   a. Japan
   b. Peninsula
   c. Korean War
   d. Kobe

3. A _____ or geophysical hazards is a threat of an event that will have a negative effect on people or the environment. Many natural hazards are related, e.g. earthquakes can result in tsunamis, drought can lead directly to famine and disease. A concrete example of the division between hazard and disaster is that the 1906 San Francisco earthquake was a disaster, whereas earthquakes are a hazard.
   a. 1700 Cascadia earthquake
   b. 1703 Genroku earthquake
   c. 1509 Istanbul earthquake
   d. Natural hazard

4. An _____ is the result from the sudden release of stored energy in the Earth's crust that creates seismic waves. At the Earth's surface, earthquakes may manifest themselves by a shaking or displacement of the ground. An _____ is caused by tectonic plates getting stuck and putting a strain on the ground. The strain becomes so great that rocks give way by breaking and sliding along fault planes.
   a. AASHTO Soil Classification System
   b. Earthquake
   c. AL 129-1
   d. AL 333

5. In meteorology, _____ are an area of low atmospheric pressure characterized by inward spiraling winds that rotate counter clockwise in the northern hemisphere and clockwise in the southern hemisphere of the Earth.
   a. Cyclones
   b. 1703 Genroku earthquake
   c. 1509 Istanbul earthquake
   d. 1700 Cascadia earthquake

6. Faults are planar rock fractures, which show evidence of relative movement. Large faults within the Earth's crust are the result of shear motion and active _____ zones are the causal locations of most earthquakes. Earthquakes are caused by energy release during rapid slippage along faults.
   a. 1703 Genroku earthquake
   b. 1509 Istanbul earthquake
   c. 1700 Cascadia earthquake
   d. Fault

7. _____ is an unconsolidated tectonite (a rock formed by tectonic forces) with a very small grain size. _____ has no cohesion, it is normally an unconsolidated rock type, unless cementation took place at a later stage. _____ forms in the same way as fault breccia, the latter also having larger clasts.

Chapter 4. Natural Hazards: An Overview 43

   a. 1703 Genroku earthquake
   c. 1700 Cascadia earthquake
   b. Fault gouge
   d. 1509 Istanbul earthquake

8. A _____ is an opening in a planet's surface or crust, which allows hot, molten rock, ash, and gases to escape from below the surface. Volcanic activity involving the extrusion of rock tends to form mountains or features like mountains over a period of time.

Volcanoes are generally found where tectonic plates are diverging or converging.

   a. 1703 Genroku earthquake
   c. 1509 Istanbul earthquake
   b. 1700 Cascadia earthquake
   d. Volcano

9. A popular way of classifying magmatic volcanoes goes by their frequency of eruption, or _____, with those that erupt regularly called active, those that have erupted in historical times but are now quiet called dormant, and those that have not erupted in historical times called extinct.

   a. 1700 Cascadia earthquake
   c. 1509 Istanbul earthquake
   b. 1703 Genroku earthquake
   d. Volcanic activity

10. A _____ is a statement or claim that a particular event will occur in the future in more certain terms than a forecast. The etymology of this word is Latin (from præ- 'before' plus dicere 'to say'.) In regards to predicting the future Howard H. Stevenson Says, ' _____ is at least two things: Important and hard.' Important, because we have to act, and hard because we have to realize the future we want, and what is the best way to get there.

   a. Prediction
   c. 1703 Genroku earthquake
   b. 1700 Cascadia earthquake
   d. 1509 Istanbul earthquake

11. _____ is a state on the West Coast of the United States, along the Pacific Ocean. It is bordered by Oregon to the north, Nevada to the east, Arizona to the southeast, and to the south the Mexican state of Baja _____. _____ is the most populous U.S. state.

   a. 1700 Cascadia earthquake
   c. 1509 Istanbul earthquake
   b. California
   d. 1703 Genroku earthquake

12. A _____ is a body of water, not part of the ocean, that is larger and deeper than a pond.

   a. 1703 Genroku earthquake
   c. 1509 Istanbul earthquake
   b. 1700 Cascadia earthquake
   d. Lake

13. A _____ is any of a number of an extinct genus of proboscidean, often with long curved tusks and, in northern species, a covering of long hair. They lived from the Pliocene epoch from to around 4,000 years ago.

   a. 1509 Istanbul earthquake
   c. Mammoth
   b. 1703 Genroku earthquake
   d. 1700 Cascadia earthquake

14. _____ is an incorporated town in Mono County, California, United States. The population was 7,093 at the 2000 census. _____ resides on the edge of the Long Valley Caldera. The area around the town is geologically active, with hot springs and rhyolite domes that are less than 1000 years old.

   a. 1509 Istanbul earthquake
   c. Mammoth Lakes
   b. 1703 Genroku earthquake
   d. 1700 Cascadia earthquake

Chapter 4. Natural Hazards: An Overview

15. The _____ occurred on January 17, 1994 at 4:30:55 AM Pacific Standard Time in the city of Los Angeles, California. It had a "moderate" moment magnitude of 6.7, but the ground acceleration was the highest ever instrumentally recorded in an urban area in North America. Seventy-two people died as a result of the earthquake and over 11,000 were injured. In addition, the earthquake caused an estimated $12.5 billion in damage, making it one of the costliest natural disasters in U.S. history.
   a. 1509 Istanbul earthquake
   b. Northridge earthquake
   c. 1703 Genroku earthquake
   d. 1700 Cascadia earthquake

16. In demographics and ecology, Population growth rate (PGR) is the fractional rate at which the number of individuals in a _____. Specifically, PGR ordinarily refers to the change in population over a unit time period, often expressed as a percentage of the number of individuals in the population at the beginning of that period. This can be written as the formula:

$$\text{Growth rate} = \frac{(\text{population at end of period} - \text{population at beginning of period})}{\text{population at beginning of period}}$$

(In the limit of a sufficiently small time period.)

   a. 1700 Cascadia earthquake
   b. 1703 Genroku earthquake
   c. 1509 Istanbul earthquake
   d. Population increases

17. A _____ is a bipedal primate belonging to the mammalian species Homo sapiens in the family Hominidae. Compared to other living organisms on Earth, a _____ has a highly developed brain capable of abstract reasoning, language, and introspection.
   a. 1509 Istanbul earthquake
   b. Human
   c. 1703 Genroku earthquake
   d. 1700 Cascadia earthquake

18. _____ is a concept that denotes the precise probability of specific eventualities. Technically, the notion of _____ is independent from the notion of value and, as such, eventualities may have both beneficial and adverse consequences. However, in general usage the convention is to focus only on potential negative impact to some characteristic of value that may arise from a future event.
   a. Risk
   b. 1700 Cascadia earthquake
   c. 1509 Istanbul earthquake
   d. 1703 Genroku earthquake

19. _____ is a qualitative or quantitative evaluation of the environmental and health risk resulting from exposure to a chemical agent. It combines exposure assessment results with toxicity assessment results to estimate risk.
   a. 1700 Cascadia earthquake
   b. 1509 Istanbul earthquake
   c. 1703 Genroku earthquake
   d. Risk assessment

20. A _____ is an urban area with a high population and a particular administrative, legal, or historical status.

Large industrialized cities generally have advanced systems for sanitation, utilities, land usage, housing, and transportation and more. This close proximity greatly facilitates interaction between people and firms, benefiting both parties in the process.

a. City
b. 1509 Istanbul earthquake
c. 1703 Genroku earthquake
d. 1700 Cascadia earthquake

21. In the _____ phase of emergency management, emergency managers develop plans of action for when the disaster strikes.
   a. 1509 Istanbul earthquake
   b. 1703 Genroku earthquake
   c. Disaster preparedness
   d. 1700 Cascadia earthquake

22. _____, in law and economics, is a form of risk management primarily used to hedge against the risk of a contingent loss. _____ is defined as the equitable transfer of the risk of a loss, from one entity to another, in exchange for a premium, and can be thought of as a guaranteed small loss to prevent a large, possibly devastating loss. An insurer is a company selling the _____; an insured is the person or entity buying the _____.
   a. AL 333
   b. AASHTO Soil Classification System
   c. AL 129-1
   d. Insurance

23. The United Mexican States, commonly known as _____, is a federal constitutional republic in North America. It is bordered on the north by the United States; on the south and west by the North Pacific Ocean; on the southeast by Guatemala, Belize, and the Caribbean Sea; and on the east by the Gulf of _____. The United Mexican States are a federation comprising thirty-one states and a federal district, the capital _____ City, whose metropolitan area is one of the world's most populous.
   a. Amblypoda
   b. Andrija Mohorovičić
   c. Ambulocetus
   d. Mexico

24. _____ is the capital city of Mexico. It is the most important economic, industrial and cultural center in the country, and the most populous city with over 8,836,045 inhabitants in 2008. Greater _____ incorporates 59 adjacent municipalities of Mexico State and 1 municipality of the state of Hidalgo, according to the most recent definition agreed upon by the federal and state governments.
   a. Mexico City
   b. 1700 Cascadia earthquake
   c. 1509 Istanbul earthquake
   d. 1703 Genroku earthquake

25. _____ is the average and variations of weather over long periods of time. _____ zones can be defined using parameters such as temperature and rainfall.
   a. 1703 Genroku earthquake
   b. Climate
   c. 1509 Istanbul earthquake
   d. 1700 Cascadia earthquake

26. In biology a _____ is the collection of inter-breeding organisms of a particular species; in sociology, a collection of human beings. A _____ shares a particular characteristic of interest, most often that of living in a given geographic area. In taxonomy _____ is a low-level taxonomic rank.
   a. Metapopulation
   b. 1700 Cascadia earthquake
   c. 1509 Istanbul earthquake
   d. Population

27. _____ was one of the most powerful hurricanes on record in the Atlantic basin, with maximum sustained winds of 180 mph (285 km/h.) The storm was the thirteenth tropical storm, ninth hurricane, and third major hurricane of the 1998 Atlantic hurricane season. At the time, _____ was the strongest Atlantic hurricane observed in the month of October, though it has since been surpassed by Hurricane Wilma of the 2005 season.

a. Helium
b. Hippocrates
c. Francium
d. Hurricane Mitch

28. _____ is an Andean stratovolcano in Caldas Department, Colombia. It is the northernmost and highest Colombian volcano with historical activity. Its 1985 eruption produced a lahar which completely buried Armero and caused an estimated 23,000 deaths.
   a. Nevado del Ruiz
   b. 1509 Istanbul earthquake
   c. 1703 Genroku earthquake
   d. 1700 Cascadia earthquake

29. The _____ is the longest river in Asia and the third longest in the world, after the Nile in Africa, and the Amazon in South America. The river is about 6,380 km long and flows from its source in Qinghai Province, eastwards into the East China Sea at Shanghai. It has traditionally been considered a dividing line between North and South China.
   a. 1509 Istanbul earthquake
   b. 1703 Genroku earthquake
   c. 1700 Cascadia earthquake
   d. Yangtze River

30. _____ usually commence with phreatomagmatic eruptions which can be extremely noisy due the rising magma heating water in the ground. This is usually followed by the explosive throat clearing of the vent and the eruption column is dirty grey to black as old weathered rocks are blasted out of the vent. As the vent clears, further ash clouds become grey-white and creamy in colour, with convulations of the ash similar to those of plinian eruptions.
   a. 1703 Genroku earthquake
   b. 1509 Istanbul earthquake
   c. Vulcanian eruptions
   d. 1700 Cascadia earthquake

Chapter 5. Rivers and Flooding

1. A _____ is flat or nearly flat land adjacent to a stream or river that experiences occasional or periodic flooding. It includes the floodway, which consists of the stream channel and adjacent areas that carry flood flows, and the flood fringe, which are areas covered by the flood, but which do not experience a strong current.
    a. 1509 Istanbul earthquake
    b. Floodplain
    c. 1703 Genroku earthquake
    d. 1700 Cascadia earthquake

2. The _____ of a river or stream is the lowest point to which it can flow, often referred to as the 'mouth' of the river. For large rivers, sea level is usually the _____, but a large river or lake is likewise the _____ for tributary streams.
    a. Base level
    b. 1509 Istanbul earthquake
    c. 1703 Genroku earthquake
    d. 1700 Cascadia earthquake

3. _____ is a term to describe the larger particles, relative to the suspended load, that are carried along the bottom of a stream.
    a. Bed load
    b. 1700 Cascadia earthquake
    c. 1509 Istanbul earthquake
    d. 1703 Genroku earthquake

4. The ways in which sediments are transported by streams, or the stream load is comprised of three types: Bed Loads, _____, Suspended Loads.
    a. 1509 Istanbul earthquake
    b. 1700 Cascadia earthquake
    c. 1703 Genroku earthquake
    d. Dissolved loads

5. _____ is the natural or artificial removal of surface and sub-surface water from a given area. Many agricultural soils need _____ to improve production or to manage water supplies.
    a. 1703 Genroku earthquake
    b. 1509 Istanbul earthquake
    c. Drainage
    d. 1700 Cascadia earthquake

6. A _____ is a body of water with a current, confined within a bed and banks. Streams are important as conduits in the water cycle, instruments in aquifer recharge, and corridors for fish and wildlife migration.
    a. 1700 Cascadia earthquake
    b. 1703 Genroku earthquake
    c. Stream
    d. 1509 Istanbul earthquake

7. _____ is the term for the fine particles that are light enough to be carried in a stream without touching the stream bed. These particles are generally of the sand, silt and clay size, although they can be larger, especially in cases of high discharge, such as during floods. This is in contrast to bed load which is carried along the bottom of the stream.
    a. 1703 Genroku earthquake
    b. 1700 Cascadia earthquake
    c. Suspended load
    d. 1509 Istanbul earthquake

8. _____ was an employee at Limerick nuclear power plant who set off the radiation alarms on his way to work in 1984. Other employees searched his house and found that he had radon poisoning in his basement that was unrelated to the nuclear power plant. It was calculated that about 100,000 Bq/m³ (2,700 pCi/L) was contaminating his house and the risk of living there was equal to that of smoking 135 packs of cigarettes a day.
    a. 1703 Genroku earthquake
    b. 1700 Cascadia earthquake
    c. 1509 Istanbul earthquake
    d. Stanley Watras

9. In vector calculus, the _____ of a scalar field is a vector field which points in the direction of the greatest rate of increase of the scalar field, and whose magnitude is the greatest rate of change.

A generalization of the _____ for functions on a Euclidean space which have values in another Euclidean space is the Jacobian. A further generalization for a function from one Banach space to another is the Fréchet derivative.

- a. 1509 Istanbul earthquake
- b. 1703 Genroku earthquake
- c. Gradient
- d. 1700 Cascadia earthquake

10. _____ is any particulate matter that can be transported by fluid flow and which eventually is deposited as a layer of solid particles on the bed or bottom of a body of water or other liquid.
- a. 1509 Istanbul earthquake
- b. 1700 Cascadia earthquake
- c. 1703 Genroku earthquake
- d. Sediment

11. In electromagnetic theory, the _____ is derived from two of Maxwell's equations. It states that the divergence of the current density is equal to the negative rate of change of the charge density.
- a. Continuity equation
- b. 1509 Istanbul earthquake
- c. 1703 Genroku earthquake
- d. 1700 Cascadia earthquake

12. In physics, _____ is defined as the rate of change of displacement or the rate of displacement. Simply put, it is distance per units of time.
- a. Velocity
- b. Supersaturation
- c. Supercritical fluid
- d. Redshift

13. _____ is displacement of solids by the agents of ocean currents, wind, water, or ice by downward or down-slope movement in response to gravity or by living organisms.
- a. AASHTO Soil Classification System
- b. AL 129-1
- c. AL 333
- d. Erosion

14. A _____ is a landform where the mouth of a river flows into an ocean, sea, desert, estuary or lake. It builds up sediment outwards into the flat area which the river's flow encounters transported by the water and set down as the currents slow.
- a. Delta
- b. 1703 Genroku earthquake
- c. 1509 Istanbul earthquake
- d. 1700 Cascadia earthquake

15. _____ are networks of small channels that are ever-changing and interlacing. They make up one large river or stream.
- a. 1509 Istanbul earthquake
- b. 1703 Genroku earthquake
- c. 1700 Cascadia earthquake
- d. Braided channels

16. A _____ is a bend in a river. A stream or river flowing through a wide valley or flat plain will tend to form a meandering stream course as it alternatively erodes and deposits sediments along its course. The result is a snaking pattern.
- a. 1700 Cascadia earthquake
- b. 1509 Istanbul earthquake
- c. 1703 Genroku earthquake
- d. Meander

Chapter 5. Rivers and Flooding

17. The _____ (1968) is a book written by Paul R. Ehrlich. A best-selling work, it predicted disaster for humanity due to overpopulation and the 'population explosion'. The book predicted that 'in the 1970s and 1980s hundreds of millions of people will starve to death', that nothing can be done to avoid mass famine greater than any in the history, and radical action is needed to limit the overpopulation.
    a. Andrija Mohorovičić
    b. Ambulocetus
    c. Population bomb
    d. Amblypoda

18. A _____ is a depositional feature of streams. Point bars are found in abundance in mature or meandering streams, they are located on the inside of a stream bend, known as a meander.
    a. 1703 Genroku earthquake
    b. 1700 Cascadia earthquake
    c. 1509 Istanbul earthquake
    d. Point bar

19. The _____ environment consists of all navigable rivers of interest.
    a. 1509 Istanbul earthquake
    b. Riverine
    c. 1700 Cascadia earthquake
    d. 1703 Genroku earthquake

20. _____ is the point at which the surface of a river, creek, or other body of water has risen to a sufficient level to cause damage or affects use of man-made structures. When a body of water rises to this level, it is considered a flood event.

Definition

_____ means a manmade feature is underwater.

    a. 1700 Cascadia earthquake
    b. 1703 Genroku earthquake
    c. 1509 Istanbul earthquake
    d. Flood stage

21. _____ is the measurement of the number of occurrences of a repeated event per unit of time. It is also defined as the rate of change of phase of a sinusoidal waveform.
    a. 1703 Genroku earthquake
    b. 1700 Cascadia earthquake
    c. Frequency
    d. 1509 Istanbul earthquake

22. _____ is the increase in the population of cities in proportion to the region's rural population. _____ is studied in terms of its effects on the ecology and economy of a region.
    a. AASHTO Soil Classification System
    b. AL 129-1
    c. AL 333
    d. Urbanization

23. The _____ of an edge is $c_f(u, v) = c(u, v) - f(u, v)$. This defines a residual network denoted $G_f(V, E_f)$, giving the amount of available capacity. See that there can be an edge from u to v in the residual network, even though there is no edge from u to v in the original network.
    a. Residual capacity
    b. 1703 Genroku earthquake
    c. 1700 Cascadia earthquake
    d. 1509 Istanbul earthquake

24. _____ refers to the phenomena of the physical world, and also to life in general. _____ is also generally distinguished from the supernatural. It ranges in scale from the subatomic to the galactic.

a. 1700 Cascadia earthquake
b. 1703 Genroku earthquake
c. 1509 Istanbul earthquake
d. Nature

25. An _____ is a usually dry creek bed or gulch that temporarily fills with water after a heavy rain, or seasonally, natural or man-made and usually applies to a mountainous desert environment.
   a. AL 129-1
   b. AL 333
   c. AASHTO Soil Classification System
   d. Arroyo

26. _____ secures a definite available depth for navigation; and the discharge of the river generally is amply sufficient for maintaining the impounded waterlevel, as well as providing the necessary water for locking.
   a. 1509 Istanbul earthquake
   b. 1703 Genroku earthquake
   c. 1700 Cascadia earthquake
   d. Channelization

27. A _____ is a rapid flooding of geomorphic low-lying areas, rivers and streams, caused by the intense rainfall associated with a thunderstorm, or multiple training thunderstorms.
   a. 1509 Istanbul earthquake
   b. 1703 Genroku earthquake
   c. Flash flood
   d. 1700 Cascadia earthquake

28. _____ is the total length of all the streams and rivers in a drainage basin divided by the total area of the drainage basin.
   a. 1509 Istanbul earthquake
   b. 1703 Genroku earthquake
   c. Drainage density
   d. 1700 Cascadia earthquake

29. The _____ is the second-longest named river in North America, with a length of 2320 miles from Lake Itasca to the Gulf of Mexico. It drains most of the area between the Rocky Mountains and the Appalachian Mountains, except for the areas drained by Hudson Bay via the Red River of the North, the Great Lakes and the Rio Grande.
   a. 1703 Genroku earthquake
   b. 1700 Cascadia earthquake
   c. 1509 Istanbul earthquake
   d. Mississippi River

30. The _____ is a federal agency made up of some 34,600 civilian and 650 military men and women. The Corps' mission is to provide engineering services to the United States. The _____. The _____ is organized geographically into eight permanent divisions, one provisional division, and one provisional district. They are defined by watershed boundaries for civil works projects, and by political boundaries for military projects.
   a. Amblypoda
   b. Ambulocetus
   c. U.S. Army Corps of Engineers
   d. Andrija Mohorovičić

31. The _____ of a material is defined as its mass per unit volume:

$$\rho = \frac{m}{V}$$

Different materials usually have different densities, so _____ is an important concept regarding buoyancy, metal purity and packaging.

In some cases _____ is expressed as the dimensionless quantities specific gravity or relative _____, in which case it is expressed in multiples of the _____ of some other standard material, usually water or air.

Chapter 5. Rivers and Flooding 51

In a well-known story, Archimedes was given the task of determining whether King Hiero's goldsmith was embezzling gold during the manufacture of a wreath dedicated to the gods and replacing it with another, cheaper alloy.

- a. 1700 Cascadia earthquake
- b. Density
- c. 1509 Istanbul earthquake
- d. Particle density

32. _____ is a general term for the plant life of a region; it refers to the ground cover provided by plants, and is, by far, the most abundant biotic element of the biosphere. Primeval redwood forests, coastal mangrove stands, sphagnum bogs, desert soil crusts, roadside weed patches, wheat fields, cultivated gardens and lawns; are all encompassed by the term _____.

- a. 1700 Cascadia earthquake
- b. 1509 Istanbul earthquake
- c. 1703 Genroku earthquake
- d. Vegetation

33. The State of _____ is a state located in the southwestern region of the United States. The capital and largest city is Phoenix. The second largest city is Tucson, followed by the four Phoenix-area conurbation cities of Mesa, Glendale, Chandler, and Scottsdale.

- a. AL 129-1
- b. Kaibab Plateau
- c. AASHTO Soil Classification System
- d. Arizona

34. _____ is a term used in urban planning for a system of land-use regulation in various parts of the world, including North America, the United Kingdom, and Australia.

- a. 1703 Genroku earthquake
- b. 1700 Cascadia earthquake
- c. 1509 Istanbul earthquake
- d. Zoning

35. _____ (December 16, 1863, Madrid - September 26, 1952, Rome), was a philosopher, essayist, poet, and novelist.

A lifelong Spanish citizen, Santayana was raised and educated in the United States, wrote in English and is generally considered an American man of letters, although, of his nearly 89 years, he spent only 39 in the U.S. He is perhaps best known as an aphorist, and for the oft-misquoted remark, 'Those who cannot remember the past, are condemned to repeat it,' (hence, 'Santayana's Aphorism on Repetitive Consequences') from Reason in Common Sense, the first volume of his The Life of Reason.

Born Jorge Agustín Nicolás Ruíz de Santayana y Borrás, he spent his early childhood in Ávila, Spain.

- a. Milutin Milankovié‡
- b. Pinochet
- c. Cecil John Rhodes
- d. George Santayana

36. The _____ is a river in Ventura County, California. The river forms at the confluence of Matilija Creek and North Fork Matilija Creek, 15 miles upstream from the Pacific Ocean. San Antonio Creek joins the river halfway to the ocean and Coyote Creek does the same a couple of miles downstream.

- a. 1509 Istanbul earthquake
- b. 1703 Genroku earthquake
- c. 1700 Cascadia earthquake
- d. Ventura River

Chapter 5. Rivers and Flooding

37. _____ is the study of the past, particularly using written records. New technology, such as photography, and computer text files now sometimes complement traditional archival sources. _____ is a field of research producing a continuous narrative and a systematic analysis of past events of importance to the human race.
   a. 1700 Cascadia earthquake
   b. History
   c. Absolute time
   d. 1509 Istanbul earthquake

38. _____ ecology is the study of renewing a degraded, damaged, or destroyed ecosystem through active human intervention. It specifically refers to the scientific study that has evolved as recently as the 1980's.
   a. Restoration
   b. 1509 Istanbul earthquake
   c. 1700 Cascadia earthquake
   d. 1703 Genroku earthquake

39. The _____ is a river in south-central Florida, USA.
   a. 1703 Genroku earthquake
   b. 1700 Cascadia earthquake
   c. 1509 Istanbul earthquake
   d. Kissimmee River

40. _____ is rock or other material used to armor shorelines or stream banks against water erosion
   a. 1509 Istanbul earthquake
   b. 1700 Cascadia earthquake
   c. 1703 Genroku earthquake
   d. Riprap

41. A _____ is a natural or artificial slope or wall, usually earthen and often parallels the course of a river.
   a. 1509 Istanbul earthquake
   b. Levee
   c. 1700 Cascadia earthquake
   d. 1703 Genroku earthquake

42. The _____ is an agency of the United States Department of Homeland Security, initially created by Presidential Order on April 1, 1979.) The purpose of _____ is to coordinate the response to a disaster which has occurred in the United States and which overwhelms the resources of local and state authorities. The governor of the state in which the disaster occurred must declare a state of emergency and formally request from the President that _____ and the federal government respond to the disaster.
   a. FEMA
   b. 1700 Cascadia earthquake
   c. 1703 Genroku earthquake
   d. 1509 Istanbul earthquake

43. The _____ is an agency of the United States Department of Homeland Security. It's purpose is to coordinate the response to a disaster which has occurred in the United States and which overwhelms the resouces of local ands state authorities.
   a. Ambulocetus
   b. Andrija MohoroviÄ iÄ‡
   c. Federal Emergency Management Agency
   d. Amblypoda

44. _____ is the process of breaking a complex topic or substance into smaller parts to gain a better understanding of it. The technique has been applied in the study of mathematics and logic since before Aristotle, though _____ as a formal concept is a relatively recent development.

As a formal concept, the method has variously been ascribed by Ibn al-Haytham, Descartes (Discourse on the Method), Galileo, and Isaac Newton, as a practical method of physical discovery.

a. AL 129-1 b. Analysis
c. AASHTO Soil Classification System d. AL 333

Chapter 6. Landslides and Related Phenomena

1. A _____ is a geological phenomenon which includes a wide range of ground movement, such as rock falls, deep failure of slopes and shallow debris flows. Although gravity's action on an over-steepened slope is the primary reason for a _____, there are other contributing factors affecting the original slope stability.
   a. 1703 Genroku earthquake
   b. 1700 Cascadia earthquake
   c. 1509 Istanbul earthquake
   d. Landslide

2. _____ is the geomorphic process by which soil, regolith, and rock move downslope under the force of gravity. Types of _____ include creep, slides, flows, topples, and falls, each with their own characteristic features, and take place over timescales from seconds to years. _____ occurs on both terrestrial and submarine slopes, and has been observed on Earth, Mars, and Venus.
   a. 1509 Istanbul earthquake
   b. 1700 Cascadia earthquake
   c. 1703 Genroku earthquake
   d. Mass wasting

3. In geology, engineering, and surveying, _____ is the motion of a surface as it shifts downward relative to a datum such as sea-level. The opposite of _____ is uplift, which results in an increase in elevation. In meteorology, _____ refers to the downward movement of air.
   a. 1700 Cascadia earthquake
   b. 1509 Istanbul earthquake
   c. 1703 Genroku earthquake
   d. Subsidence

4. _____ are very large slides of snow or rock down a mountainside, caused when a buildup of snow is released down a slope, and is one of the major dangers faced in the mountains.
   a. AL 333
   b. Avalanches
   c. AL 129-1
   d. AASHTO Soil Classification System

5. _____, is the slow downward progression of rock and soil down a low grade slope; it can also refer to slow deformation of such materials as a result of prolonged pressure and stress.
   a. Creep
   b. 1509 Istanbul earthquake
   c. 1703 Genroku earthquake
   d. 1700 Cascadia earthquake

6. _____ refers to quantities of rock falling freely from a cliff face.
   a. 1509 Istanbul earthquake
   b. 1703 Genroku earthquake
   c. 1700 Cascadia earthquake
   d. Rockfall

7. The field of _____ encompasses the analysis of static and dynamic stability of slopes of earth and rock-fill dams, slopes of other types of embankments, excavated slopes, and natural slopes in soil and soft rock.
   a. Slope stability
   b. 1509 Istanbul earthquake
   c. 1703 Genroku earthquake
   d. 1700 Cascadia earthquake

8. _____ is a form of mass wasting event that occurs when loosely consolidated materials or rock layers move a short distance down a slope. When the movement occurs in soil, there is often a distinctive rotational movement to the mass, that cuts vertically through bedding planes.
   a. 1700 Cascadia earthquake
   b. Slump
   c. 1509 Istanbul earthquake
   d. 1703 Genroku earthquake

9. An _____ is a usually dry creek bed or gulch that temporarily fills with water after a heavy rain, or seasonally, natural or man-made and usually applies to a mountainous desert environment.

Chapter 6. Landslides and Related Phenomena

a. AASHTO Soil Classification System
b. AL 129-1
c. Arroyo
d. AL 333

10. In physics, a _____ is that which can cause an object with mass to accelerate. _____ has both magnitude and direction, making it a vector quantity. According to Newton's second law, an object with constant mass will accelerate in proportion to the net _____ acting upon it and in inverse proportion to its mass.
   a. Newton
   b. 1509 Istanbul earthquake
   c. Force
   d. 1700 Cascadia earthquake

11. _____ (FoS) can mean either the fraction of structural capability over that required torque, bending moment or a combination) to which a component or assembly will be subjected. The two senses of the term are completely different in that the first is a measure of the reliability of a particular design, while the second is a requirement imposed by law, standard, specification, contract or custom. Careful engineers refer to the first sense as a _____, or, to be explicit, a realized _____, and the second sense as a design factor, but usage is inconsistent and confusing, so engineers need to be aware of both.
   a. 1703 Genroku earthquake
   b. Factor of safety
   c. 1509 Istanbul earthquake
   d. 1700 Cascadia earthquake

12. _____ is the name for loose bodies of sediment that have been deposited or built up at the bottom of a low grade slope or against a barrier on that slope, transported by gravity. The deposits that collect at the foot of a steep slope or cliff are also known by the same name.
   a. 1509 Istanbul earthquake
   b. 1703 Genroku earthquake
   c. 1700 Cascadia earthquake
   d. Colluvium

13. _____ are downslope, viscous flows of saturated, fine-grained materials, that move at any speed from slow to fast. Typically, they can move at speeds from .17 to 20 km/h. Though these are a lot like mudflows, overall they are slower moving and are covered with solid material carried along by flow from within.
   a. Earthflows
   b. AASHTO Soil Classification System
   c. AL 333
   d. AL 129-1

14. _____ is a fine-grained sedimentary rock whose original constituents were clays or muds. It is characterized by thin laminae breaking with an irregular curving fracture, often splintery and usually parallel to the often-indistinguishable bedding plane.
   a. 1703 Genroku earthquake
   b. 1509 Istanbul earthquake
   c. 1700 Cascadia earthquake
   d. Shale

15. _____ is the process of breaking a complex topic or substance into smaller parts to gain a better understanding of it. The technique has been applied in the study of mathematics and logic since before Aristotle, though _____ as a formal concept is a relatively recent development.

As a formal concept, the method has variously been ascribed by Ibn al-Haytham, Descartes (Discourse on the Method), Galileo, and Isaac Newton, as a practical method of physical discovery.

   a. AASHTO Soil Classification System
   b. AL 129-1
   c. AL 333
   d. Analysis

Chapter 6. Landslides and Related Phenomena

16. _____ is the third or vertical dimension of land surface. When _____ is described underwater, the term bathymetry is used.
    a. 1509 Istanbul earthquake
    b. Terrain
    c. 1700 Cascadia earthquake
    d. 1703 Genroku earthquake

17. _____ is the study of Earth's surface features or those of other planets, moons, and asteroids
    a. 1509 Istanbul earthquake
    b. 1703 Genroku earthquake
    c. 1700 Cascadia earthquake
    d. Topography

18. _____ often refers to mudslides, mudflows, jökulhlaups, or debris avalanches. They consist primarily of geological material mixed with water. They may be generated when hillside colluvium or landslide material becomes rapidly saturated with water and flows into a channel.
    a. 1700 Cascadia earthquake
    b. 1703 Genroku earthquake
    c. 1509 Istanbul earthquake
    d. Debris flow

19. A _____ is the most rapid up to 80 km/h and fluid type of downhill mass wasting.
    a. Mudflow
    b. 1703 Genroku earthquake
    c. 1509 Istanbul earthquake
    d. 1700 Cascadia earthquake

20. The _____ of an edge is $c_f(u, v) = c(u, v) - f(u, v)$. This defines a residual network denoted $G_f(V, E_f)$, giving the amount of available capacity. See that there can be an edge from u to v in the residual network, even though there is no edge from u to v in the original network.
    a. 1509 Istanbul earthquake
    b. Residual capacity
    c. 1703 Genroku earthquake
    d. 1700 Cascadia earthquake

21. The _____ is the surface where the water pressure is equal to atmospheric pressure. A large amount of water within a body of sand or rock below the _____ is called an aquifer, and the ability of rocks to store such groundwater is dependent on their porosity and permeability.
    a. Water table
    b. 1703 Genroku earthquake
    c. 1509 Istanbul earthquake
    d. 1700 Cascadia earthquake

22. A _____ is a section of a river of relatively steep gradient causing an increase in water flow and turbulence. A _____ is a hydrological feature between a run and a cascade. It is characterized by the river becoming shallower and having some rocks exposed above the flow surface.
    a. 1700 Cascadia earthquake
    b. 1509 Istanbul earthquake
    c. Rapid
    d. 1703 Genroku earthquake

23. _____ can be a change from a gas to a liquid through condensation, usually by cooling, or a change from a solid to a liquid through melting, usually by heating or by grinding and blending with another liquid to induce dissolution.
    a. Liquefaction
    b. 1509 Istanbul earthquake
    c. 1703 Genroku earthquake
    d. 1700 Cascadia earthquake

24. _____ is a unique form of highly sensitive marine clay, with the tendency to change from a relatively stiff condition to a liquid mass when it is disturbed.

Chapter 6. Landslides and Related Phenomena 57

Undisturbed _____ resembles a water-saturated gel. When a mass of _____ undergoes sufficient stress, however, it instantly turns into a flowing ooze, a process known as liquefaction.

a. 1700 Cascadia earthquake
b. 1509 Istanbul earthquake
c. 1703 Genroku earthquake
d. Quick clay

25. _____ is a term used to describe a group of hydrous aluminium phyllosilicate minerals, that are typically less than 2 micrometres in diameter. _____ consists of a variety of phyllosilicate minerals rich in silicon and aluminium oxides and hydroxides which include variable amounts of structural water. Clays are generally formed by the chemical weathering of silicate-bearing rocks by carbonic acid but some are formed by hydrothermal activity.

a. 1700 Cascadia earthquake
b. 1703 Genroku earthquake
c. 1509 Istanbul earthquake
d. Clay

26. There are two distinct views on the meaning of _____. One view is that _____ is part of the fundamental structure of the universe, a dimension in which events occur in sequence, and _____ itself is something that can be measured. A contrasting view is that _____ is part of the fundamental intellectual structure in which _____, rather than being an objective thing to be measured, is part of the mental measuring system.

a. Time
b. 1703 Genroku earthquake
c. 1700 Cascadia earthquake
d. 1509 Istanbul earthquake

27. _____ , officially the Republic of _____ , is a country in western South America. It is bordered on the north by Ecuador and Colombia, on the east by Brazil, on the southeast by Bolivia, on the south by Chile, and on the west by the Pacific Ocean.

Peruvian territory was home to the Norte Chico civilization, one of the oldest in the world, and to the Inca Empire, the largest state in Pre-Columbian America.

a. Peru
b. Plug-in hybrid electric vehicle
c. Norman Borlaug
d. Kingdom of Cambodia

28. A _____ is a bipedal primate belonging to the mammalian species Homo sapiens in the family Hominidae. Compared to other living organisms on Earth, a _____ has a highly developed brain capable of abstract reasoning, language, and introspection.

a. 1509 Istanbul earthquake
b. 1700 Cascadia earthquake
c. 1703 Genroku earthquake
d. Human

29. _____ , is the second largest city of Brazil, behind São Paulo, and the third largest city in the continent, behind São Paulo and Buenos Aires. The city is capital of the state of _____. It was the capital of Brazil for almost two centuries, from 1763 to 1822 while it was a Portuguese colony and from 1822 to 1960 as an independent nation.

a. Rio de Janeiro
b. Andrija Mohorovičić
c. Amblypoda
d. Ambulocetus

Chapter 6. Landslides and Related Phenomena

30. In agriculture, _____ is the process of gathering mature crops from the fields. Reaping is the _____ of grain crops. The harvest marks the end of the growing season, or the growing cycle for a particular crop. _____ in general usage includes an immediate post-harvest handling, all of the actions taken immediately after removing the crop—cooling, sorting, cleaning, packing—up to the point of further on-farm processing, or shipping to the wholesale or consumer market.
    a. Harvesting
    b. 1703 Genroku earthquake
    c. 1509 Istanbul earthquake
    d. 1700 Cascadia earthquake

31. _____ is the increase in the population of cities in proportion to the region's rural population. _____ is studied in terms of its effects on the ecology and economy of a region.
    a. AASHTO Soil Classification System
    b. AL 333
    c. Urbanization
    d. AL 129-1

32. A _____ is a barrier across flowing water that obstructs, directs or slows down the flow, often creating a reservoir, lake or impoundment.
    a. 1700 Cascadia earthquake
    b. 1703 Genroku earthquake
    c. 1509 Istanbul earthquake
    d. Dam

33. _____ is a concept that denotes the precise probability of specific eventualities. Technically, the notion of _____ is independent from the notion of value and, as such, eventualities may have both beneficial and adverse consequences. However, in general usage the convention is to focus only on potential negative impact to some characteristic of value that may arise from a future event.
    a. 1703 Genroku earthquake
    b. 1700 Cascadia earthquake
    c. 1509 Istanbul earthquake
    d. Risk

34. _____ is the natural or artificial removal of surface and sub-surface water from a given area. Many agricultural soils need _____ to improve production or to manage water supplies.
    a. 1703 Genroku earthquake
    b. 1509 Istanbul earthquake
    c. 1700 Cascadia earthquake
    d. Drainage

35. The _____ region is the largest area of natural vegetation remaining on the Palos Verdes Peninsula. Though once slated for development (and in fact the projected route of Crenshaw Boulevard through the area still shows on many maps), the area is geologically unstable and is unsuitable for building.

    The geographical location and geological history of the peninsula make the remaining habitat extremely valuable for ecological and other scientific reasons.

    a. Portuguese Bend
    b. 1509 Istanbul earthquake
    c. 1700 Cascadia earthquake
    d. 1703 Genroku earthquake

36. The _____ is the largest area of natural vegetation remaining on the Palos Verdes Peninsula. Though once slated for development, the area is geologically unstable and is unsuitable for building.
    a. 1509 Istanbul earthquake
    b. 1703 Genroku earthquake
    c. 1700 Cascadia earthquake
    d. Portuguese Bend landslide

Chapter 6. Landslides and Related Phenomena

37. A _____ is any system of biological or technical nature deployed by an individual or group to inform of a future danger. Its purpose is to enable the deployer of the _____ to prepare for the danger and act accordingly to mitigate against or avoid it.
   a. 1509 Istanbul earthquake
   b. 1700 Cascadia earthquake
   c. 1703 Genroku earthquake
   d. Warning system

38. _____ is the largest state of the United States of America by area; it is situated in the northwest extremity of the North American continent, with Canada to the east, the Arctic Ocean to the north, and the Pacific Ocean to the west and south, with Russia further west across the Bering Strait. As of 2007, the population was 683,478 with approximately 50% residing along the Anchorage metropolitan areas.

    The area that became _____ was purchased from the Russian Empire after Western Union discontinued construction of its first electric telegraph line which ran from California, up the coast of North America, across the Bering Strait, continuing to Moscow and into the European Telegraph network.

   a. Alaska
   b. AASHTO Soil Classification System
   c. AL 129-1
   d. Prudhoe Bay

39. A _____ is a natural depression or hole in the surface topography caused by the removal of soil or bedrock, often both, by water. They may vary in size from less than a meter to several hundred meters both in diameter and depth, and vary in form from soil-lined bowls to bedrock-edged chasms.
   a. 1703 Genroku earthquake
   b. 1700 Cascadia earthquake
   c. 1509 Istanbul earthquake
   d. Sinkhole

40. The _____ is a diverse scientific, social, and political movement for addressing the concerns of environmentalism. The _____ is represented by a range of organizations, from the large to grassroots. Due to its large membership, varying and strong beliefs, and occasionally speculative nature, the _____ is not always united in its goals.
   a. Ambulocetus
   b. Amblypoda
   c. Andrija Mohorovičić
   d. Environmental movement

41. _____ is a fossil fuel formed in swamp ecosystems where plant remains were saved by water and mud from oxidization and biodegradation. It is a sedimentary rock, but the harder forms, such as anthracite _____, can be regarded as metamorphic rocks because of later exposure to elevated temperature and pressure. It is composed primarily of carbon along with assorted other elements, including sulfur.
   a. 1509 Istanbul earthquake
   b. 1703 Genroku earthquake
   c. 1700 Cascadia earthquake
   d. Coal

42. _____ is commonly practiced where a coal seam outcrops a hilly terrain. It removes the overburden above the coal seam and then creates a bench arounf the hill.
   a. 1700 Cascadia earthquake
   b. 1703 Genroku earthquake
   c. 1509 Istanbul earthquake
   d. Contour strip mining

43. _____ is the extraction of valuable minerals or other geological materials from the earth, usually from an ore body, vein, or seam. Any material that cannot be grown from agricultural processes, or created artificially in a laboratory or factory, is usually extracted from the earth by this method.

Chapter 6. Landslides and Related Phenomena

a. 1509 Istanbul earthquake
c. Mining
b. 1703 Genroku earthquake
d. 1700 Cascadia earthquake

44. A _____ is a body of water, not part of the ocean, that is larger and deeper than a pond.
a. Lake
c. 1703 Genroku earthquake
b. 1700 Cascadia earthquake
d. 1509 Istanbul earthquake

Chapter 7. Earthquakes and Related Phenomena

1. _____ is a state on the West Coast of the United States, along the Pacific Ocean. It is bordered by Oregon to the north, Nevada to the east, Arizona to the southeast, and to the south the Mexican state of Baja _____. _____ is the most populous U.S. state.
   - a. 1700 Cascadia earthquake
   - b. 1703 Genroku earthquake
   - c. 1509 Istanbul earthquake
   - d. California

2. A _____ is an urban area with a high population and a particular administrative, legal, or historical status.

   Large industrialized cities generally have advanced systems for sanitation, utilities, land usage, housing, and transportation and more. This close proximity greatly facilitates interaction between people and firms, benefiting both parties in the process.
   - a. 1703 Genroku earthquake
   - b. 1700 Cascadia earthquake
   - c. 1509 Istanbul earthquake
   - d. City

3. An _____ is the result from the sudden release of stored energy in the Earth's crust that creates seismic waves. At the Earth's surface, earthquakes may manifest themselves by a shaking or displacement of the ground. An _____ is caused by tectonic plates getting stuck and putting a strain on the ground. The strain becomes so great that rocks give way by breaking and sliding along fault planes.
   - a. AASHTO Soil Classification System
   - b. Earthquake
   - c. AL 333
   - d. AL 129-1

4. _____ (æ—¥æœ¬ Nihon or Nippon making it an archipelago. The largest islands are HonshÅ«, HokkaidÅ, KyÅ«shÅ« and Shikoku, together accounting for 97% of _____'s land area. Most of the islands are mountainous, many volcanic; for example, _____'s highest peak, Mount Fuji, is a volcano.
   - a. Kenya
   - b. Kabul
   - c. Java
   - d. Japan

5. _____ (ç¥žæˆ¸ã‚, KÅ be-shi For most of its history the area was never a single political entity, even during the Tokugawa Period, when the port was controlled directly by the Tokugawa Shogunate. _____ did not exist in its current form until its founding in 1889. Its name comes from 'kanbe' HyÅ go Port in the 19th century The Bund in _____ around 1890

   Stone artifacts and tools found in western _____ demonstrate that the area was populated at least from the JÅ mon period.
   - a. Peninsula
   - b. Japan
   - c. Kobe
   - d. Korean War

6. The United Mexican States, commonly known as _____, is a federal constitutional republic in North America. It is bordered on the north by the United States; on the south and west by the North Pacific Ocean; on the southeast by Guatemala, Belize, and the Caribbean Sea; and on the east by the Gulf of _____. The United Mexican States are a federation comprising thirty-one states and a federal district, the capital _____ City, whose metropolitan area is one of the world's most populous.
   - a. Amblypoda
   - b. Andrija MohoroviÄiÄ‡
   - c. Ambulocetus
   - d. Mexico

Chapter 7. Earthquakes and Related Phenomena

7. _____ is the capital city of Mexico. It is the most important economic, industrial and cultural center in the country, and the most populous city with over 8,836,045 inhabitants in 2008. Greater _____ incorporates 59 adjacent municipalities of Mexico State and 1 municipality of the state of Hidalgo, according to the most recent definition agreed upon by the federal and state governments.
   a. 1703 Genroku earthquake
   b. Mexico City
   c. 1509 Istanbul earthquake
   d. 1700 Cascadia earthquake

8. Faults are planar rock fractures, which show evidence of relative movement. Large faults within the Earth's crust are the result of shear motion and active _____ zones are the causal locations of most earthquakes. Earthquakes are caused by energy release during rapid slippage along faults.
   a. Fault
   b. 1509 Istanbul earthquake
   c. 1703 Genroku earthquake
   d. 1700 Cascadia earthquake

9. A _____ is a planar rock fracture, which show evidence of relative movement. Large ones within the Earth's crust are the result of shear motion and active fault zones are the causal locations of most earthquakes. Earthquakes are caused by energy release during rapid slippage along a fault.
   a. Geologic fault
   b. 1509 Istanbul earthquake
   c. 1703 Genroku earthquake
   d. 1700 Cascadia earthquake

10. Although the theory of plate tectonics well describes the mechanisms for interplate earthquakes very large _____, earthquake within plates can inflict heavy damage on towns and cities.
    a. AL 129-1
    b. Intraplate earthquakes
    c. AL 333
    d. AASHTO Soil Classification System

11. _____ is a Northern California mountain with elevation 3,786 feet and located at approximately 37.114° N, 121.846 W in the Santa Cruz Mountains. The peak is located on private property, about 11 miles west of Morgan Hill and within the boundaries of Santa Clara County.
    a. 1703 Genroku earthquake
    b. Loma Prieta
    c. 1509 Istanbul earthquake
    d. 1700 Cascadia earthquake

12. The _____ was a major earthquake affecting the greater San Francisco Bay Area of California. It occurred on Tuesday October 17, 1989 at 5:04 p.m. and measured 6.9 on the Moment magnitude scale. It lasted approximately 15 seconds and its epicenter was at located in Forest of Nisene Marks State Park, in the Santa Cruz Mountains.
    a. Loma Prieta earthquake
    b. 1509 Istanbul earthquake
    c. 1703 Genroku earthquake
    d. 1700 Cascadia earthquake

13. The _____ occurred on January 17, 1994 at 4:30:55 AM Pacific Standard Time in the city of Los Angeles, California. It had a "moderate" moment magnitude of 6.7, but the ground acceleration was the highest ever instrumentally recorded in an urban area in North America. Seventy-two people died as a result of the earthquake and over 11,000 were injured. In addition, the earthquake caused an estimated $12.5 billion in damage, making it one of the costliest natural disasters in U.S. history.
    a. 1700 Cascadia earthquake
    b. 1509 Istanbul earthquake
    c. 1703 Genroku earthquake
    d. Northridge earthquake

Chapter 7. Earthquakes and Related Phenomena

14. The _____ is a geological fault that runs a length of roughly 800 miles through western and southern California in the United States. The fault, a right-lateral strike-slip fault, marks a transform boundary between the Pacific Plate and the North American Plate.
    a. 1700 Cascadia earthquake
    b. San Andreas fault
    c. 1703 Genroku earthquake
    d. 1509 Istanbul earthquake

15. _____ is the capital and largest city of Spain. It is the third-most populous municipality in the European Union after London and Berlin, and the fourth-most populous urban area in the European Union after Paris, London, and the Ruhr Area.

    The city is located on the river Manzanares both in the centre of the country and Community of _____; this community is bordered by the autonomous communities of Castile and León and Castile-La Mancha.

    a. 1703 Genroku earthquake
    b. 1700 Cascadia earthquake
    c. Madrid
    d. 1509 Istanbul earthquake

16. The _____ is a physiographic feature in the United States. It is essentially a northward continuation of the fluvial sediments of the Mississippi River Delta to its confluence with the Ohio River. The embayment is a topographically low-lying basin that is filled with Cretaceous to recent sediments.
    a. 1509 Istanbul earthquake
    b. 1700 Cascadia earthquake
    c. 1703 Genroku earthquake
    d. Mississippi Embayment

17. Seismology is the scientific study of earthquakes and the propagation of elastic waves through the Earth. The field also includes studies of earthquake effects, such as tsunamis as well as diverse _____ sources such as volcanic, tectonic, oceanic, atmospheric, and artificial processes (such as explosions.) A related field that uses geology to infer information regarding past earthquakes is paleoseismology.
    a. 1703 Genroku earthquake
    b. 1700 Cascadia earthquake
    c. 1509 Istanbul earthquake
    d. Seismic

18. A _____ travels through the Earth, most often as the result of a tectonic earthquake, sometimes from an explosion. They are also continually excited by the pounding of ocean waves and the wind.
    a. 1700 Cascadia earthquake
    b. Seismic wave
    c. 1703 Genroku earthquake
    d. 1509 Istanbul earthquake

19. A _____ is a disturbance that propagates through space or spacetime, transferring energy and momentum and sometimes angular momentum.
    a. 1703 Genroku earthquake
    b. 1700 Cascadia earthquake
    c. 1509 Istanbul earthquake
    d. Wave

20. _____ are planar rock fractures, which show evidence of relative movement. Large faults within the Earth's crust are the result of shear motion and active fault zones are the causal locations of most earthquakes. Earthquakes are caused by energy release during rapid slippage along faults.
    a. 1703 Genroku earthquake
    b. 1509 Istanbul earthquake
    c. 1700 Cascadia earthquake
    d. Strike-slip faults

Chapter 7. Earthquakes and Related Phenomena

21. An _____ is a fault which has had displacement or seismic activity during the geologically recent period. In the United States, an _____ is generally defined as a fault which displaced earth materials during the Holocene Epoch. An _____ is the most common source of earthquakes and tectonic movements.
    a. AL 129-1
    b. AL 333
    c. AASHTO Soil Classification System
    d. Active fault

22. _____ looks at geologic sediments and rocks, for signs of ancient earthquakes. It is used to supplement seismic monitoring, for the calculation of seismic hazard. _____ is usually restricted to geologic regimes that have undergone continuous sediment creation for the last few thousand years, such as swamps, lakes, river beds and shorelines.
    a. 1509 Istanbul earthquake
    b. Paleoseismology
    c. 1703 Genroku earthquake
    d. 1700 Cascadia earthquake

23. _____ is a field of study within geology concerned generally with the structures within the crust of the Earth, or other planets, and particularly with the forces and movements that have operated in a region to create these structures.
    a. Tectonics
    b. 1700 Cascadia earthquake
    c. 1703 Genroku earthquake
    d. 1509 Istanbul earthquake

24. _____, is the slow downward progression of rock and soil down a low grade slope; it can also refer to slow deformation of such materials as a result of prolonged pressure and stress.
    a. 1700 Cascadia earthquake
    b. Creep
    c. 1703 Genroku earthquake
    d. 1509 Istanbul earthquake

25. _____ are waves that have vibrations along or parallel to their direction of travel. They include waves in which the motion of the medium is in the same direction as the motion of the wave.
    a. 1509 Istanbul earthquake
    b. Compressional waves
    c. 1703 Genroku earthquake
    d. 1700 Cascadia earthquake

26. The _____ is the point on the Earth's surface that is directly above the point where an earthquake or other underground explosion originates or focus. It is directly above the hypocenter the actual location of the energy released inside the earth and usually suffers the maximum destruction.
    a. AASHTO Soil Classification System
    b. AL 129-1
    c. AL 333
    d. Epicenter

27. _____ are essentially horizontally polarized shear waves guided by an elastic layer, which is "welded" to an elastic half space on one side and borders vacuum on the other side.
    a. Love waves
    b. 1700 Cascadia earthquake
    c. 1703 Genroku earthquake
    d. 1509 Istanbul earthquake

28. _____ are a type of surface wave. They are associated on the Earth with earthquakes and subterranean movement of magma, or with any other source of seismic energy, such as an explosion or even a sledgehammer impact, and are also the form of ocean waves.
    a. 1700 Cascadia earthquake
    b. 1509 Istanbul earthquake
    c. 1703 Genroku earthquake
    d. Rayleigh waves

29. In physics, _____ can refer to a mechanical wave that propagates along the interface between differing media, usually two fluids with different densities. A _____ can also be an electromagnetic wave guided by a refractive index gradient.
   a. 1509 Istanbul earthquake
   b. 1703 Genroku earthquake
   c. 1700 Cascadia earthquake
   d. Surface wave

30. _____ is the measurement of the number of occurrences of a repeated event per unit of time. It is also defined as the rate of change of phase of a sinusoidal waveform.
   a. 1509 Istanbul earthquake
   b. 1700 Cascadia earthquake
   c. 1703 Genroku earthquake
   d. Frequency

31. The _____ is one of the two main types of elastic body waves, so named because they move through the body of an object, unlike surface waves. It moves as a shear or transverse wave, so motion is perpendicular to the direction of wave propagation: S-shaped, like waves in a rope, as opposed to waves moving through a slinky, the P-wave.
   a. 1703 Genroku earthquake
   b. 1509 Istanbul earthquake
   c. 1700 Cascadia earthquake
   d. S waves

32. A type of seismic wave is one of the two main types of elastic body waves, so named because they move through the body of an object, unlike surface waves. The _____ moves as a shear or transverse wave, so motion is perpendicular to the direction of wave propagation. The wave moves through elastic mediums, and the main restoring force comes from shear effects.
   a. 1703 Genroku earthquake
   b. 1700 Cascadia earthquake
   c. 1509 Istanbul earthquake
   d. S-wave

33. The _____ scale, or more correctly local magnitude ML scale, assigns a single number to quantify the amount of seismic energy released by an earthquake. It is a base-10 logarithmic scale obtained by calculating the logarithm of the combined horizontal amplitude of the largest displacement from zero on a seismometer output
   a. 1509 Istanbul earthquake
   b. 1703 Genroku earthquake
   c. Richter magnitude
   d. 1700 Cascadia earthquake

34. A _____ is used by seismologists to measure and record the size and force of seismic waves.
   a. 1509 Istanbul earthquake
   b. 1703 Genroku earthquake
   c. Seismograph
   d. 1700 Cascadia earthquake

35. Peak _____ is a measure of earthquake acceleration. Unlike the Richter magnitude scale, it is not a measure of the total size of the earthquake, but rather how hard the earth shakes in a given geographic area.
   a. 1703 Genroku earthquake
   b. 1509 Istanbul earthquake
   c. 1700 Cascadia earthquake
   d. Ground acceleration

36. The _____ is a scale used for measuring the intensity of an earthquake. The scale quantifies the effects of an earthquake on the Earth's surface, humans, objects of nature, and man-made structures on a scale of 1 through 12, with 1 denoting a weak earthquake and 12 one that causes almost complete destruction.
   a. 1703 Genroku earthquake
   b. 1509 Istanbul earthquake
   c. 1700 Cascadia earthquake
   d. Mercalli intensity scale

37. _____ was introduced in 1979 by Tom Hanks and Hiroo Kanamori as a successor to the Richter scale and is used by seismologists to compare the energy released by earthquakes.
   a. 1700 Cascadia earthquake
   b. 1703 Genroku earthquake
   c. Moment magnitude
   d. 1509 Istanbul earthquake

38. An _____ is an earthquake that occurs after a previous earthquake. An _____ is in the same region of the main shock but is always of smaller magnitude. It occurs with a pattern that follows Omori's law. Omori's law, or more correctly the modified Omori's law, is an empirical relation for the temporal decay of _____ rates.
   a. AL 129-1
   b. AL 333
   c. AASHTO Soil Classification System
   d. Aftershock

39. _____ are earthquakes in the same region of the central shock but of smaller magnitude and which occur with a pattern that follows Omori's law.
   a. AASHTO Soil Classification System
   b. AL 129-1
   c. Aftershocks
   d. AL 333

40. In geology, the _____ theory was the first theory to satisfactorily explain earthquakes. The theory is that earthquake are the result of the _____ of previously stored elastic strain energy in the rocks on either side of the fault. In an interseismic period the earth's plates move relative to each other except at most plate boundaries where they are locked.
   a. AASHTO Soil Classification System
   b. Elastic rebound
   c. AL 333
   d. AL 129-1

41. _____ is a quantity used by earthquake seismologists to measure the size of an earthquake.
   a. 1703 Genroku earthquake
   b. Seismic moment
   c. 1509 Istanbul earthquake
   d. 1700 Cascadia earthquake

42. A _____ is a smaller earthquake preceding a much larger earthquake. Many scientists hope to use them to predict upcoming earthquakes.
   a. 1700 Cascadia earthquake
   b. 1703 Genroku earthquake
   c. 1509 Istanbul earthquake
   d. Foreshock

43. _____ is the pressure at some point within a fluid, such as water or air.

_____ occurs in one of two situations:

   1. an open condition, such as the ocean, a swimming pool, or the atmosphere; or
   2. a closed condition, such as a water line or a gas line.

Pressure in open conditions usually can be approximated as the pressure in 'static' or non-moving conditions (even in the ocean where there are waves and currents), because the motions create only negligible changes in the pressure. Such conditions conform with principles of fluid statics. The pressure at any given point of a non-moving (static) fluid is called the hydrostatic pressure.

   a. 1509 Istanbul earthquake
   b. 1700 Cascadia earthquake
   c. 1703 Genroku earthquake
   d. Fluid pressure

Chapter 7. Earthquakes and Related Phenomena

44. _____ is when a mass of water in a reservoir alters the pressure in the rock below, which can trigger earthquakes.
   a. 1509 Istanbul earthquake
   b. Reservoir induced seismicity
   c. 1700 Cascadia earthquake
   d. 1703 Genroku earthquake

45. A _____ is a bipedal primate belonging to the mammalian species Homo sapiens in the family Hominidae. Compared to other living organisms on Earth, a _____ has a highly developed brain capable of abstract reasoning, language, and introspection.
   a. 1703 Genroku earthquake
   b. Human
   c. 1700 Cascadia earthquake
   d. 1509 Istanbul earthquake

46. _____ is a concept for disposing of High Level Radioactive Waste from Nuclear reactors. The system seeks to place the waste as much as five kilometers beneath the surface of the Earth and relies primarily on the immense natural geological barrier to do most of the work of confining the waste safely and permanently so that it will never pose a threat to the environment.
   a. 1700 Cascadia earthquake
   b. 1703 Genroku earthquake
   c. 1509 Istanbul earthquake
   d. Deep waste disposal

47. A _____ is a landform that extends above the surrounding terrain in a limited area. A _____ is generally steeper than a hill, but there is no universally accepted standard definition for the height of a _____ or a hill although a _____ usually has an identifiable summit.
   a. 1509 Istanbul earthquake
   b. 1700 Cascadia earthquake
   c. 1703 Genroku earthquake
   d. Mountain

48. A _____ occurs as a result of the rapid release of energy from an uncontrolled nuclear reaction. The driving reaction may be nuclear fission, nuclear fusion or a multistage cascading combination of the two.
   a. 1703 Genroku earthquake
   b. 1509 Istanbul earthquake
   c. Nuclear explosion
   d. 1700 Cascadia earthquake

49. The _____ was a United States chemical weapons manufacturing center located in the Denver Metropolitan Area in Commerce City, Colorado. The site was operated by the United States Army throughout the later 20th century and was controversial among local residents until its closure.
   a. 1700 Cascadia earthquake
   b. 1703 Genroku earthquake
   c. 1509 Istanbul earthquake
   d. Rocky Mountain Arsenal

50. An _____ is a sudden increase in volume and release of energy in an extreme manner, usually with the generation of high temperatures and the release of gases. An _____ creates a shock wave.

Explosions do not commonly occur in nature.

   a. Explosion
   b. Chemical hazard
   c. AASHTO Soil Classification System
   d. AL 129-1

51. _____ is unwanted or undesired material.

Chapter 7. Earthquakes and Related Phenomena

a. 1700 Cascadia earthquake
c. 1509 Istanbul earthquake
b. 1703 Genroku earthquake
d. Waste

52. _____ is the largest state of the United States of America by area; it is situated in the northwest extremity of the North American continent, with Canada to the east, the Arctic Ocean to the north, and the Pacific Ocean to the west and south, with Russia further west across the Bering Strait. As of 2007, the population was 683,478 with approximately 50% residing along the Anchorage metropolitan areas.

The area that became _____ was purchased from the Russian Empire after Western Union discontinued construction of its first electric telegraph line which ran from California, up the coast of North America, across the Bering Strait, continuing to Moscow and into the European Telegraph network.

a. AL 129-1
c. Alaska
b. Prudhoe Bay
d. AASHTO Soil Classification System

53. _____ can be a change from a gas to a liquid through condensation, usually by cooling, or a change from a solid to a liquid through melting, usually by heating or by grinding and blending with another liquid to induce dissolution.
a. 1700 Cascadia earthquake
c. Liquefaction
b. 1703 Genroku earthquake
d. 1509 Istanbul earthquake

54. A _____ is a series of waves created when a body of water, such as an ocean, is rapidly displaced on a massive scale. Earthquakes, mass movements above or below water, volcanic eruptions and other underwater explosions, landslides, large meteorite impacts and testing with nuclear weapons at sea all have the potential to generate a _____. The effects of a _____ can range from unnoticeable to devastating.
a. 1703 Genroku earthquake
c. 1509 Istanbul earthquake
b. Tsunami
d. 1700 Cascadia earthquake

55. A _____ is a geological phenomenon which includes a wide range of ground movement, such as rock falls, deep failure of slopes and shallow debris flows. Although gravity's action on an over-steepened slope is the primary reason for a _____, there are other contributing factors affecting the original slope stability.
a. 1700 Cascadia earthquake
c. 1509 Istanbul earthquake
b. 1703 Genroku earthquake
d. Landslide

56. When building a house, regional _____ maps are used to find the best place to locate for earthquake shaking. Although greatly confused with its sister, seismic risk, _____ is the study of expected earthquake ground motions at any point on the earth.
a. 1703 Genroku earthquake
c. Seismic hazard
b. 1509 Istanbul earthquake
d. 1700 Cascadia earthquake

57. A _____ is a visual representation of an area--a symbolic depiction highlighting relationships between elements of that space such as objects, regions, and themes.

Many maps are static two-dimensional, geometrically accurate representations of three-dimensional space, while others are dynamic or interactive, even three-dimensional. Although most commonly used to depict geography, maps may represent any space, real or imagined, without regard to context or scale; e.g. Brain mapping, DNA mapping, and extraterrestrial mapping.

Chapter 7. Earthquakes and Related Phenomena

a. 1509 Istanbul earthquake
b. Cartography
c. 1700 Cascadia earthquake
d. Map

58. _____ is a concept that denotes the precise probability of specific eventualities. Technically, the notion of _____ is independent from the notion of value and, as such, eventualities may have both beneficial and adverse consequences. However, in general usage the convention is to focus only on potential negative impact to some characteristic of value that may arise from a future event.
a. Risk
b. 1509 Istanbul earthquake
c. 1703 Genroku earthquake
d. 1700 Cascadia earthquake

59. _____ is the probability of some event A, given the occurrence of some other event B. _____ is written P(A | B), and is read 'the probability of A, given B'.

Joint probability is the probability of two events in conjunction.

a. Conditional probability
b. 1703 Genroku earthquake
c. 1509 Istanbul earthquake
d. 1700 Cascadia earthquake

60. A _____ is any system of biological or technical nature deployed by an individual or group to inform of a future danger. Its purpose is to enable the deployer of the _____ to prepare for the danger and act accordingly to mitigate against or avoid it.
a. 1703 Genroku earthquake
b. Warning system
c. 1509 Istanbul earthquake
d. 1700 Cascadia earthquake

61. The 1975 _____ measuring 7.3 on the Richter Scale occurred at 19:36 CST on February 4, 1975 in Haicheng, Liaoning, China, a city that at the time had approximately 1 million residents.

Seismologists sent out warnings about this earthquake a day. Because of this correct prediction, many lives were saved.

a. 1509 Istanbul earthquake
b. 1700 Cascadia earthquake
c. Haicheng earthquake
d. 1703 Genroku earthquake

62. A _____ is a segment of an active geologic fault or subduction zone that has not slipped in an unusually long time; they are often considered susceptible to future strong earthquakes
a. 1509 Istanbul earthquake
b. 1700 Cascadia earthquake
c. 1703 Genroku earthquake
d. Seismic gap

63. _____ is the highest mountain in the U.S. state of Idaho. It is located in the central section of the Lost River Range and within the Challis National Forest. The peak is named for William Edgar Borah, a U.S. Senator from Idaho serving from 1907 to 1940.
a. 1509 Istanbul earthquake
b. 1703 Genroku earthquake
c. 1700 Cascadia earthquake
d. Borah Peak

64. A _____ is a statement or claim that a particular event will occur in the future in more certain terms than a forecast. The etymology of this word is Latin (from præ- 'before' plus dicere 'to say'.) In regards to predicting the future Howard H. Stevenson Says, '_____ is at least two things: Important and hard.' Important, because we have to act, and hard because we have to realize the future we want, and what is the best way to get there.
   a. Prediction
   b. 1703 Genroku earthquake
   c. 1509 Istanbul earthquake
   d. 1700 Cascadia earthquake

65. A _____ is a condition or value that is not limited to a specific set of values but can vary infinitely within a continuum. The word saw its first scientific use within the field of optics to describe the rainbow of colors in visible light when separated using a prism; it has since been applied by analogy to many fields.
   a. 1509 Istanbul earthquake
   b. 1700 Cascadia earthquake
   c. 1703 Genroku earthquake
   d. Spectrum

Chapter 8. Volcanic Activity

1. A _____ is an opening in a planet's surface or crust, which allows hot, molten rock, ash, and gases to escape from below the surface. Volcanic activity involving the extrusion of rock tends to form mountains or features like mountains over a period of time.

Volcanoes are generally found where tectonic plates are diverging or converging.

   a. 1509 Istanbul earthquake
   b. 1700 Cascadia earthquake
   c. 1703 Genroku earthquake
   d. Volcano

2. A popular way of classifying magmatic volcanoes goes by their frequency of eruption, or _____, with those that erupt regularly called active, those that have erupted in historical times but are now quiet called dormant, and those that have not erupted in historical times called extinct.
   a. 1703 Genroku earthquake
   b. Volcanic activity
   c. 1509 Istanbul earthquake
   d. 1700 Cascadia earthquake

3. _____ is a common gray to black extrusive volcanic rock. It is usually fine-grained due to rapid cooling of lava on the Earth's surface. It may be porphyritic containing larger crystals in a fine matrix, or vesicular, or frothy scoria.
   a. 1509 Istanbul earthquake
   b. 1703 Genroku earthquake
   c. 1700 Cascadia earthquake
   d. Basalt

4. A _____ is a fragment of cooled pyroclastic material, lava or magma.
   a. 1703 Genroku earthquake
   b. 1700 Cascadia earthquake
   c. 1509 Istanbul earthquake
   d. Cinder

5. _____ are steep, conical hills of volcanic fragments that accumulate around and downwind from a volcanic vent. The rock fragments, often called cinders are glassy and contain numerous gas bubbles "frozen" into place as magma exploded into the air and then cooled quickly.
   a. Cinder cones
   b. 1700 Cascadia earthquake
   c. 1703 Genroku earthquake
   d. 1509 Istanbul earthquake

6. _____ is molten rock expelled by a volcano during an eruption. When first extruded from a volcanic vent, it is a liquid at temperatures from 700 °C to 1,200 °C.
   a. 1700 Cascadia earthquake
   b. 1509 Istanbul earthquake
   c. 1703 Genroku earthquake
   d. Lava

7. _____ is molten rock located beneath the surface of the Earth, and which often collects in a _____ chamber. _____ is a complex high-temperature fluid substance. Most are silicate solutions. It is capable of intrusion into adjacent rocks or of extrusion onto the surface as lava or ejected explosively as tephra to form pyroclastic rock. Environments of _____ formation include subduction zones, continental rift zones, mid-oceanic ridges, and hotspots, some of which are interpreted as mantle plumes.
   a. 1509 Istanbul earthquake
   b. 1700 Cascadia earthquake
   c. Magma
   d. 1703 Genroku earthquake

8. _____ are clastic rocks composed solely or primarily of volcanic materials.
   a. 1509 Istanbul earthquake
   b. 1703 Genroku earthquake
   c. 1700 Cascadia earthquake
   d. Pyroclastics

Chapter 8. Volcanic Activity

9. A _____ is generally a large area of exposed Precambrian crystalline igneous and high-grade metamorphic rocks that form tectonically stable areas.
   - a. 1700 Cascadia earthquake
   - b. 1703 Genroku earthquake
   - c. Shield
   - d. 1509 Istanbul earthquake

10. A _____ is a large volcano with shallowly-sloping sides. A _____ is formed by lava flows of low viscosity — lava that flows easily. Consequently, a volcanic mountain having a broad profile is built up over time by flow after flow of relatively fluid basaltic lava issuing from vents or fissures on the surface of the volcano.
    - a. 1703 Genroku earthquake
    - b. 1700 Cascadia earthquake
    - c. Shield volcano
    - d. 1509 Istanbul earthquake

11. _____ is air-fall material produced by a volcanic eruption regardless of composition or fragment size. It is typically rhyolitic in composition as most explosive volcanoes are the product of the more viscous felsic or high silica magmas.
    - a. 1703 Genroku earthquake
    - b. 1700 Cascadia earthquake
    - c. 1509 Istanbul earthquake
    - d. Tephra

12. In geology, _____ is a naturally occurring aggregate of minerals and/or mineraloids.

The Earth's outer solid layer, the lithosphere, is made of _____. In general rocks are of three types, namely, igneous, sedimentary, and metamorphic.

   - a. 1700 Cascadia earthquake
   - b. 1509 Istanbul earthquake
   - c. 1703 Genroku earthquake
   - d. Rock

13. _____ is a measure of the resistance of a fluid to deform under shear stress. It is commonly perceived as "thickness", or resistance to flow. _____ describes a fluid's internal resistance to flow and may be thought of as a measure of fluid friction.
    - a. 1509 Istanbul earthquake
    - b. 1703 Genroku earthquake
    - c. 1700 Cascadia earthquake
    - d. Viscosity

14. Motto: Fluctuat nec mergitur The Eiffel Tower and the skyscrapers of Paris' suburban La Défense business district. _____ Time Zone CET Coordinates °52'0"N 2°19'59"E">48°52'0"N 2°19'59"Eï»¿ / ï»¿48.86667, 2.33306 Administration Country France Region Île-de-France Department Paris Subdivisions 20 arrondissements Mayor Bertrand Delanoë
City Statistics Land area km) Urban Spread Urban Area 2,723 km The Paris unité urbaine extends well beyond the administrative city limits and has an estimated population of 9.93 million. The Paris aire urbaine has a population of nearly 12 million, and is one of the most populated metropolitan areas in Europe.

An important settlement for more than two millennia, Paris is today one of the world's leading business and cultural centres, and its influence in politics, education, entertainment, media, fashion, science and the arts all contribute to its status as one of the world's major global cities.

   - a. 1509 Istanbul earthquake
   - b. 1700 Cascadia earthquake
   - c. 1703 Genroku earthquake
   - d. Location

15. _____ is an igneous, volcanic rock, of intermediate composition, with aphanitic to porphyritic texture.

Chapter 8. Volcanic Activity

a. Andesite
c. AL 333
b. AASHTO Soil Classification System
d. AL 129-1

16. The _____ is an engineering property of granular materials. The _____ is the maximum angle of a stable slope determined by friction, cohesion and the shapes of the particles.
a. AL 333
c. AL 129-1
b. Angle of repose
d. AASHTO Soil Classification System

17. A _____, is a tall, conical volcano composed of many layers of hardened lava, tephra, and volcanic ash. These volcanoes are characterized by a steep profile and periodic, explosive eruptions. The lava that flows from them is viscous, and cools and hardens before spreading very far.
a. Stratovolcano
c. 1703 Genroku earthquake
b. 1700 Cascadia earthquake
d. 1509 Istanbul earthquake

18. _____ is a stratovolcano in Pierce County, Washington, located 54 miles .
a. 1509 Istanbul earthquake
c. 1700 Cascadia earthquake
b. 1703 Genroku earthquake
d. Mount Rainier

19. _____ is an active stratovolcano in Skamania County, Washington, in the Pacific Northwest region of the United States. It is located 96 miles northeast of Portland, Oregon.
a. 1509 Istanbul earthquake
c. 1700 Cascadia earthquake
b. Mount St. Helens
d. 1703 Genroku earthquake

20. In geology, a _____ is a deformational feature consisting of symmetrically-dipping anticlines; their general outline on a geologic map is circular or oval.
a. 1509 Istanbul earthquake
c. 1703 Genroku earthquake
b. 1700 Cascadia earthquake
d. Dome

21. The _____ is the southernmost active volcano in the Cascade Range. It is part of the Cascade Volcanic Arc which is an arc that stretches from northern California to southwestern British Columbia. Located in the Shasta Cascade region of Northern California, Lassen rises 2,000 feet above the surrounding terrain and has a volume of half a cubic mile, making it one of the largest lava domes on Earth.
a. 1509 Istanbul earthquake
c. 1703 Genroku earthquake
b. Lassen Peak
d. 1700 Cascadia earthquake

22. _____ is an igneous, volcanic rock, of felsic composition. It may have any texture from aphanitic to porphyritic. The mineral assemblage is usually quartz, alkali feldspar and plagioclase. Biotite and pyroxene are common accessory minerals.
a. 1703 Genroku earthquake
c. 1700 Cascadia earthquake
b. 1509 Istanbul earthquake
d. Rhyolite

23. _____ are volcanic features formed by the collapse of land following a volcanic eruption. They are often confused with volcanic craters.
a. 1700 Cascadia earthquake
c. 1509 Istanbul earthquake
b. Calderas
d. 1703 Genroku earthquake

Chapter 8. Volcanic Activity

24. _____ usually commence with phreatomagmatic eruptions which can be extremely noisy due the rising magma heating water in the ground. This is usually followed by the explosive throat clearing of the vent and the eruption column is dirty grey to black as old weathered rocks are blasted out of the vent. As the vent clears, further ash clouds become grey-white and creamy in colour, with convulations of the ash similar to those of plinian eruptions.
   a. 1703 Genroku earthquake
   b. Vulcanian eruptions
   c. 1509 Istanbul earthquake
   d. 1700 Cascadia earthquake

25. A _____ is an approximately circular depression in the surface of a planet, moon or other solid body in the Solar System, formed by the hyper-velocity impact of a smaller body with the surface. Impact craters typically have raised rims, and they range from small, simple, bowl-shaped depressions to large, complex, multi-ringed, impact basins.
   a. 1509 Istanbul earthquake
   b. 1700 Cascadia earthquake
   c. 1703 Genroku earthquake
   d. Crater

26. A _____ is a type of hot spring that erupts periodically, ejecting a column of hot water and steam into the air.
   a. 1703 Genroku earthquake
   b. 1509 Istanbul earthquake
   c. 1700 Cascadia earthquake
   d. Geyser

27. A _____ is a spring that is produced by the emergence of geothermally-heated groundwater from the earth's crust. They are all over the earth, on every continent and even under the oceans and seas.
   a. 1509 Istanbul earthquake
   b. 1703 Genroku earthquake
   c. 1700 Cascadia earthquake
   d. Hot spring

28. A _____ column is a column of rizing air in the lower altitudes of the Earth's atmosphere. Thermals are created by the uneven heating of the Earth's surface from solar radiation, and are an example of convection. The Sun warms the ground, which in turn warms the air directly above it.
   a. 1509 Istanbul earthquake
   b. 1703 Genroku earthquake
   c. 1700 Cascadia earthquake
   d. Thermal

29. _____ is a town on the Island of Hawaiʻi in the Hawaiian Islands that was destroyed and partly buried by the eruptive flow of lava from the Puʻu ʻŌʻō vent of the Kīlauea volcano in 1990. A nearby housing subdivision, Royal Gardens, was also largely destroyed, though some of its structures remain untouched to the present day. The lava flow that destroyed _____ erupted from the southeast rift zone of Kīlauea.
   a. 1509 Istanbul earthquake
   b. 1703 Genroku earthquake
   c. 1700 Cascadia earthquake
   d. Kalapana

30. The _____ of an edge is $c_f(u, v) = c(u, v) - f(u, v)$. This defines a residual network denoted $G_f(V, E_f)$, giving the amount of available capacity. See that there can be an edge from u to v in the residual network, even though there is no edge from u to v in the original network.
   a. 1509 Istanbul earthquake
   b. 1700 Cascadia earthquake
   c. 1703 Genroku earthquake
   d. Residual capacity

31. _____ is an active volcano in the Hawaiian Islands, one of five shield volcanoes that together form the Island of Hawai'i. In Hawaiian, the word _____ means "spewing" or "much spreading", in reference to the mountain's frequent outpouring of lava. It is presently the most active volcano and one of the most visited active volcanoes on the planet.

Chapter 8. Volcanic Activity

a. 1700 Cascadia earthquake
b. 1703 Genroku earthquake
c. 1509 Istanbul earthquake
d. Kilauea

32. _____ is a depression in eastern California that is adjacent to Mammoth Mountain. The valley is one of the largest calderas on earth, measuring about 32 kilometres long and 17 kilometres wide.
a. 1703 Genroku earthquake
b. 1509 Istanbul earthquake
c. Long Valley caldera
d. 1700 Cascadia earthquake

33. In geology, a _____ is a depression with predominant extent in one direction. The terms U-shaped and V-shaped are descriptive terms of geography to characterize the form of valleys. Most valleys belong to one of these two main types or a mixture of them, at least with respect of the cross section of the slopes or hillsides.
a. 1700 Cascadia earthquake
b. 1509 Istanbul earthquake
c. 1703 Genroku earthquake
d. Valley

34. _____ is a state on the West Coast of the United States, along the Pacific Ocean. It is bordered by Oregon to the north, Nevada to the east, Arizona to the southeast, and to the south the Mexican state of Baja _____. _____ is the most populous U.S. state.
a. 1700 Cascadia earthquake
b. 1509 Istanbul earthquake
c. 1703 Genroku earthquake
d. California

35. A _____ is a body of water, not part of the ocean, that is larger and deeper than a pond.
a. 1700 Cascadia earthquake
b. 1509 Istanbul earthquake
c. 1703 Genroku earthquake
d. Lake

36. A _____ is any of a number of an extinct genus of proboscidean, often with long curved tusks and, in northern species, a covering of long hair. They lived from the Pliocene epoch from to around 4,000 years ago.
a. 1509 Istanbul earthquake
b. 1700 Cascadia earthquake
c. 1703 Genroku earthquake
d. Mammoth

37. _____ is an incorporated town in Mono County, California, United States. The population was 7,093 at the 2000 census. _____ resides on the edge of the Long Valley Caldera. The area around the town is geologically active, with hot springs and rhyolite domes that are less than 1000 years old.
a. 1700 Cascadia earthquake
b. 1703 Genroku earthquake
c. 1509 Istanbul earthquake
d. Mammoth Lakes

38. _____ consists of very fine rock and mineral particles less than 2 mm in diameter that are ejected from a volcanic vent. The very fine particles may be carried for many miles, settling out as a dust-like layer across the landscape
a. AL 333
b. AASHTO Soil Classification System
c. AL 129-1
d. Ash fall

39. _____ was first recognised after the Taal Volcano eruption of 1965, where a visiting volcanologist recognised the phenomenon as congruent to _____ in atomic explosions. The USGS defines _____ as turbulent, low-density cloud of rock debris and water and (or) steam that moves over the ground surface at high speed. Base surges are generated by explosions.

Chapter 8. Volcanic Activity

a. 1509 Istanbul earthquake
b. 1700 Cascadia earthquake
c. Base surge
d. 1703 Genroku earthquake

40. The Republic of _____ is a unitary republic of central and western Africa. It is bordered by Nigeria to the west; Chad to the northeast; the Central African Republic to the east; and Equatorial Guinea, Gabon, and the Republic of the Congo to the south. _____'s coastline lies on the Bight of Bonny, part of the Gulf of Guinea and the Atlantic Ocean.
   a. Swaziland
   b. Cameroon
   c. Somaliland
   d. Guinea

41. _____ is the chemical element in the periodic table that has the symbol F and atomic number 9. Atomic _____ is univalent and is the most chemically reactive and electronegative of all the elements. In its pure form, it is a poisonous, pale, yellow-green gas. Like other halogens, molecular _____ is highly dangerous; it causes severe chemical burns on contact with skin.
   a. 1703 Genroku earthquake
   b. Fluorine
   c. 1509 Istanbul earthquake
   d. 1700 Cascadia earthquake

42. _____ is a volcanic pyroclastic rock, often of dacitic or rhyolitic composition. It forms as the result of immense explosions of pyroclastic dust/ash flowing down the sides of volcanic cones or mountains.
   a. AL 129-1
   b. AL 333
   c. AASHTO Soil Classification System
   d. Ignimbrite

43. _____ is a crater lake in the Northwest Province of Cameroon. It is a deep lake high on the flank of an inactive volcano near Mount Oku, along the Cameroon line of volcanic activity. A natural dam of volcanic rock hems in the lake waters.
   a. 1509 Istanbul earthquake
   b. 1703 Genroku earthquake
   c. 1700 Cascadia earthquake
   d. Lake Nyos

44. _____ is a common and devastating result of some volcanic eruptions. The flows are fast-moving fluidized bodies of hot gas, ash and rock which can travel away from the vent at up to 700 km/h. The gas is usually at a temperature of up to 1000 degrees Celsius. The flows normally hug the ground and travel downhill under gravity, their speed depending upon the gradient of the slope and the size of the flow.
   a. 1703 Genroku earthquake
   b. 1509 Istanbul earthquake
   c. 1700 Cascadia earthquake
   d. Nuee ardente

45. A _____ is a common and devastating result of some volcanic eruptions. The flows are fast-moving fluidized bodies of hot gas, ash and rock. The flows normally hug the ground and travel downhill under gravity, their speed depending upon the gradient of the slope and the size of the flow.
   a. Pyroclastic flow
   b. 1700 Cascadia earthquake
   c. 1703 Genroku earthquake
   d. 1509 Istanbul earthquake

46. _____ are very large slides of snow or rock down a mountainside, caused when a buildup of snow is released down a slope, and is one of the major dangers faced in the mountains.
   a. AASHTO Soil Classification System
   b. AL 333
   c. AL 129-1
   d. Avalanches

47. _____ is the largest island in the Vestmannaeyjar cluster, approximately 4 nautical miles off the south coast of Iceland. It is the only island in Vestmannaeyjar that is populated, and currently there are around 4,500 inhabitants.

Chapter 8. Volcanic Activity

a. 1509 Istanbul earthquake
b. 1700 Cascadia earthquake
c. 1703 Genroku earthquake
d. Heimaey

48. _____, officially the Republic of _____, is an island country in Northern Europe, located in the North Atlantic Ocean between mainland Europe and Greenland. It has a population of about 320,000 and a total area of 103,000 km Its capital and largest city is Reykjavík.

Located on the Mid-Atlantic Ridge, _____ is volcanically and geologically active on a large scale; this defines the landscape.

a. Ireland
b. Iron Curtain
c. Independence
d. Iceland

49. An _____ is any piece of land that is completely surrounded by water, above high tide. There are two main types of islands: continental islands and oceanic islands. There are also artificial islands. A grouping of geographically and/or geologically related islands is called an archipelago.

a. AL 333
b. AASHTO Soil Classification System
c. AL 129-1
d. Island

50. _____ often refers to mudslides, mudflows, jökulhlaups, or debris avalanches. They consist primarily of geological material mixed with water. They may be generated when hillside colluvium or landslide material becomes rapidly saturated with water and flows into a channel.

a. 1700 Cascadia earthquake
b. 1703 Genroku earthquake
c. Debris flow
d. 1509 Istanbul earthquake

51. A _____ is a type of mudflow composed of pyroclastic material and water that flows down from a volcano, typically along a river valley.

a. Lahar
b. 1700 Cascadia earthquake
c. 1703 Genroku earthquake
d. 1509 Istanbul earthquake

52. A _____ is the most rapid up to 80 km/h and fluid type of downhill mass wasting.

a. 1700 Cascadia earthquake
b. Mudflow
c. 1703 Genroku earthquake
d. 1509 Istanbul earthquake

53. _____ is an active volcanic complex of several overlapping stratovolcanoes near the city of Shimabara, Nagasaki Prefecture, on the island of Kyûshû, Japan's southernmost main island.

a. AASHTO Soil Classification System
b. AL 129-1
c. AL 333
d. Unzen volcano

54. _____ is an Andean stratovolcano in Caldas Department, Colombia. It is the northernmost and highest Colombian volcano with historical activity. Its 1985 eruption produced a lahar which completely buried Armero and caused an estimated 23,000 deaths.

a. 1703 Genroku earthquake
b. 1700 Cascadia earthquake
c. 1509 Istanbul earthquake
d. Nevado del Ruiz

55. _____ is an active stratovolcano located on the island of Luzon in the Philippines, at the intersection of the borders of the provinces of Zambales, Tarlac, and Pampanga.
- a. 1509 Istanbul earthquake
- b. 1703 Genroku earthquake
- c. 1700 Cascadia earthquake
- d. Mount Pinatubo

56. A _____ is a statement or claim that a particular event will occur in the future in more certain terms than a forecast. The etymology of this word is Latin (from præ- 'before' plus dicere 'to say'.) In regards to predicting the future Howard H. Stevenson Says, '_____ is at least two things: Important and hard.' Important, because we have to act, and hard because we have to realize the future we want, and what is the best way to get there.
- a. 1703 Genroku earthquake
- b. 1509 Istanbul earthquake
- c. 1700 Cascadia earthquake
- d. Prediction

57. Seismology is the scientific study of earthquakes and the propagation of elastic waves through the Earth. The field also includes studies of earthquake effects, such as tsunamis as well as diverse _____ sources such as volcanic, tectonic, oceanic, atmospheric, and artificial processes (such as explosions.) A related field that uses geology to infer information regarding past earthquakes is paleoseismology.
- a. 1700 Cascadia earthquake
- b. 1509 Istanbul earthquake
- c. 1703 Genroku earthquake
- d. Seismic

58. _____ include a variety of substances given off by active volcanos. These include gases trapped in cavities in volcanic rocks, dissolved or dissociated gases in magma and lava, or gases emanating directly from lava or indirectly through ground water heated by volcanic action.
- a. 1703 Genroku earthquake
- b. Volcanic gases
- c. 1509 Istanbul earthquake
- d. 1700 Cascadia earthquake

59. _____ is the science and study of the solid matter that constitute the Earth. Encompassing such things as rocks, soil, and gemstones, _____ studies the composition, structure, physical properties, history, and the processes that shape Earth's components.
- a. 1700 Cascadia earthquake
- b. 1703 Genroku earthquake
- c. 1509 Istanbul earthquake
- d. Geology

60. _____ is the study of the past, particularly using written records. New technology, such as photography, and computer text files now sometimes complement traditional archival sources. _____ is a field of research producing a continuous narrative and a systematic analysis of past events of importance to the human race.
- a. 1509 Istanbul earthquake
- b. 1700 Cascadia earthquake
- c. Absolute time
- d. History

61. A _____ is any system of biological or technical nature deployed by an individual or group to inform of a future danger. Its purpose is to enable the deployer of the _____ to prepare for the danger and act accordingly to mitigate against or avoid it.
- a. 1703 Genroku earthquake
- b. 1700 Cascadia earthquake
- c. 1509 Istanbul earthquake
- d. Warning system

Chapter 9. Coastal Hazards

1. In meteorology, _____ are an area of low atmospheric pressure characterized by inward spiraling winds that rotate counter clockwise in the northern hemisphere and clockwise in the southern hemisphere of the Earth.
   a. Cyclones
   b. 1700 Cascadia earthquake
   c. 1703 Genroku earthquake
   d. 1509 Istanbul earthquake

2. A _____ is a storm system characterized by a low pressure center and numerous thunderstorms that produce strong winds and flooding rain. Tropical cyclones feed on heat released when moist air rises, resulting in condensation of water vapour contained in the moist air. They are fueled by a different heat mechanism than other cyclonic windstorms such as nor'easters, European windstorms, and polar lows, leading to their classification as 'warm core' storm systems.
   a. Persia
   b. Khmer Empire
   c. Tropical cyclone
   d. Kenya

3. The Tropics, seated in the equatorial regions of the world, are limited in latitude by the Tropic of Cancer in the northern hemisphere at approximately 23°26' N latitude, and the Tropic of Capricorn in the southern hemisphere at 23°26' S latitude. The Tropics are also referred to as the _____ zone and the torrid zone. A noontime scene from the Philippines on a day when the Sun is almost directly overhead.

   The Tropics includes all the areas on the Earth where the sun reaches a point directly overhead at least once during the solar year.
   a. 1700 Cascadia earthquake
   b. 1703 Genroku earthquake
   c. 1509 Istanbul earthquake
   d. Tropical

4. _____ are storm systems characterized by a low pressure center and thunderstorms that produces strong wind and flooding rain. They feed on the heat released when moist air rises and the water vapor it contains condenses.
   a. 1703 Genroku earthquake
   b. 1700 Cascadia earthquake
   c. 1509 Istanbul earthquake
   d. Tropical cyclones

5. _____ is displacement of solids by the agents of ocean currents, wind, water, or ice by downward or down-slope movement in response to gravity or by living organisms.
   a. AL 333
   b. AASHTO Soil Classification System
   c. Erosion
   d. AL 129-1

6. _____ is the second-most-destructive hurricane in U.S. history, and the last of three Category 5 hurricanes that made U.S. landfall during the 20th century, after the Labor Day Hurricane of 1935 and Hurricane Camille in 1969. The storm caused 65 deaths.
   a. Hurricane Andrew
   b. 1703 Genroku earthquake
   c. 1700 Cascadia earthquake
   d. 1509 Istanbul earthquake

7. A _____ is any disturbed state of an astronomical body's atmosphere, especially affecting its surface, and strongly implying severe weather. It may be marked by strong wind, thunder and lightning, heavy precipitation, such as ice, or wind transporting some substance through the atmosphere.
   a. Storm
   b. 1509 Istanbul earthquake
   c. 1700 Cascadia earthquake
   d. 1703 Genroku earthquake

Chapter 9. Coastal Hazards

8. A _____ is an offshore rise of water associated with a low pressure weather system, typically a tropical cyclone. _____ is caused primarily by high winds pushing on the ocean's surface, causing the water to pile up higher than the ordinary sea level.
   a. 1700 Cascadia earthquake
   b. 1703 Genroku earthquake
   c. 1509 Istanbul earthquake
   d. Storm surge

9. _____ is a term for the length of water over which a given wind has blown. It is used in geography and meteorology and is usually associated with coastal erosion. It plays a large part in longshore drift as well.
   a. 1703 Genroku earthquake
   b. 1700 Cascadia earthquake
   c. 1509 Istanbul earthquake
   d. Fetch

10. A _____ is a disturbance that propagates through space or spacetime, transferring energy and momentum and sometimes angular momentum.
    a. 1703 Genroku earthquake
    b. 1509 Istanbul earthquake
    c. 1700 Cascadia earthquake
    d. Wave

11. The _____ is a major river flowing through southern England. While best known because its lower reaches flow through central London, the river flows through several other towns and cities, including Oxford, Reading and Windsor.

    The river gives its name to the _____ Valley, a region of England centred around the river between Oxford and West London, the _____ Gateway, the area centred around the tidal _____, and the _____ Estuary to the east of London.

    a. Amblypoda
    b. Ambulocetus
    c. Andrija Mohorovičić
    d. Thames

12. _____ is a flood control structure on the River Thames, constructed between 1974 and 1984 at Woolwich Reach, and first used defensively in 1983. It is the world's second largest movable flood barrier (the largest is the Maeslantkering in The Netherlands.)

    Located downstream of central London, the barrier's purpose is to prevent London from being flooded by an exceptionally high tide moving up from the sea, often exacerbated by a storm surge.

    a. 1700 Cascadia earthquake
    b. 1703 Genroku earthquake
    c. 1509 Istanbul earthquake
    d. Thames barrier

13. Fullerenes are a family of carbon allotropes, molecules composed entirely of carbon, in the form of a hollow sphere, ellipsoid, tube, or plane. Spherical fullerenes are also called buckyballs, and cylindrical ones are called carbon nanotubes or buckytubes. Graphene is an example of a planar _____ sheet.
    a. 1509 Istanbul earthquake
    b. 1703 Genroku earthquake
    c. 1700 Cascadia earthquake
    d. Fullerene

14. _____ is the change in direction of a wave due to a change in its speed. This is most commonly seen when a wave passes from one medium to another.

Chapter 9. Coastal Hazards

a. 1703 Genroku earthquake
b. 1509 Istanbul earthquake
c. 1700 Cascadia earthquake
d. Refraction

15. With _____ the crest undergoes deformation and destabilizes, resulting in it spilling over the front of the wave. This wave tends to create a frothy appearance. It occurs most often on gentle beaches.
a. 1703 Genroku earthquake
b. 1700 Cascadia earthquake
c. 1509 Istanbul earthquake
d. Spilling breakers

16. _____ are level spaces, shelves or raised barriers separating two areas.
a. 1509 Istanbul earthquake
b. 1703 Genroku earthquake
c. 1700 Cascadia earthquake
d. Berms

17. As ocean surface waves come closer to shore they break, forming the foamy, bubbly surface we call surf. The region of breaking waves defines the _____.
a. 1509 Istanbul earthquake
b. 1700 Cascadia earthquake
c. 1703 Genroku earthquake
d. Surf zone

18. In geology, a _____ generally refers to a linear structural depression that extends laterally over a distance, while being less steep than a trench. It can be a narrow basin or a geologic rift. In meteorolology a _____ is an elongated region of relatively low atmospheric pressure, often associated with fronts.
a. Wilson cycle
b. Riparian zone
c. Trough
d. Shelf break

19. The _____ is defined as the area between the high water and low water marks, or the portion of the lake that is less than 15 feet in depth.
a. 1703 Genroku earthquake
b. 1700 Cascadia earthquake
c. 1509 Istanbul earthquake
d. Littoral

20. At times when larger waves attack the beach berm, some of the beach material is redistributed offshore to become a _____ possibly visible at low tide.
a. 1700 Cascadia earthquake
b. 1703 Genroku earthquake
c. 1509 Istanbul earthquake
d. Longshore bar

21. _____ is a geological process by which sediments such as sand or other materials, move along a beach shore.
a. 1703 Genroku earthquake
b. 1509 Istanbul earthquake
c. 1700 Cascadia earthquake
d. Longshore drift

22. _____ is a 16-ton, manned deep-ocean research submersible owned by the United States Navy and operated by the Woods Hole Oceanographic Institution in Woods Hole, Massachusetts. The three-person vessel allows for two scientists and one pilot to dive for up to nine hours at 4500 metersor 15,000 feet.
a. Alvin
b. AL 129-1
c. AASHTO Soil Classification System
d. AL 333

23. A _____ is a steep-sided valley on the sea floor of the continental slope. They are formed by powerful turbidity currents, volcanic and earthquake activity. Many continue as submarine channels across continental rise areas and may extend for hundreds of kilometers.

a. 1700 Cascadia earthquake
b. 1509 Istanbul earthquake
c. 1703 Genroku earthquake
d. Submarine canyon

24. A _____ is a deep valley between cliffs often carved from the landscape by a river. Most were formed by a process of long-time erosion from a plateau level. The cliffs form because harder rock strata that are resistant to erosion and weathering remain exposed on the valley walls.
a. 1700 Cascadia earthquake
b. 1509 Istanbul earthquake
c. 1703 Genroku earthquake
d. Canyon

25. _____ is the average and variations of weather over long periods of time. _____ zones can be defined using parameters such as temperature and rainfall.
a. 1700 Cascadia earthquake
b. 1703 Genroku earthquake
c. 1509 Istanbul earthquake
d. Climate

26. Ocean _____ are any more or less continuous, directed movement of ocean water that flows in one of the Earth's oceans. They are rivers of hot or cold water within the ocean. They are generated from the forces acting upon the water like the earth's rotation, the wind, the temperature and salinity differences and the gravitation of the moon.
a. 1703 Genroku earthquake
b. 1509 Istanbul earthquake
c. 1700 Cascadia earthquake
d. Currents

27. A _____ is a macro-scale storm whose winds come from the northeast, especially in the coastal areas of the Northeastern United States and Atlantic Canada. More specifically, it describes a low pressure area whose center of rotation is just off the coast and whose leading winds in the left forward quadrant rotate onto land from the northeast.
a. 1509 Istanbul earthquake
b. 1703 Genroku earthquake
c. Nor'easter
d. 1700 Cascadia earthquake

28. _____ refers to a member of any human group whose adult males grow to less than 150 cm in average height or less than 155 cm. A member of a slightly taller group is termed pygmoid. The best known _____ are the Aka, Efe and Mbuti of central Africa.
a. 1703 Genroku earthquake
b. Pygmies
c. 1700 Cascadia earthquake
d. 1509 Istanbul earthquake

29. _____ comprises a beach, an estate and a harbor. It lies 4 miles east of North Berwick, East Lothian, Scotland.
a. 1509 Istanbul earthquake
b. 1700 Cascadia earthquake
c. 1703 Genroku earthquake
d. Seacliff

30. A _____ is a landform where the mouth of a river flows into an ocean, sea, desert, estuary or lake. It builds up sediment outwards into the flat area which the river's flow encounters transported by the water and set down as the currents slow.
a. 1700 Cascadia earthquake
b. 1703 Genroku earthquake
c. 1509 Istanbul earthquake
d. Delta

31. Mean _____ is the average height of the sea, with reference to a suitable reference surface.
a. 1700 Cascadia earthquake
b. 1703 Genroku earthquake
c. Sea level
d. 1509 Istanbul earthquake

Chapter 9. Coastal Hazards

32. A _____ is a deliberate process for transforming one or more inputs into one or more results, with variable change.
   a. 1700 Cascadia earthquake
   b. 1509 Istanbul earthquake
   c. 1703 Genroku earthquake
   d. Calculation

33. A _____ is a structure constructed on coasts as part of coastal defense or to protect an anchorage from the effects of weather and longshore drift.
   a. Breakwater
   b. 1509 Istanbul earthquake
   c. 1703 Genroku earthquake
   d. 1700 Cascadia earthquake

34. A _____ is a rigid hydraulic structure built out from the shore or from the bank and interrupts the flow of water and sediment. Groynes serve a multitude of functions.
   a. 1703 Genroku earthquake
   b. 1509 Istanbul earthquake
   c. 1700 Cascadia earthquake
   d. Groyne

35. _____ are a form of hard coastal defense constructed on the inland part of a coast to reduce the effects of strong waves and to defend the coast around a town or harbor from erosion. The walls can be sloping, vertical or curved to reflect wave power.
   a. 1509 Istanbul earthquake
   b. 1700 Cascadia earthquake
   c. 1703 Genroku earthquake
   d. Seawalls

36. _____ is a complimentary term that describes a process by which sediment, usually sand, lost through longshore drift or erosion is replaced on a beach
   a. 1509 Istanbul earthquake
   b. 1700 Cascadia earthquake
   c. 1703 Genroku earthquake
   d. Beach nourishment

37. The term _____ signifyies something thrown out, is applied to a variety of structures employed in river, dock, and maritime works which are generally carried out in pairs from river banks, or in continuation of river channels at their outlets into deep water; or out into docks, and outside their entrances; or for forming basins along the sea-coast for ports in tideless seas.
   a. 1703 Genroku earthquake
   b. 1509 Istanbul earthquake
   c. Jetty
   d. 1700 Cascadia earthquake

38. A _____ is an urban area with a high population and a particular administrative, legal, or historical status.

Large industrialized cities generally have advanced systems for sanitation, utilities, land usage, housing, and transportation and more. This close proximity greatly facilitates interaction between people and firms, benefiting both parties in the process.

   a. 1509 Istanbul earthquake
   b. 1703 Genroku earthquake
   c. 1700 Cascadia earthquake
   d. City

39. _____ is a state located in the southeastern region of the United States, bordering Alabama to the northwest and Georgia to the northeast. Much of the land mass of the state is a large peninsula with the Gulf of Mexico to the west and the Atlantic Ocean to the east. Most of _____ has a humid subtropical climate; southern _____ has a tropical climate.

a. 1509 Istanbul earthquake
b. 1703 Genroku earthquake
c. Florida
d. 1700 Cascadia earthquake

40. _____ is a global city in southeastern Florida, in the United States. _____ is the county seat of _____-Dade County, the most populous county in Florida. With a population of more than 409,719, _____ is the largest city within the _____ metropolitan area, which is the seventh-largest metro area in the United States with over 5.4 million residents.
   a. Florida
   b. Ambulocetus
   c. Amblypoda
   d. Miami

41. _____ is a city in Cape May County, New Jersey, United States.
   a. AASHTO Soil Classification System
   b. AL 129-1
   c. AL 333
   d. Ocean City

42. The _____ is a federal agency made up of some 34,600 civilian and 650 military men and women. The Corps' mission is to provide engineering services to the United States. The _____. The _____ is organized geographically into eight permanent divisions, one provisional division, and one provisional district. They are defined by watershed boundaries for civil works projects, and by political boundaries for military projects.
   a. Amblypoda
   b. Andrija Mohorović ić
   c. Ambulocetus
   d. U.S. Army Corps of Engineers

43. _____ is a state located in the South Central United States nicknamed the Lone Star State. Austin is the state capital. _____--the second largest U.S. state in both area and population--spans 268,820 square miles (696,200 km Due to its long history as a center of the American cattle industry, _____ is associated throughout much of the world with the image of the cowboy.
   a. 1700 Cascadia earthquake
   b. Texas
   c. Comal Springs
   d. 1509 Istanbul earthquake

44. An _____ is any piece of land that is completely surrounded by water, above high tide. There are two main types of islands: continental islands and oceanic islands. There are also artificial islands. A grouping of geographically and/or geologically related islands is called an archipelago.
   a. AASHTO Soil Classification System
   b. AL 129-1
   c. AL 333
   d. Island

45. The _____ are a 100-mile long string of narrow barrier islands off the coast of North Carolina on the East Coast of the United States. They cover approximately the northern half of North Carolina's coastline, separating the Albemarle Sound and Pamlico Sound from the Atlantic Ocean.
   a. AASHTO Soil Classification System
   b. AL 129-1
   c. AL 333
   d. Outer Banks

46. The _____ is defined as the part of the land adjoining or near the ocean. A coastline is properly a line on a map indicating the disposition of a _____, but the word is often used to refer to the _____ itself. The adjective coastal describes something as being on, near to, or associated with a _____.
   a. Coast
   b. 1703 Genroku earthquake
   c. 1700 Cascadia earthquake
   d. 1509 Istanbul earthquake

Chapter 9. Coastal Hazards

47. A _____ is a bipedal primate belonging to the mammalian species Homo sapiens in the family Hominidae. Compared to other living organisms on Earth, a _____ has a highly developed brain capable of abstract reasoning, language, and introspection.
   a. 1509 Istanbul earthquake
   b. 1703 Genroku earthquake
   c. 1700 Cascadia earthquake
   d. Human

48. The Laurentian _____ are a group of five large lakes in North America on or near the Canada-United States border. They are the largest group of fresh water lakes on Earth.
   a. 1703 Genroku earthquake
   b. Great Lakes
   c. 1509 Istanbul earthquake
   d. 1700 Cascadia earthquake

49. The _____ region of the United States comprises the coasts of states which border the Gulf of Mexico. The states of Texas, Louisiana, Mississippi, Alabama, and Florida are known as the Gulf States. All Gulf States are located in the Southern region of the United States.
   a. 1703 Genroku earthquake
   b. Gulf coast
   c. 1700 Cascadia earthquake
   d. 1509 Istanbul earthquake

50. A _____ is a body of water, not part of the ocean, that is larger and deeper than a pond.
   a. Lake
   b. 1509 Istanbul earthquake
   c. 1703 Genroku earthquake
   d. 1700 Cascadia earthquake

51. A _____ is a piece of land that is nearly surrounded by water but connected to mainland via an isthmus.

A _____ can also be a headland, cape, island promontory, bill, point, or spit.

A beach on the Mornington _____

- Beecraft _____, New South Wales
- Bellarine _____, Victoria
- Cape York _____, Queensland
- Cobourg _____, Northern Territory
- Cronulla sand dunes, Kurnell _____
- Dampier _____, Western Australia
- Eyre _____, South Australia
- Fleurieu _____, South Australia
- Freycinet _____, Tasmania
- Inskip _____, Queensland.
- Jervis Bay Territory
- Mornington _____, Victoria
- Redcliffe, Queensland
- Stockton, New South Wales
- Tasman _____, Tasmania
- Tasmania itself was one a _____ connected to Australia during the great Ice Ages
- Wilsons Promontory, Victoria
- Woy Woy, New South Wales
- Yorke _____, South Australia
- Younghusband _____, South Australia

Looking north over the Kurnell _____.

- Aupouri _____, North Island
- Banks _____, South Island
- Bluff _____, South Island
- Bream Head, North Island
- Cape Brett, North Island
- Cape Campbell, South Island
- Cape Foulwind, South Island
- Cape Kidnappers, North Island
- Cape Turnagain, North Island
- Coromandel _____, North Island
- Farewell Spit, South Island
- Kaikoura _____, South Island
- Karikari _____, North Island
- Mahia _____, North Island
- Miramar _____, North Island
- Mount Maunganui, North Island
- North Auckland _____, North Island
- Otago _____, South Island
- Tiwai Point, South Island

- Gazelle _____, New Britain
- Huon _____

- Europe is composed of many peninsulas, such as the Iberian _____, Scandinavian, etc.

Chapter 9. Coastal Hazards

The Balkans is a _____ including the Republic of Macedonia, Greece, Bosnia and Herzegovina, Bulgaria, Croatia, Serbia, Albania, and Montenegro.

a. Peninsula
b. Japan
c. Kinmen
d. Human beings

52. _____ is the wearing away of land or the removal of beach or dune sediments by wave action, tidal currents, wave currents, or drainage. Waves, generated by storms or fast moving moter craft, cause _____, which may take the form of long-term losses of sediment and rocks, or merely in the temporary redistribution of coastal sediments; erosion in one location may result in accretion nearby.

a. 1509 Istanbul earthquake
b. 1700 Cascadia earthquake
c. 1703 Genroku earthquake
d. Beach erosion

53. _____ is rock or other material used to armor shorelines or stream banks against water erosion

a. 1700 Cascadia earthquake
b. 1703 Genroku earthquake
c. 1509 Istanbul earthquake
d. Riprap

54. The _____ is an agency of the United States Department of Homeland Security, initially created by Presidential Order on April 1, 1979.) The purpose of _____ is to coordinate the response to a disaster which has occurred in the United States and which overwhelms the resources of local and state authorities. The governor of the state in which the disaster occurred must declare a state of emergency and formally request from the President that _____ and the federal government respond to the disaster.

a. 1509 Istanbul earthquake
b. 1700 Cascadia earthquake
c. 1703 Genroku earthquake
d. FEMA

55. The _____ is an agency of the United States Department of Homeland Security. It's purpose is to coordinate the response to a disaster which has occurred in the United States and which overwhelms the resouces of local ands state authorities.

a. Amblypoda
b. Federal Emergency Management Agency
c. Andrija Mohorovi̇Ä iÄ‡
d. Ambulocetus

56. The _____ of the USA is the working arm of the United States National Academy of Sciences and the United States National Academy of Engineering, carrying out most of the studies done in their names.

a. Andrija Mohorovi̇Ä iÄ‡
b. Ambulocetus
c. National Research Council
d. Amblypoda

57. Due to shore erosion in the Outer Bank of North Carolina a navagational lighthouse had to be moved leading to the _____.

a. 1509 Istanbul earthquake
b. 1700 Cascadia earthquake
c. Cape Hatteras Lighthouse controversy
d. 1703 Genroku earthquake

Chapter 10. Water: Process, Supply, and Use

1. _____ in chemistry is the intermolecular attraction between like-molecules. It explains phenomena such as surface tension.
   - a. 1700 Cascadia earthquake
   - b. 1509 Istanbul earthquake
   - c. 1703 Genroku earthquake
   - d. Cohesion

2. A _____ bond is a form of chemical bonding that is characterized by the sharing of pairs of electrons between atoms, or between atoms and other _____ bonds. In short, attraction-to-repulsion stability that forms between atoms when they share electrons is known as _____ bonding.
   - a. 1700 Cascadia earthquake
   - b. 1509 Istanbul earthquake
   - c. Covalent
   - d. 1703 Genroku earthquake

3. _____ polarization is a polarization that is particular to polar molecules. This polarization results from permanent dipoles, which retain polarization in the absence of an external electric field. The assembly of these forms a macroscopic polarization.
   - a. 1700 Cascadia earthquake
   - b. Dipolar
   - c. 1509 Istanbul earthquake
   - d. 1703 Genroku earthquake

4. _____ is a term used to describe the flow of water, from rain, snowmelt, or other sources, over the land surface, and is a major component of the water cycle.
   - a. 1509 Istanbul earthquake
   - b. 1700 Cascadia earthquake
   - c. 1703 Genroku earthquake
   - d. Surface runoff

5. In thermodynamics, the _____ of a substance is the temperature and pressure at which three phases (for example, gas, liquid, and solid) of that substance coexist in thermodynamic equilibrium. For example, the _____ of mercury occurs at a temperature of −38.8344 °C and a pressure of 0.2 mPa.

   In addition to the _____ between solid, liquid, and gas, there can be triple points involving more than one solid phase, for substances with multiple polymorphs.

   - a. Triple point
   - b. 1700 Cascadia earthquake
   - c. 1703 Genroku earthquake
   - d. 1509 Istanbul earthquake

6. The Earth's water is always in movement, and the _____, describes the continuous movement of water on, above, and below the surface of the Earth. Since the _____ is truly a "cycle," there is no beginning or end. Water can change states among liquid, vapor, and ice at various places in the _____, with these processes happening in the blink of an eye and over millions of years. Although the balance of water on Earth remains fairly constant over time, individual water molecules can come and go in a hurry.
   - a. 1700 Cascadia earthquake
   - b. 1509 Istanbul earthquake
   - c. Hydrologic cycle
   - d. 1703 Genroku earthquake

7. A _____ substance is a material with a definite _____ composition. It is a concept that became firmly established in the late eighteenth century after work by the chemist Joseph Proust on the composition of some pure _____ compounds such as basic copper carbonate.
   - a. 1509 Istanbul earthquake
   - b. 1700 Cascadia earthquake
   - c. 1703 Genroku earthquake
   - d. Chemical

Chapter 10. Water: Process, Supply, and Use

8. _____ is the physical process responsible for the attractive interactions between atoms and molecules, and that which confers stability to diatomic and polyatomic chemical compounds.
   a. 1703 Genroku earthquake
   b. 1700 Cascadia earthquake
   c. 1509 Istanbul earthquake
   d. Chemical Bonding

9. _____ is energy transferred from one body or system to another due to a difference in temperature or can be defined as the absolute temperature of an object multiplied by the differential quantity of a system's entropy measured at the boundary of the object.
   a. Heat
   b. 1703 Genroku earthquake
   c. 1700 Cascadia earthquake
   d. 1509 Istanbul earthquake

10. In chemistry, a _____ is defined as a sufficiently stable electrically neutral group of at least two atoms in a definite arrangement held together by strong chemical bonds.
    a. 1509 Istanbul earthquake
    b. Molecule
    c. 1703 Genroku earthquake
    d. 1700 Cascadia earthquake

11. _____ is the natural or artificial removal of surface and sub-surface water from a given area. Many agricultural soils need _____ to improve production or to manage water supplies.
    a. 1703 Genroku earthquake
    b. 1509 Istanbul earthquake
    c. 1700 Cascadia earthquake
    d. Drainage

12. _____ was an employee at Limerick nuclear power plant who set off the radiation alarms on his way to work in 1984. Other employees searched his house and found that he had radon poisoning in his basement that was unrelated to the nuclear power plant. It was calculated that about 100,000 Bq/mÂ³ (2,700 pCi/L) was contaminating his house and the risk of living there was equal to that of smoking 135 packs of cigarettes a day.
    a. 1703 Genroku earthquake
    b. 1700 Cascadia earthquake
    c. 1509 Istanbul earthquake
    d. Stanley Watras

13. _____ is the total length of all the streams and rivers in a drainage basin divided by the total area of the drainage basin.
    a. 1700 Cascadia earthquake
    b. 1509 Istanbul earthquake
    c. 1703 Genroku earthquake
    d. Drainage density

14. _____ is the third or vertical dimension of land surface. When _____ is described underwater, the term bathymetry is used.
    a. 1700 Cascadia earthquake
    b. Terrain
    c. 1703 Genroku earthquake
    d. 1509 Istanbul earthquake

15. The _____ of a material is defined as its mass per unit volume:

$$\rho = \frac{m}{V}$$

Different materials usually have different densities, so _____ is an important concept regarding buoyancy, metal purity and packaging.

In some cases _____ is expressed as the dimensionless quantities specific gravity or relative _____, in which case it is expressed in multiples of the _____ of some other standard material, usually water or air.

In a well-known story, Archimedes was given the task of determining whether King Hiero's goldsmith was embezzling gold during the manufacture of a wreath dedicated to the gods and replacing it with another, cheaper alloy.

- a. 1700 Cascadia earthquake
- b. Density
- c. Particle density
- d. 1509 Istanbul earthquake

16. _____ is water located beneath the ground surface in soil pore spaces and in the fractures of geologic formations. _____ is recharged from, and eventually flows to, the surface naturally; natural discharge often occurs at springs and seeps, streams and can often form oases or wetlands.
- a. 1700 Cascadia earthquake
- b. 1509 Istanbul earthquake
- c. 1703 Genroku earthquake
- d. Groundwater

17. Groundwater models are computer models of _____ systems, and are used by hydrogeologists. Groundwater models are used to simulate and predict aquifer conditions.
- a. 1703 Genroku earthquake
- b. 1700 Cascadia earthquake
- c. 1509 Istanbul earthquake
- d. Groundwater flow

18. _____ is any particulate matter that can be transported by fluid flow and which eventually is deposited as a layer of solid particles on the bed or bottom of a body of water or other liquid.
- a. Sediment
- b. 1703 Genroku earthquake
- c. 1700 Cascadia earthquake
- d. 1509 Istanbul earthquake

19. In Hydrology, _____ is the movement of water horizontally beneath the land surface. It occurs once water has infiltrated the soil, the water moves downwards under gravity and because the soil becomes more compact and less permeable with increasing depth, water will begin to move sideways at speeds of between 0.005 to 0.3 m/h. It usually happens when the soil is completely saturated with water. This water then flows underground until it reaches a river, lake, or ocean.
- a. Throughflow
- b. 1700 Cascadia earthquake
- c. 1703 Genroku earthquake
- d. 1509 Istanbul earthquake

20. A _____ is a body of water with a current, confined within a bed and banks. Streams are important as conduits in the water cycle, instruments in aquifer recharge, and corridors for fish and wildlife migration.
- a. Stream
- b. 1509 Istanbul earthquake
- c. 1700 Cascadia earthquake
- d. 1703 Genroku earthquake

21. The _____ is the subsurface layer in which groundwater seeps up from a water table by capillary action to fill pores. Pores at the base of the _____ are filled with water due to tension saturation. This saturated portion of the _____ is less than total capillary rise because of the presence of a mix in pore size.
- a. 1509 Istanbul earthquake
- b. Capillary fringe
- c. 1703 Genroku earthquake
- d. 1700 Cascadia earthquake

Chapter 10. Water: Process, Supply, and Use

22. The _____ is the portion of Earth between the land surface and the phreatic zone or zone of saturation.
    a. 1703 Genroku earthquake
    b. 1700 Cascadia earthquake
    c. Vadose zone
    d. 1509 Istanbul earthquake

23. The _____ is the surface where the water pressure is equal to atmospheric pressure. A large amount of water within a body of sand or rock below the _____ is called an aquifer, and the ability of rocks to store such groundwater is dependent on their porosity and permeability.
    a. 1700 Cascadia earthquake
    b. 1703 Genroku earthquake
    c. 1509 Istanbul earthquake
    d. Water table

24. The _____ is the area in an aquifer, below the water table, which relatively all pores and fractures are saturated with water. It may fluctuate with changes in seasons and during wet and dry periods.
    a. 1509 Istanbul earthquake
    b. 1700 Cascadia earthquake
    c. Zone of saturation
    d. 1703 Genroku earthquake

25. An _____ is an underground layer of water-bearing permeable rock or unconsolidated materials from which groundwater can be usefully extracted using a water well.
    a. Aquifer
    b. AL 333
    c. AASHTO Soil Classification System
    d. AL 129-1

26. An _____ is a zone within the earth that restricts the flow of groundwater from one aquifer to another.
    a. AL 129-1
    b. AASHTO Soil Classification System
    c. Aquitard
    d. AL 333

27. An _____ occurs in recharging aquifers, this happens because the water table at its recharge zone is at a higher elevation than the head of the well.
    a. AL 129-1
    b. AL 333
    c. AASHTO Soil Classification System
    d. Artesian well

28. A _____ has the water table above their upper boundary and is typically found below unconfined aquifers. It has very low storativity values, which means that the aquifer is storing water using the mechanisms of aquifer matrix expansion and the compressibility of water, which typically are both quite small quantities.
    a. 1703 Genroku earthquake
    b. 1700 Cascadia earthquake
    c. 1509 Istanbul earthquake
    d. Confined aquifer

29. _____ is the volumetric flow rate of groundwater through an aquifer.

Total _____, as reported through a specified area, is similarly expressed as:

$$Q = \frac{dh}{dl} KA$$

where

> Q is the total _____ ([L³T⁻¹]; m³/s), and
> A is the area which the groundwater is flowing through ([L²]; m²)

For example, this can be used to determine the flow rate of water flowing along a plane with known geometry.

- Groundwater flow equation
- Groundwater energy balance
- Submarine _____
- Discharge (hydrology) - for rivers
- volumetric flow rate
- flux (transport definition)
- Darcy's Law

a. 1700 Cascadia earthquake
b. 1509 Istanbul earthquake
c. 1703 Genroku earthquake
d. Groundwater discharge

30. _____ or deep drainage or deep percolation is a hydrologic process where water moves downward from surface water to groundwater. This process usually occurs in the vadose zone below plant roots and is often expressed as a flux to the water table surface. Recharge occurs both naturally (through the water cycle) and anthropologically (i.e., 'artificial _____'), where rainwater and or reclaimed water is routed to the subsurface.
    a. 1700 Cascadia earthquake
    b. 1509 Istanbul earthquake
    c. 1703 Genroku earthquake
    d. Groundwater recharge

31. _____ refers to a member of any human group whose adult males grow to less than 150 cm in average height or less than 155 cm. A member of a slightly taller group is termed pygmoid. The best known _____ are the Aka, Efe and Mbuti of central Africa.
    a. 1700 Cascadia earthquake
    b. 1703 Genroku earthquake
    c. Pygmies
    d. 1509 Istanbul earthquake

32. _____ flow beneath the water table and gain water froman outflow, groundwater or the water table which creates an increased flow.
    a. AL 333
    b. Effluent streams
    c. AASHTO Soil Classification System
    d. AL 129-1

33. _____, symbolically represented as K, is a property of vascular plants, soil or rock, that describes the ease with which water can move through pore spaces or fractures
    a. Hydraulic conductivity
    b. 1700 Cascadia earthquake
    c. 1509 Istanbul earthquake
    d. 1703 Genroku earthquake

Chapter 10. Water: Process, Supply, and Use

34. _____ or piezometric head is a specific measurement of water pressure above a geodetic datum. It is usually measured as a water surface elevation, expressed in units of length, at the entrance (or bottom) of a piezometer. In an aquifer, it can be calculated from the depth to water in a piezometric well (a specialized water well), and given information of the piezometer's elevation and screen depth.
    a. 1509 Istanbul earthquake
    b. 1700 Cascadia earthquake
    c. Hydraulic head
    d. 1703 Genroku earthquake

35. In the earth sciences, _____ is a measure of the ability of a material to transmit fluids. It is of great importance in determining the flow characteristics of hydrocarbons in oil and gas reservoirs, and of groundwater in aquifers.
    a. 1700 Cascadia earthquake
    b. 1703 Genroku earthquake
    c. 1509 Istanbul earthquake
    d. Permeability

36. _____ is a measure of the void spaces in a material, and is measured as a fraction, between 0–1, or as a percentage between 0–100%.
    a. 1703 Genroku earthquake
    b. 1700 Cascadia earthquake
    c. 1509 Istanbul earthquake
    d. Porosity

37. Water collecting on the ground or in a stream, river, lake, or wetland is called _____; as opposed to groundwater. _____ is naturally replenished by precipitation and naturally lost through discharge to the oceans, evaporation, and sub-surface seepage into the groundwater. _____ is the largest source of fresh water.
    a. 1700 Cascadia earthquake
    b. 1703 Genroku earthquake
    c. 1509 Istanbul earthquake
    d. Surface water

38. In vector calculus, the _____ of a scalar field is a vector field which points in the direction of the greatest rate of increase of the scalar field, and whose magnitude is the greatest rate of change.

A generalization of the _____ for functions on a Euclidean space which have values in another Euclidean space is the Jacobian. A further generalization for a function from one Banach space to another is the Fréchet derivative.

   a. Gradient
   b. 1703 Genroku earthquake
   c. 1700 Cascadia earthquake
   d. 1509 Istanbul earthquake

39. A _____ is a deliberate process for transforming one or more inputs into one or more results, with variable change.
    a. 1703 Genroku earthquake
    b. 1700 Cascadia earthquake
    c. 1509 Istanbul earthquake
    d. Calculation

40. _____ is an infection of the digestive system that results in severe diarrhea containing mucus and blood in the feces and is typically the result of unsanitary water containing micro-organisms which cause significant inflammation of the intestinal lining.
    a. Dysentery
    b. 1700 Cascadia earthquake
    c. 1509 Istanbul earthquake
    d. 1703 Genroku earthquake

41. _____ refers to any of several processes that remove excess salt and other minerals from water in order to obtain fresh water suitable for animal consumption or irrigation, and if almost all of the salt is removed, for human consumption.

Chapter 10. Water: Process, Supply, and Use

a. 1700 Cascadia earthquake
b. 1509 Istanbul earthquake
c. 1703 Genroku earthquake
d. Desalination

42. _____ refers to a water body or system that is not located in a streambed or does not receive significant natural flows.
   a. AL 333
   b. AL 129-1
   c. AASHTO Soil Classification System
   d. Offstream water

43. _____ is a state on the West Coast of the United States, along the Pacific Ocean. It is bordered by Oregon to the north, Nevada to the east, Arizona to the southeast, and to the south the Mexican state of Baja _____. _____ is the most populous U.S. state.
   a. California
   b. 1509 Istanbul earthquake
   c. 1700 Cascadia earthquake
   d. 1703 Genroku earthquake

44. _____ is the process of self-provision or provision by third parties of water of various qualities to different users.
   a. 1509 Istanbul earthquake
   b. 1700 Cascadia earthquake
   c. 1703 Genroku earthquake
   d. Water supply

45. A _____ is an urban area with a high population and a particular administrative, legal, or historical status.

Large industrialized cities generally have advanced systems for sanitation, utilities, land usage, housing, and transportation and more. This close proximity greatly facilitates interaction between people and firms, benefiting both parties in the process.

   a. City
   b. 1509 Istanbul earthquake
   c. 1703 Genroku earthquake
   d. 1700 Cascadia earthquake

46. The City of New York, most often called _____, is the most populous city in the United States, in a metropolitan area that ranks among the world's most-populous urban areas. It is a leading global city, exerting a powerful influence over worldwide commerce, finance, culture, and entertainment. The city is also an important center for international affairs, hosting the United Nations headquarters.
   a. New York City
   b. 1509 Istanbul earthquake
   c. 1703 Genroku earthquake
   d. 1700 Cascadia earthquake

47. The principal body of law currently in effect is based on the Federal Water Pollution Control Amendments of 1972, which significantly expanded and strengthened earlier legislation. Major amendments were enacted in the Clean Water Act of 1977 enacted by the 95th United States Congress and the _____ of 1987 enacted by the 100th United States Congress.

The Act governs discharges to waters of the United States. Older statutory language used the term 'navigable waters,' but this term was expanded in the 1972 law:

The term 'navigable waters' means the waters of the United States, including the territorial seas.

   a. NEPA
   b. Water Quality Act
   c. Fish and Wildlife Coordination Act
   d. Mediation

Chapter 10. Water: Process, Supply, and Use

48. The _____ is a diverse scientific, social, and political movement for addressing the concerns of environmentalism. The _____ is represented by a range of organizations, from the large to grassroots. Due to its large membership, varying and strong beliefs, and occasionally speculative nature, the _____ is not always united in its goals.
   a. Environmental movement
   b. Andrija Mohorovičić
   c. Amblypoda
   d. Ambulocetus

49. The _____ is a river in the southwestern United States and northwestern Mexico, approximately 1,450 mi long, draining a part of the arid regions on the western slope of the Rocky Mountains. The natural course of the river flows into the Gulf of California, but the heavy use of the river as an irrigation source for the Imperial Valley has desiccated the lower course of the river in Mexico such that it no longer consistently reaches the sea.
   a. 1703 Genroku earthquake
   b. Colorado River
   c. 1509 Istanbul earthquake
   d. 1700 Cascadia earthquake

50. _____ (October 8, 1915 in Albuquerque, New Mexico - February 23, 2006 in Berkeley, California) was a leading U.S. geomorphologist, and son of Aldo Leopold.

A famous U.S. hydrologist, he suggested that a new philosophy of water management is needed, one based on geologic, geographic, and climatic factors as well as traditional economic, social, and political factors. He argued that the management of water resources cannot be successful as long as it is naïvely perceived from an economic and political standpoint, as it is in the status quo.

   a. Hambali
   b. Roald Amundsen
   c. Luna Bergere Leopold
   d. Hafez Al-Assad

51. The _____ is a 1922 agreement among seven U.S. states in the basin of the Colorado River in the American Southwest governing the allocation of the river's water among the parties of the interstate compact.
   a. 1703 Genroku earthquake
   b. Colorado River Compact
   c. 1509 Istanbul earthquake
   d. 1700 Cascadia earthquake

52. Most often, a _____ refers to an artificial lake, used to store water for various uses. Reservoirs are created first by building a sturdy dam, usually out of cement, earth, rock, or a mixture. Once the dam is completed, a stream is allowed to flow behind it and eventually fill it to capacity.
   a. 1703 Genroku earthquake
   b. 1509 Istanbul earthquake
   c. Reservoir
   d. 1700 Cascadia earthquake

53. A _____ is a barrier across flowing water that obstructs, directs or slows down the flow, often creating a reservoir, lake or impoundment.
   a. 1700 Cascadia earthquake
   b. 1703 Genroku earthquake
   c. 1509 Istanbul earthquake
   d. Dam

54. _____ are artificial channels for water. There are two main types of _____: irrigation _____, which are used for the delivery of water, and waterways, which are transportation _____ used for passage of goods and people, often connected to existing lakes, rivers, or oceans.

Chapter 10. Water: Process, Supply, and Use

    a. 1700 Cascadia earthquake
    b. 1509 Istanbul earthquake
    c. 1703 Genroku earthquake
    d. Canals

55. A _____ is a region where the atmospheric pressure is greater than the surrounding area.
    a. 1700 Cascadia earthquake
    b. 1509 Istanbul earthquake
    c. 1703 Genroku earthquake
    d. High

56. An _____ is a natural unit consisting of all plants, animals and micro organisms in an area functioning together with all the non living physical factors of the environment.
    a. AL 129-1
    b. AASHTO Soil Classification System
    c. AL 333
    d. Ecosystem

57. A _____ is a deep valley between cliffs often carved from the landscape by a river. Most were formed by a process of long-time erosion from a plateau level. The cliffs form because harder rock strata that are resistant to erosion and weathering remain exposed on the valley walls.
    a. 1700 Cascadia earthquake
    b. 1703 Genroku earthquake
    c. Canyon
    d. 1509 Istanbul earthquake

58. _____ is a dam on the Colorado River at Page, Arizona, operated by the United States Bureau of Reclamation. The purpose of the dam is to provide water storage for the arid southwestern United States, and to generate electricity for the region's growing population.
    a. Glen Canyon Dam
    b. 1509 Istanbul earthquake
    c. 1703 Genroku earthquake
    d. 1700 Cascadia earthquake

59. The _____ is a very colorful, steep-sided gorge, carved by the Colorado River in the U.S. state of Arizona. It is one of the first national parks in the United States.
    a. 1700 Cascadia earthquake
    b. 1509 Istanbul earthquake
    c. 1703 Genroku earthquake
    d. Grand Canyon

60. In physical geography, a _____ is an environment "at the interface between truly terrestrial ecosystems and aquatic systems making them inherently different from each other yet highly dependent on both". In essence, they are ecotones.
    a. 1509 Istanbul earthquake
    b. 1700 Cascadia earthquake
    c. Wetland
    d. 1703 Genroku earthquake

Chapter 11. Water Pollution and Treatment

1. _____ is a large set of adverse effects upon water bodies such as lakes, rivers, oceans, and groundwater caused by human activities. Although natural phenomena such as volcanoes, algae blooms, storms, and earthquakes also cause major changes in water quality and the ecological status of water, these are not deemed to be pollution. _____ has many causes and characteristics.
   a. Water pollution
   b. 1509 Istanbul earthquake
   c. 1700 Cascadia earthquake
   d. 1703 Genroku earthquake

2. _____ is the introduction of substances or energy into the environment, resulting in deleterious effects of such a nature as to endanger human health, harm living resources and ecosystems, and impair or interfere with amenities and other legitimate uses of the environment.
   a. 1700 Cascadia earthquake
   b. 1509 Istanbul earthquake
   c. 1703 Genroku earthquake
   d. Pollution

3. _____ is a broadly useful concept that expresses how fast something moves through a system in equilibrium. It is the average time a substance spends within a specified region of space, such as a reservoir.
   a. 1509 Istanbul earthquake
   b. 1700 Cascadia earthquake
   c. 1703 Genroku earthquake
   d. Residence time

4. There are two distinct views on the meaning of _____. One view is that _____ is part of the fundamental structure of the universe, a dimension in which events occur in sequence, and _____ itself is something that can be measured. A contrasting view is that _____ is part of the fundamental intellectual structure in which _____, rather than being an objective thing to be measured, is part of the mental measuring system.
   a. 1509 Istanbul earthquake
   b. Time
   c. 1703 Genroku earthquake
   d. 1700 Cascadia earthquake

5. _____ is a layer of gases surrounding the planet Earth and retained by the Earth's gravity, protecting life on Earth by absorbing ultraviolet solar radiation and reducing temperature extremes between day and night.
   a. AL 333
   b. AL 129-1
   c. Earths atmosphere
   d. AASHTO Soil Classification System

6. _____ is a chemical, physical, or biological agent that modifies the natural characteristics of the atmosphere. The atmosphere is a complex, dynamic natural gaseous system that is essential to support life on planet Earth. Stratospheric ozone depletion due to _____ has long been recognized as a threat to human health as well as to the Earth's ecosystems. Worldwide _____ is responsible for large numbers of deaths and cases of respiratory disease.
   a. AL 333
   b. AASHTO Soil Classification System
   c. AL 129-1
   d. Air pollution

7. _____ are unicellular microorganisms. They are typically a few micrometres long and have many shapes including curved rods, spheres, rods, and spirals.
   a. 1703 Genroku earthquake
   b. 1509 Istanbul earthquake
   c. Bacteria
   d. 1700 Cascadia earthquake

8. _____ is a chemical procedure for determining how fast biological organisms use up oxygen in a body of water.
   a. 1509 Istanbul earthquake
   b. 1703 Genroku earthquake
   c. 1700 Cascadia earthquake
   d. Biochemical oxygen demand

9. _____ bacteria are a commonly-used bacterial indicator of sanitary quality of foods and water.

Chapter 11. Water Pollution and Treatment

   a. 1700 Cascadia earthquake
   c. 1703 Genroku earthquake
   b. 1509 Istanbul earthquake
   d. Coliform

10. _____ are the commonly-used bacterial indicator of sanitary quality of foods and water. They are defined as rod-shaped Gram-negative non-spore forming organisms that ferment lactose with the production of acid and gas when incubated at 35-37°C. Coliforms are abundant in the feces of warm-blooded animals, but can also be found in the aquatic environment, in soil and on vegetation.
   a. 1509 Istanbul earthquake
   c. 1703 Genroku earthquake
   b. 1700 Cascadia earthquake
   d. Coliform bacteria

11. The _____ is a division of the White House that coordinates federal environmental efforts in the United States and works closely with agencies and other White House offices in the development of environmental and energy policies and initiatives.
   a. 1703 Genroku earthquake
   c. 1509 Istanbul earthquake
   b. 1700 Cascadia earthquake
   d. Council on Environmental Quality

12. _____ is a parasitic disease affecting the intestines of mammals. It is a disease spread through the fecal-oral route; the main symptom is self-limiting diarrhea in people with intact immune system.
   a. Cryptosporidiosis
   c. 1703 Genroku earthquake
   b. 1509 Istanbul earthquake
   d. 1700 Cascadia earthquake

13. _____ is one of the main species of bacteria living in the lower intestines of mammals, known as gut flora. When located in the large intestine, it actually assists with waste processing, vitamin K production, and food absorption.
   a. AL 129-1
   c. AL 333
   b. AASHTO Soil Classification System
   d. Escherichia coli

14. In epidemiology, an infection that is _____ appears as new cases in a given human population, during a given period, at a rate that substantially exceeds what is 'expected,' based on recent experience. In recent usages, the disease is not required to be communicable.

Defining an _____ can be subjective, depending in part on what is 'expected'.

   a. AASHTO Soil Classification System
   c. Epidemic
   b. AL 129-1
   d. Environmental factor

15. _____ is a facultatively-anaerobic, rod-shaped, gram-negative, non-sporulating bacteria. They are capable of growth in the presence of bile salts or similar surface agents, oxidase negative, and produce acid and gas from lactose within 48 hours at 44 ± 0.5°C.
   a. 1700 Cascadia earthquake
   c. 1509 Istanbul earthquake
   b. 1703 Genroku earthquake
   d. Fecal coliform bacteria

16. _____ refers to food waste and dead plant and animal tissue that consumes oxygen dissolved in water during its degradation and depleting oxygen required for survival of marine animals ans marine plants.
   a. Oxygen-demanding waste
   c. AL 333
   b. AASHTO Soil Classification System
   d. AL 129-1

Chapter 11. Water Pollution and Treatment

17. A _____ is a biological agent that causes disease or illness to its host.
   a. Pathogen
   b. 1509 Istanbul earthquake
   c. 1700 Cascadia earthquake
   d. 1703 Genroku earthquake

18. Pollution is the introduction of contaminants into an environment that causes instability, disorder, harm or discomfort to the physical systems or living organisms. Pollution can take the form of chemical substances, or energy, such as noise, heat, or light energy. _____, the elements of pollution, can be foreign substances or energies, or naturally occurring; when naturally occurring, they are considered contaminants when they exceed natural levels.
   a. 1700 Cascadia earthquake
   b. 1703 Genroku earthquake
   c. 1509 Istanbul earthquake
   d. Pollutants

19. _____ refers to the reduction of the body of a formerly living organism into simpler forms of matter.
   a. 1509 Istanbul earthquake
   b. Decomposition
   c. 1700 Cascadia earthquake
   d. 1703 Genroku earthquake

20. A _____ or medical condition is an abnormal condition of an organism that impairs bodily functions and can be deadly. It is also defined as a way of the body harming itself in an abnormal way, associated with specific symptoms and signs.

   In human beings,'_____' is often used more broadly to refer to any condition that causes extreme pain, dysfunction, distress, social problems, and/or death to the person afflicted, or similar problems for those in contact with the person.

   a. Black lung disease
   b. 1700 Cascadia earthquake
   c. Disease
   d. 1509 Istanbul earthquake

21. In biology and ecology, an _____ is a living complex adaptive system of organs that influence each other in such a way that they function in some way as a stable whole.
   a. AL 333
   b. AASHTO Soil Classification System
   c. Organism
   d. AL 129-1

22. _____ is a chemical element in the periodic table. It has the symbol O and atomic number 8. _____ is the second most common element on Earth, composing around 46% of the mass of Earth's crust and 28% of the mass of Earth as a whole, and is the third most common element in the universe.
   a. AL 333
   b. Oxygen
   c. AASHTO Soil Classification System
   d. AL 129-1

23. _____ is unwanted or undesired material.
   a. 1700 Cascadia earthquake
   b. Waste
   c. 1703 Genroku earthquake
   d. 1509 Istanbul earthquake

24. _____ diseases are pathogenic microorganisms which are directly transmitted when contaminated drinking water is consumed.
   a. 1509 Istanbul earthquake
   b. 1700 Cascadia earthquake
   c. Waterborne
   d. 1703 Genroku earthquake

Chapter 11. Water Pollution and Treatment

25. A _____ is a substance used in an organism's metabolism which must be taken in from the environment. Non-autotrophic organisms typically acquire nutrients by the ingestion of foods. Methods for _____ intake vary, with animals and protists having an internal digestive system, while plants digest nutrients externally and then ingested. The effects of nutrients are dose-dependent.
- a. 1509 Istanbul earthquake
- b. 1700 Cascadia earthquake
- c. 1703 Genroku earthquake
- d. Nutrient

26. _____ was the original name of an oil tanker owned by the former Exxon Corporation. It gained widespread infamy after the March 24, 1989 oil spill in which the tanker, captained by Joseph Hazelwood, hit Prince William Sound's Bligh Reef and spilled an estimated 11 million gallons of crude oil.
- a. AASHTO Soil Classification System
- b. AL 129-1
- c. AL 333
- d. Exxon Valdez

27. The _____ was one of the largest manmade environmental disasters ever to occur at sea, seriously affecting plants and wildlife. Its remote location made government and industry response efforts difficult, and severely taxed existing plans for response.
- a. AL 129-1
- b. AASHTO Soil Classification System
- c. Exxon Valdez oil spill
- d. AL 333

28. Some of the _____ can be found in nature. It is an naturally occuring toxin found in certain plants and some wild mushrooms and berries. It refers to any chemical or mixture that may be harmful to the environment and to human health if inhaled, swalled, or absorbed through the skin.
- a. 1703 Genroku earthquake
- b. 1509 Istanbul earthquake
- c. Toxic substance
- d. 1700 Cascadia earthquake

29. An _____ is the unintentional release of liquid petroleum hydrocarbon into the environment as a result of human activity.
- a. AL 333
- b. AL 129-1
- c. AASHTO Soil Classification System
- d. Oil spill

30. _____ is any particulate matter that can be transported by fluid flow and which eventually is deposited as a layer of solid particles on the bed or bottom of a body of water or other liquid.
- a. 1509 Istanbul earthquake
- b. 1703 Genroku earthquake
- c. Sediment
- d. 1700 Cascadia earthquake

31. A _____ column is a column of rizing air in the lower altitudes of the Earth's atmosphere. Thermals are created by the uneven heating of the Earth's surface from solar radiation, and are an example of convection. The Sun warms the ground, which in turn warms the air directly above it.
- a. 1703 Genroku earthquake
- b. Thermal
- c. 1509 Istanbul earthquake
- d. 1700 Cascadia earthquake

32. _____ is a temperature change in natural water bodies caused by human influence. The main cause of _____ is the use of water as a coolant, especially in power plants. Water used as a coolant is returned to the natural environment at a higher temperature.

Chapter 11. Water Pollution and Treatment 101

a. Thermal pollution
b. 1700 Cascadia earthquake
c. 1509 Istanbul earthquake
d. 1703 Genroku earthquake

33. The _____ is located in Northeast Ohio in the United States. Outside of Ohio, the river is most famous for being "the river that caught on fire"—which has actually happened more than once—helping to spur the environmental movement.
a. 1700 Cascadia earthquake
b. 1509 Istanbul earthquake
c. 1703 Genroku earthquake
d. Cuyahoga River

34. _____ is the largest city in the U.S. state of Michigan and the seat of Wayne County. _____ is a major port city on the _____ River, in the Midwest region of the United States. Located north of Windsor, Ontario, _____ is the only major U.S. city that looks south to Canada.
a. 1700 Cascadia earthquake
b. 1703 Genroku earthquake
c. Detroit
d. 1509 Istanbul earthquake

35. _____ comes from many unidentifiable sources with no specific solution to rectify the proble, making it difficult to regulate. An example would be urban runoff of items like oil, fertilizers, and lawn chemicals. As rainfall or snowmelt moves over and through the ground, it picks up and carries away natural and human-made pollutants.
a. 1703 Genroku earthquake
b. 1700 Cascadia earthquake
c. 1509 Istanbul earthquake
d. Nonpoint sources

36. An _____ is traditionally considered any chemical compound that, when dissolved in water, gives a solution with a hydrogen ion activity greater than in pure water, i.e. a pH less than 7.0. That approximates the modern definition of Johannes Nicolaus Brønsted and Martin Lowry, who independently defined an _____ as a compound which donates a hydrogen ion to another compound. Common examples include acetic _____ and sulfuric _____. _____/base systems are different from redox reactions in that there is no change in oxidation state.
a. AL 333
b. AASHTO Soil Classification System
c. AL 129-1
d. Acid

37. _____ refers to the outflow of acidic water from abandoned metal mines. However, other areas where the earth has been disturbed may also contribute _____ to the environment
a. AL 333
b. AASHTO Soil Classification System
c. AL 129-1
d. Acid mine drainage

38. _____ are artificial channels for water. There are two main types of _____: irrigation _____, which are used for the delivery of water, and waterways, which are transportation _____ used for passage of goods and people, often connected to existing lakes, rivers, or oceans.
a. Canals
b. 1509 Istanbul earthquake
c. 1703 Genroku earthquake
d. 1700 Cascadia earthquake

39. A _____ is a body of water with a current, confined within a bed and banks. Streams are important as conduits in the water cycle, instruments in aquifer recharge, and corridors for fish and wildlife migration.
a. 1700 Cascadia earthquake
b. Stream
c. 1703 Genroku earthquake
d. 1509 Istanbul earthquake

Chapter 11. Water Pollution and Treatment

40. _____ is water located beneath the ground surface in soil pore spaces and in the fractures of geologic formations. _____ is recharged from, and eventually flows to, the surface naturally; natural discharge often occurs at springs and seeps, streams and can often form oases or wetlands.
    a. Groundwater
    b. 1700 Cascadia earthquake
    c. 1703 Genroku earthquake
    d. 1509 Istanbul earthquake

41. _____ is a neighborhood in Niagara Falls, New York, United States of America. It officially covers 36 square blocks in the far southeastern corner of the city, along 99th Street and Read Avenue. Two bodies of water define the northern and southern boundaries of the neighborhood: Bergholtz Creek to the north and the Niagara River one-quarter mile to the south.
    a. Love Canal
    b. 1509 Istanbul earthquake
    c. 1700 Cascadia earthquake
    d. 1703 Genroku earthquake

42. _____ is a quantity expressing the two-dimensional size of a defined part of a surface, typically a region bounded by a closed curve. The term surface _____ refers to the total _____ of the exposed surface of a 3-dimensional solid, such as the sum of the areas of the exposed sides of a polyhedron. _____ is an important invariant in the differential geometry of surfaces.
    a. AASHTO Soil Classification System
    b. AL 129-1
    c. Area
    d. AL 333

43. _____ is the natural or artificial removal of surface and sub-surface water from a given area. Many agricultural soils need _____ to improve production or to manage water supplies.
    a. 1703 Genroku earthquake
    b. Drainage
    c. 1509 Istanbul earthquake
    d. 1700 Cascadia earthquake

44. _____, officially the Republic of _____ , is a country in Central America, bordered by Nicaragua to the north, Panama to the east and south, the Pacific Ocean to the west and south and the Caribbean Sea to the east. _____ was the first country in the world to constitutionally abolish its army. Among Latin American countries, _____ ranks 4th in terms of the 2007 Human Development Index.
    a. Costa Rica
    b. 1509 Istanbul earthquake
    c. 1700 Cascadia earthquake
    d. 1703 Genroku earthquake

45. The _____ in Mahican, is a river that runs through the eastern portion of New York State and, along its southern terminus, demarcates the border between the states of New York and New Jersey. It is named for Henry Hudson, an Englishman sailing for the Netherlands, who explored it in 1609.
    a. 1509 Istanbul earthquake
    b. Hudson River
    c. 1703 Genroku earthquake
    d. 1700 Cascadia earthquake

46. _____ is a natural process that occurs in virtually all coastal aquifers. It consists in salt water flowing inland in freshwater aquifers. This behavior is caused by the fact that sea water has a higher density than freshwater.
    a. 1509 Istanbul earthquake
    b. Saltwater intrusion
    c. 1703 Genroku earthquake
    d. 1700 Cascadia earthquake

47. An _____ is a body of igneous rock that has crystallized from a molten magma below the surface of the Earth.

Chapter 11. Water Pollution and Treatment

a. AL 333
b. AASHTO Soil Classification System
c. Intrusion
d. AL 129-1

48. An _____ is any piece of land that is completely surrounded by water, above high tide. There are two main types of islands: continental islands and oceanic islands. There are also artificial islands. A grouping of geographically and/or geologically related islands is called an archipelago.
a. AL 333
b. AASHTO Soil Classification System
c. Island
d. AL 129-1

49. _____ is an island located in southeastern New York, USA, just east of Manhattan. Stretching northeast into the Atlantic Ocean, _____ contains four counties, two of which are boroughs of New York City, and two of which are mainly suburban. Numerous bridges and tunnels through Queens and Brooklyn connect _____ to the three other boroughs of New York City.
a. 1703 Genroku earthquake
b. 1509 Istanbul earthquake
c. Long Island
d. 1700 Cascadia earthquake

50. _____ can be defined as any process that uses microorganisms, fungi, green plants or their enzymes to return the environment altered by contaminants to its original condition.
a. Bioremediation
b. 1509 Istanbul earthquake
c. 1703 Genroku earthquake
d. 1700 Cascadia earthquake

51. _____ is the gas phase component of a another state of matter which does not completely fill its container. It is distinguished from the pure gas phase by the presence of the same substance in another state of matter. Hence when a liquid has completely evaporated, it is said that the system has been completely transformed to the gas phase.
a. 1700 Cascadia earthquake
b. 1509 Istanbul earthquake
c. 1703 Genroku earthquake
d. Vapor

52. _____ is water that is intended to be ingested by humans. Water of sufficient quality to serve as _____ is termed potable water whether it is used as such or not.
a. 1703 Genroku earthquake
b. Drinking Water
c. 1509 Istanbul earthquake
d. 1700 Cascadia earthquake

53. The U.S. _____ (_____ or sometimes USEPA) is an agency of the federal government of the United States charged to regulate chemicals and protect human health by safeguarding the natural environment: air, water, and land. The _____ was proposed by President Richard Nixon and began operation on December 2, 1970, when its establishment was passed by Congress, and signed into law by President Nixon, and has since been chiefly responsible for the environmental policy of the United States. It is led by its Administrator, who is appointed by the President of the United States.
a. AASHTO Soil Classification System
b. AL 129-1
c. AL 333
d. EPA

54. The _____ is an agency of the federal government of the United States charged with protecting human health and with safeguarding the natural environment: air, water, and land.
a. Amblypoda
b. Ambulocetus
c. Andrija Mohorovičić
d. Environmental Protection Agency

Chapter 11. Water Pollution and Treatment

55. A _____ is a standard that is set by the United States Environmental Protection Agency for drinking water quality. It is the legal threshold limit on the amount of a hazardous substance that is allowed in drinking water under the Safe Drinking Water Act. The limit is usually expressed as a concentration in milligrams or micrograms per liter of water.
    a. Maximum Contaminant Level
    b. 1509 Istanbul earthquake
    c. 1703 Genroku earthquake
    d. 1700 Cascadia earthquake

56. A _____ is a salt of nitric acid with an ion composed of one nitrogen and three oxygen atoms. In freshwater or estuarine systems close to land, _____ can reach high levels that can potentially cause the death of fish. Water quality may also be affected through ground water resources that have a high number of septic systems in a watershed.
    a. 1509 Istanbul earthquake
    b. 1700 Cascadia earthquake
    c. 1703 Genroku earthquake
    d. Nitrate

57. _____ is any water that has been adversely affected in quality by anthropogenic influence.
    a. 1700 Cascadia earthquake
    b. 1509 Istanbul earthquake
    c. Wastewater
    d. 1703 Genroku earthquake

58. _____ is the physical, chemical and biological characteristics of water, characterized through the methods of hydrometry.
    a. 1700 Cascadia earthquake
    b. 1703 Genroku earthquake
    c. Water quality
    d. 1509 Istanbul earthquake

59. A _____, the key component of a septic system, is a small scale sewage treatment system common in areas with no connection to main sewerage pipes provided by private corporations or local governments.
    a. 1700 Cascadia earthquake
    b. 1509 Istanbul earthquake
    c. Septic tank
    d. 1703 Genroku earthquake

60. _____ is a process dealing with the treatment of sewage and industrial wastewaters. Atmospheric air or pure oxygen is bubbled through primary treated sewage combined with organisms to develop a biological floc which reduces the organic content of the sewage. The combination of raw sewage and biological mass is commonly known as Mixed Liquor.
    a. AASHTO Soil Classification System
    b. AL 333
    c. Activated sludge
    d. AL 129-1

61. _____, sometimes called recycled water, is former wastewater (sewage) that has been treated to remove solids and certain impurities, and then allowed to recharge the aquifer rather than being discharged to surface water. This recharging is often done by using the treated wastewater for irrigation. In most locations, it is only intended to be used for nonpotable uses, such as irrigation, dust control, and fire suppression, and there is controversy about possible health and environmental effects for those uses.
    a. 1509 Istanbul earthquake
    b. 1703 Genroku earthquake
    c. 1700 Cascadia earthquake
    d. Reclaimed water

62. _____ is the residual semi-solid material left from industrial, water treatment, or wastewater treatment processes.
    a. 1700 Cascadia earthquake
    b. 1703 Genroku earthquake
    c. 1509 Istanbul earthquake
    d. Sludge

Chapter 11. Water Pollution and Treatment

63. _____ are a major group of living things including familiar organisms such as trees, flowers, herbs, bushes, grasses, vines, ferns, and mosses.
    a. 1703 Genroku earthquake
    b. 1700 Cascadia earthquake
    c. 1509 Istanbul earthquake
    d. Plants

64. _____ is the process of improving a structure. Two prominent types of renovations are commercial and residential.

The process of a _____, however complex, can usually be broken down into several processes.

    a. 1703 Genroku earthquake
    b. 1509 Istanbul earthquake
    c. Renovation
    d. 1700 Cascadia earthquake

65. _____ is a West Germanic language originating in England and is the first language for most people in the United Kingdom, the United States, Canada, Australia, New Zealand, Ireland and the Anglophone Caribbean. It is used extensively as a second language and as an official language throughout the world, especially in Commonwealth countries and in many international organisations.

Modern _____, sometimes described as the first global lingua franca, is the dominant international language in communications, science, business, aviation, entertainment, radio and diplomacy.

    a. AL 129-1
    b. AL 333
    c. AASHTO Soil Classification System
    d. English

66. A _____ is a body of water, not part of the ocean, that is larger and deeper than a pond.
    a. 1700 Cascadia earthquake
    b. Lake
    c. 1509 Istanbul earthquake
    d. 1703 Genroku earthquake

67. _____ is an alkaline and hypersaline lake in California, United States that is a critical nesting habitat for several bird species and is an unusually productive ecosystem.
    a. 1509 Istanbul earthquake
    b. 1700 Cascadia earthquake
    c. Mono Lake
    d. 1703 Genroku earthquake

68. The _____ is a diverse scientific, social, and political movement for addressing the concerns of environmentalism. The _____ is represented by a range of organizations, from the large to grassroots. Due to its large membership, varying and strong beliefs, and occasionally speculative nature, the _____ is not always united in its goals.
    a. Andrija Mohorovičić
    b. Ambulocetus
    c. Environmental movement
    d. Amblypoda

69. _____ is the process that speeds up natural eutrophication because of human activity. Due to clearing of land and building of towns and cities, run - off water is accelerated and more nutrients such as phosphates and nitrate are supplied to the lakes and ponds
    a. 1700 Cascadia earthquake
    b. 1703 Genroku earthquake
    c. 1509 Istanbul earthquake
    d. Cultural eutrophication

Chapter 11. Water Pollution and Treatment

70. _____ may refer to either the private sector or the public sector. In the public sector it generally refers to a government's use and creation of the laws, regulations, and other policy mechanisms concerning environmental issues and sustainability. In the private sector it usually refers to the compliance with those tools, or the independent development of self-regulation and rule-making that may go beyond what is required by governments.
   a. AL 129-1
   b. AASHTO Soil Classification System
   c. Environmental Policy
   d. AL 333

71. The _____ (FWCA) provides the basic authority for the United States Fish and Wildlife Service's (FWS) involvement in evaluating impacts to fish and wildlife from proposed water resource development projects. It requires that fish and wildlife resources receive equal consideration to other project features. It also requires Federal agencies involved with water resource development projects to first consult with the FWS and State fish and wildlife agencies regarding the impacts on fish and wildlife resources, and provide for measures to mitigate these impacts.
   a. Water Quality Act
   b. Mediation
   c. NEPA
   d. Fish and Wildlife Coordination Act

72. The _____ (_____) is a United States environmental law that was signed into law on January 1, 1970 by U.S. President Richard Nixon. The law established a U.S. national policy promoting the enhancement of the environment and also established the President's Council on Environmental Quality (CEQ.) But _____'s most significant effect was to set up procedural requirements for all federal government agencies to prepare Environmental Assessments (EAs) and Environmental Impact Statements (EISs.)
   a. Fish and Wildlife Coordination Act
   b. Mediation
   c. Water Quality Act
   d. NEPA

73. The _____ is a United States environmental law that was signed into law on January 1, 1970 by U.S. President Richard Nixon. The law applies only to federal agencies and the programs they fund. Essentially it requires that, prior to taking any "major" or "significant" action, the agency must consider the environmental impacts of that action.
   a. 1700 Cascadia earthquake
   b. 1703 Genroku earthquake
   c. 1509 Istanbul earthquake
   d. National Environmental Policy Act

74. The United States _____ of 1899 is a long-ignored federal statute. It prohibits all industrial discharges into bodies of water.
   a. 1703 Genroku earthquake
   b. 1700 Cascadia earthquake
   c. 1509 Istanbul earthquake
   d. Refuse Act

75. The _____ enacted in 1976, is a Federal law of the United States It states that RCRA's goals are:to protect the public from harm caused by waste disposal to encourage reuse, reduction, and recycling to clean up spilled or improperly stored wastes.
   a. Resource Conservation and Recovery Act
   b. 1700 Cascadia earthquake
   c. 1509 Istanbul earthquake
   d. 1703 Genroku earthquake

76. The _____ is a United States federal law passed by the U.S. Congress on December 16, 1974. It is the main federal law that ensures safe drinking water for Americans.
   a. Safe Drinking Water Act
   b. 1509 Istanbul earthquake
   c. 1703 Genroku earthquake
   d. 1700 Cascadia earthquake

Chapter 11. Water Pollution and Treatment

77. _____ is a waste type that includes predominantly household waste with sometimes the addition of commercial wastes collected by a municipality within a given area. They are in either solid or semisolid form and generally exclude industrial hazardous wastes.
   a. 1509 Istanbul earthquake
   b. Solid Waste
   c. 1703 Genroku earthquake
   d. 1700 Cascadia earthquake

78. The principal body of law currently in effect is based on the Federal Water Pollution Control Amendments of 1972, which significantly expanded and strengthened earlier legislation. Major amendments were enacted in the Clean Water Act of 1977 enacted by the 95th United States Congress and the _____ of 1987 enacted by the 100th United States Congress.

The Act governs discharges to waters of the United States. Older statutory language used the term 'navigable waters,' but this term was expanded in the 1972 law:

   The term 'navigable waters' means the waters of the United States, including the territorial seas.

   a. Fish and Wildlife Coordination Act
   b. Mediation
   c. NEPA
   d. Water Quality Act

79. _____ includes all non-domesticated plants, animals, and other organisms.
   a. 1509 Istanbul earthquake
   b. 1703 Genroku earthquake
   c. 1700 Cascadia earthquake
   d. Wildlife

80. _____ refers to an increase in the primary productivity of any ecosystem. _____ is caused by the increase of chemical nutrients, typically compounds containing nitrogen or phosphorus. It may occur on land or in water.
   a. Eutrophication
   b. AASHTO Soil Classification System
   c. AL 333
   d. AL 129-1

81. _____ refers to a member of any human group whose adult males grow to less than 150 cm in average height or less than 155 cm. A member of a slightly taller group is termed pygmoid. The best known _____ are the Aka, Efe and Mbuti of central Africa.
   a. 1703 Genroku earthquake
   b. 1700 Cascadia earthquake
   c. Pygmies
   d. 1509 Istanbul earthquake

82. _____ is the science and study of the solid matter that constitute the Earth. Encompassing such things as rocks, soil, and gemstones, _____ studies the composition, structure, physical properties, history, and the processes that shape Earth's components.
   a. 1703 Genroku earthquake
   b. 1700 Cascadia earthquake
   c. 1509 Istanbul earthquake
   d. Geology

Chapter 12. Waste Management

1. _____ is the collection, transport, processing, recycling or disposal of waste materials, usually ones produced by human activity, in an effort to reduce their effect on human health or local aesthetics or amenity.
   a. 1700 Cascadia earthquake
   b. 1509 Istanbul earthquake
   c. 1703 Genroku earthquake
   d. Waste management

2. _____ is a stream and freshwater estuary in the western portion of the New York City borough of Staten Island. It is the site of the _____ Landfill, formerly New York City's principal landfill.
   a. 1703 Genroku earthquake
   b. 1509 Istanbul earthquake
   c. Fresh Kills
   d. 1700 Cascadia earthquake

3. A _____ is a body of water with a current, confined within a bed and banks. Streams are important as conduits in the water cycle, instruments in aquifer recharge, and corridors for fish and wildlife migration.
   a. 1703 Genroku earthquake
   b. 1509 Istanbul earthquake
   c. 1700 Cascadia earthquake
   d. Stream

4. A _____, is a site for the disposal of waste materials by burial and is the oldest form of waste treatment.
   a. 1703 Genroku earthquake
   b. 1509 Istanbul earthquake
   c. 1700 Cascadia earthquake
   d. Landfill

5. _____ is the shifting of industrial process from linear systems, in which resource and capital investments move through the system to become waste, to a closed loop system where wastes become inputs for new processes.
   a. AASHTO Soil Classification System
   b. AL 129-1
   c. AL 333
   d. Industrial ecology

6. _____ is the branch of logistics that deals with the tangible components of a supply chain. Specifically, this covers the acquisition of spare parts and replacements, quality control of purchasing and ordering such parts, and the standards involved in ordering, shipping, and warehousing the said parts.

   _____ is just managing all types of materials in an organization.

   a. 1703 Genroku earthquake
   b. Materials management
   c. 1509 Istanbul earthquake
   d. 1700 Cascadia earthquake

7. A _____ substance is a material with a definite _____ composition. It is a concept that became firmly established in the late eighteenth century after work by the chemist Joseph Proust on the composition of some pure _____ compounds such as basic copper carbonate.
   a. 1703 Genroku earthquake
   b. 1700 Cascadia earthquake
   c. 1509 Istanbul earthquake
   d. Chemical

8. _____ is a waste that is made from harmful chemicals (mostly produced by large factories.) _____ may fall under regulations such as COSHH in the UK, or the Clean Water Act and Resource Conservation and Recovery Act in the US. _____ may or may not be classed as hazardous waste.
   a. 1509 Istanbul earthquake
   b. Metalloid
   c. Transferability
   d. Chemical waste

9. _____ is the scientific study of the distribution and abundance of living organisms and how the distribution and abundance are affected by interactions between the organisms and their environment.

Chapter 12. Waste Management

a. AL 129-1
b. AL 333
c. AASHTO Soil Classification System
d. Ecology

10. _____ is the reprocessing of materials into new products. It prevents useful material resources being wasted, reduces the consumption of raw materials and reduces energy usage, and hence greenhouse gas emissions, compared to virgin production.
   a. 1700 Cascadia earthquake
   b. 1703 Genroku earthquake
   c. 1509 Istanbul earthquake
   d. Recycling

11. _____ is using an item more than once. This includes conventional _____ where the item is used again for the same function, and new-life _____ where it is used for a new function. In contrast, recycling is the breaking down of the used item into raw materials which are used to make new items.
   a. 1509 Istanbul earthquake
   b. 1703 Genroku earthquake
   c. Reuse
   d. 1700 Cascadia earthquake

12. _____ is unwanted or undesired material.
   a. 1700 Cascadia earthquake
   b. 1703 Genroku earthquake
   c. 1509 Istanbul earthquake
   d. Waste

13. _____ is the aerobic decomposition of biodegradable organic matter, producing compost.
   a. 1509 Istanbul earthquake
   b. 1703 Genroku earthquake
   c. 1700 Cascadia earthquake
   d. Composting

14. _____ is a waste treatment technology that involves the combustion of waste at high temperatures.
   a. Incineration
   b. AASHTO Soil Classification System
   c. AL 333
   d. AL 129-1

15. _____ is the liquid produced when water percolates through any permeable material. It can contain either dissolved or suspended material, or usually both. This liquid is most commonly found in association with landfills, where rain percolates through the waste and reacts with the products of decomposition, chemicals and other materials in the waste to produce the _____.
   a. 1509 Istanbul earthquake
   b. 1703 Genroku earthquake
   c. 1700 Cascadia earthquake
   d. Leachate

16. _____ is a chemical compound with the molecular formula CH_4. It is the simplest alkane, and the principal component of natural gas. Burning one molecule of _____ in the presence of oxygen releases one molecule. _____'s relative abundance and clean burning process makes it a very attractive fuel.
   a. 1703 Genroku earthquake
   b. 1509 Istanbul earthquake
   c. 1700 Cascadia earthquake
   d. Methane

17. _____ is an uncovered site used for disposal of waste without environmental controls.
   a. AL 333
   b. AASHTO Soil Classification System
   c. Open dump
   d. AL 129-1

18. _____ is a method of controlled disposal of refuse on land. _____ involves natural fermentation brought by microorganisms. It is often employed to reclaim otherwise useless land.

a. 1703 Genroku earthquake
b. Sanitary landfill
c. 1700 Cascadia earthquake
d. 1509 Istanbul earthquake

19. The U.S. _____ (_____ or sometimes USEPA) is an agency of the federal government of the United States charged to regulate chemicals and protect human health by safeguarding the natural environment: air, water, and land. The _____ was proposed by President Richard Nixon and began operation on December 2, 1970, when its establishment was passed by Congress, and signed into law by President Nixon, and has since been chiefly responsible for the environmental policy of the United States. It is led by its Administrator, who is appointed by the President of the United States.
   a. AL 129-1
   b. EPA
   c. AL 333
   d. AASHTO Soil Classification System

20. The _____ is an agency of the federal government of the United States charged with protecting human health and with safeguarding the natural environment: air, water, and land.
   a. Andrija Mohorovičić
   b. Ambulocetus
   c. Environmental Protection Agency
   d. Amblypoda

21. _____ are dangerous compounds that cause contamination and are dangerous to human health and the environement.
   a. 1703 Genroku earthquake
   b. 1700 Cascadia earthquake
   c. 1509 Istanbul earthquake
   d. Hazardous chemicals

22. _____ are artificial channels for water. There are two main types of _____: irrigation _____, which are used for the delivery of water, and waterways, which are transportation _____ used for passage of goods and people, often connected to existing lakes, rivers, or oceans.
   a. 1509 Istanbul earthquake
   b. 1703 Genroku earthquake
   c. 1700 Cascadia earthquake
   d. Canals

23. _____ is a neighborhood in Niagara Falls, New York, United States of America. It officially covers 36 square blocks in the far southeastern corner of the city, along 99th Street and Read Avenue. Two bodies of water define the northern and southern boundaries of the neighborhood: Bergholtz Creek to the north and the Niagara River one-quarter mile to the south.
   a. Love Canal
   b. 1703 Genroku earthquake
   c. 1700 Cascadia earthquake
   d. 1509 Istanbul earthquake

24. The _____ is a diverse scientific, social, and political movement for addressing the concerns of environmentalism. The _____ is represented by a range of organizations, from the large to grassroots. Due to its large membership, varying and strong beliefs, and occasionally speculative nature, the _____ is not always united in its goals.
   a. Ambulocetus
   b. Andrija Mohorovičić
   c. Amblypoda
   d. Environmental movement

25. The _____ enacted in 1976, is a Federal law of the United States It states that RCRA's goals are:to protect the public from harm caused by waste disposal to encourage reuse, reduction, and recycling to clean up spilled or improperly stored wastes.

Chapter 12. Waste Management

a. 1700 Cascadia earthquake
c. 1509 Istanbul earthquake
b. 1703 Genroku earthquake
d. Resource Conservation and Recovery Act

26. The _____ was a nuclear reactor accident in the Chernobyl Nuclear Power Plant in the Soviet Union. It was the worst nuclear power plant disaster ever and the only level 7 instance on the International Nuclear Event Scale. It resulted in a severe release of radioactivity into the environment following a massive power excursion which destroyed the reactor.
a. 1509 Istanbul earthquake
c. 1700 Cascadia earthquake
b. 1703 Genroku earthquake
d. Chernobyl disaster

27. The _____ was enacted by the United States Congress in response to the Love Canal disaster. The Act was created to protect people, families, communities and others from heavily contaminated toxic waste sites that have been abandoned. It paid for toxic waste cleanups at sites where no other responsible parties could pay for a cleanup by assessing a tax on petroleum and chemical industries.
a. 1703 Genroku earthquake
c. Comprehensive Environmental Response, Compensation, and Liability Act
b. 1700 Cascadia earthquake
d. 1509 Istanbul earthquake

28. _____ is waste that poses substantial or potential threats to public health or the environment. Many types of businesses generate _____. Some are small companies that may be located in a community.
a. 1700 Cascadia earthquake
c. 1509 Istanbul earthquake
b. 1703 Genroku earthquake
d. Hazardous waste

29. _____ is a type of waste, typically originating from plant or animal sources, which may be broken down by other living organisms.
a. Biodegradable waste
c. 1509 Istanbul earthquake
b. 1703 Genroku earthquake
d. 1700 Cascadia earthquake

30. _____ is a concept for disposing of High Level Radioactive Waste from Nuclear reactors. The system seeks to place the waste as much as five kilometers beneath the surface of the Earth and relies primarily on the immense natural geological barrier to do most of the work of confining the waste safely and permanently so that it will never pose a threat to the environment.
a. 1703 Genroku earthquake
c. 1509 Istanbul earthquake
b. 1700 Cascadia earthquake
d. Deep waste disposal

31. _____ are waste types containing radioactive chemical elements that do not have a practical purpose. It is sometimes the product of a nuclear process, such as nuclear fission. However, other industries not directly connected to the nuclear industry can produce large quantities of _____.
a. Radioactive waste
c. 1509 Istanbul earthquake
b. 1700 Cascadia earthquake
d. 1703 Genroku earthquake

32. _____ is the administrative and technical functions necessary for the treatment, disposal, storage, manipulation, and evacuation of radioactive materials in order to protect the environment and people.
a. 1703 Genroku earthquake
c. 1509 Istanbul earthquake
b. 1700 Cascadia earthquake
d. Radioactive waste management

33. The _____ of a quantity, subject to exponential decay, is the time required for the quantity to decay to half of its initial value. The concept originated in the study of radioactive decay, but applies to many other fields as well, including phenomena which are described by non-exponential decays.
   a. 1509 Istanbul earthquake
   b. 1703 Genroku earthquake
   c. Half-life
   d. 1700 Cascadia earthquake

34. A _____ is a landform that extends above the surrounding terrain in a limited area. A _____ is generally steeper than a hill, but there is no universally accepted standard definition for the height of a _____ or a hill although a _____ usually has an identifiable summit.
   a. 1703 Genroku earthquake
   b. 1700 Cascadia earthquake
   c. 1509 Istanbul earthquake
   d. Mountain

35. _____ are waste types containing radioactive chemical elements that do not have a practical purpose. It is sometimes the product of a nuclear process, such as nuclear fission. However, other industries not directly connected to the nuclear industry can produce large quantities of _____.
   a. Nuclear Waste
   b. 1509 Istanbul earthquake
   c. 1703 Genroku earthquake
   d. 1700 Cascadia earthquake

36. The _____ is a United States federal law enacted in 1982. It established a national program for disposal of highly radioactive wastes, and resulted in the studying of Yucca Mountain as a possible site for long-term disposal of radioactive waste.
   a. 1700 Cascadia earthquake
   b. 1509 Istanbul earthquake
   c. 1703 Genroku earthquake
   d. Nuclear Waste Policy Act

37. _____ is a ridge line in Nye County, in the south-central part of the U.S. state of Nevada. It is composed of volcanic material ejected from a now-extinct caldera-forming supervolcano. _____ is most notable as the site of the proposed _____ Repository, a U.S. Department of Energy terminal storage facility for spent nuclear reactor fuel and other radioactive waste.
   a. 1509 Istanbul earthquake
   b. Yucca Mountain
   c. 1700 Cascadia earthquake
   d. 1703 Genroku earthquake

38. _____ and low level are terms used in classifying levels of description and goals in many fields where systems could be described from different perspectives.

A _____ description is one that describes 'top level' goals, overall systemic features, is more abstracted, and is typically more concerned with the system as a whole, and its goals.

A low level description is one that describes individual components, detail rather than overview, rudimentary functions rather than complex overall ones, and is typically more concerned with individual components within the system and how they operate.

   a. 1703 Genroku earthquake
   b. 1509 Istanbul earthquake
   c. 1700 Cascadia earthquake
   d. High level

39. _____ is a type of waste produced by industrial activity, such as that of factories, mills and mines. It has existed since the outset of the industrial revolution.

Chapter 12. Waste Management

Much _____ is neither hazardous nor toxic, such as waste fiber produced by agriculture and logging.

a. Industrial waste
c. AL 333
b. AASHTO Soil Classification System
d. AL 129-1

40. _____ is the introduction of substances or energy into the environment, resulting in deleterious effects of such a nature as to endanger human health, harm living resources and ecosystems, and impair or interfere with amenities and other legitimate uses of the environment.

a. 1700 Cascadia earthquake
c. 1509 Istanbul earthquake
b. Pollution
d. 1703 Genroku earthquake

41. Deliberate disposal of wastes at sea is called _____.

Some forms of marine debris, such as driftwood, occur naturally, and human activities have been discharging similar material into the oceans for thousands of years. Recently however, with the increasing use of plastic, human influence has become an issue as many types of plastics do not biodegrade.

a. AASHTO Soil Classification System
c. AL 333
b. AL 129-1
d. Ocean dumping

42. _____ refers to the international agreement that resulted from the third United Nations Convention on the _____ that took place from 1973 through 1982 with modifications that were made by the 1994 Agreement on Implementation. The _____ Convention is a set of rules for the use of the world's oceans, which cover 70 percent of the Earth's surface.

a. 1509 Istanbul earthquake
c. 1700 Cascadia earthquake
b. 1703 Genroku earthquake
d. Law of the Sea

43. A _____ is a cultural and social community. In as much as most members never meet each other, yet feel a common bond, it may be considered an imagined community. One of the most influential doctrines in Western Europe and the Western hemisphere since the late eighteenth century is that all humans are divided into groups called nations.

a. 1703 Genroku earthquake
c. 1509 Istanbul earthquake
b. Nation
d. 1700 Cascadia earthquake

Chapter 13. The Geologic Aspects of Environmental Health

1. _____ describes any of a group of minerals that can be fibrous, many of which are metamorphic and are hydrous magnesium silicates.
   a. AL 333
   b. Asbestos
   c. AASHTO Soil Classification System
   d. AL 129-1

2. _____ are dangerous compounds that cause contamination and are dangerous to human health and the environement.
   a. 1703 Genroku earthquake
   b. 1509 Istanbul earthquake
   c. Hazardous chemicals
   d. 1700 Cascadia earthquake

3. A _____ substance is a material with a definite _____ composition. It is a concept that became firmly established in the late eighteenth century after work by the chemist Joseph Proust on the composition of some pure _____ compounds such as basic copper carbonate.
   a. 1703 Genroku earthquake
   b. 1509 Istanbul earthquake
   c. 1700 Cascadia earthquake
   d. Chemical

4. _____ is a parasitic disease affecting the intestines of mammals. It is a disease spread through the fecal-oral route; the main symptom is self-limiting diarrhea in people with intact immune system.
   a. 1703 Genroku earthquake
   b. 1509 Istanbul earthquake
   c. 1700 Cascadia earthquake
   d. Cryptosporidiosis

5. _____ , (AmE)) and dengue hemorrhagic fever (DHF) are acute febrile diseases, found in the tropics and Africa, and caused by four closely related virus serotypes of the genus Flavivirus, family Flaviviridae. It is also known as breakbone fever. The geographical spread is similar to malaria, including northern Australia, Singapore, Malaysia, Taiwan, Thailand, Vietnam, Indonesia, Philippines, Pakistan, India, Bangladesh, Puerto Rico, Brazil, Guyana, Venezuela, Trinidad and now Samoa.
   a. 1700 Cascadia earthquake
   b. Dengue fever
   c. 1509 Istanbul earthquake
   d. 1703 Genroku earthquake

6. _____ is a genus of anaerobic flagellated protozoan parasites that colonise and reproduce in the small intestines of several vertebrates, causing giardiasis. Their life cycle alternates between an actively swimming trophozoite and an infective, resistant cyst. The genus was named after French zoologist Alfred Mathieu Giard.
   a. 1509 Istanbul earthquake
   b. Giardia
   c. 1703 Genroku earthquake
   d. 1700 Cascadia earthquake

7. An _____ is a clinically evident disease resulting from the presence of pathogenic microbial agents, including pathogenic viruses, pathogenic bacteria, fungi, protozoa, multicellular parasites, and aberrant proteins known as prions. These pathogens are able to cause disease in animals and/or plants.
   a. AASHTO Soil Classification System
   b. AL 129-1
   c. AL 333
   d. Infectious disease

8. _____ is an emerging infectious disease caused by at least three species of bacteria belonging to the genus Borrelia. Borrelia burgdorferi is the predominant cause of _____ in the United States, whereas Borrelia afzelii and Borrelia garinii are implicated in most European cases.

_____ is the most common tick-borne disease in the Northern Hemisphere.

Chapter 13. The Geologic Aspects of Environmental Health

    a. Lyme disease
    b. 1509 Istanbul earthquake
    c. 1703 Genroku earthquake
    d. 1700 Cascadia earthquake

9. _____ is a vector-borne infectious disease caused by protozoan parasites. It is widespread in tropical and subtropical regions, including parts of the Americas, Asia, and Africa. Each year, there are approximately 515 million cases of _____, killing between one and three million people, the majority of whom are young children in Sub-Saharan Africa.
    a. 1700 Cascadia earthquake
    b. Cryptosporidiosis
    c. 1509 Istanbul earthquake
    d. Malaria

10. _____ is a genus of rod-shaped Gram-negative enterobacteria that causes typhoid fever, paratyphoid fever, and the foodborne illness salmonellosis. Most _____ species are motile and produce hydrogen sulfide. There are approximately 40,000 cases of _____ infection reported in the United States each year.
    a. 1509 Istanbul earthquake
    b. Salmonella
    c. 1703 Genroku earthquake
    d. 1700 Cascadia earthquake

11. A _____ or medical condition is an abnormal condition of an organism that impairs bodily functions and can be deadly. It is also defined as a way of the body harming itself in an abnormal way, associated with specific symptoms and signs.

In human beings,'_____' is often used more broadly to refer to any condition that causes extreme pain, dysfunction, distress, social problems, and/or death to the person afflicted, or similar problems for those in contact with the person.

    a. 1509 Istanbul earthquake
    b. 1700 Cascadia earthquake
    c. Disease
    d. Black lung disease

12. _____ comprises those aspects of human health, including quality of life, that are determined by physical, chemical, biological, social, and psychosocial factors in the natural environment.
    a. AL 333
    b. AL 129-1
    c. AASHTO Soil Classification System
    d. Environmental health

13. _____ refers to a member of any human group whose adult males grow to less than 150 cm in average height or less than 155 cm. A member of a slightly taller group is termed pygmoid. The best known _____ are the Aka, Efe and Mbuti of central Africa.
    a. 1703 Genroku earthquake
    b. 1700 Cascadia earthquake
    c. 1509 Istanbul earthquake
    d. Pygmies

14. _____ is the average and variations of weather over long periods of time. _____ zones can be defined using parameters such as temperature and rainfall.
    a. 1700 Cascadia earthquake
    b. 1703 Genroku earthquake
    c. 1509 Istanbul earthquake
    d. Climate

Chapter 13. The Geologic Aspects of Environmental Health

15. _____ is a term derived from the Latin 'imperium', denoting military command within the ancient Roman government. An _____ is an extensive group of states or ethnic peoples united and ruled over by a single monarch or ruling authority; having a strong centralized political power; and a large commercial organization under the control of one person or group within this nation state. However this term has been widely applied to other quite distinct nation states such as the Holy Roman _____ and the Byzantine _____ at one end, to the Colonial Empires of the Spanish _____ and the British _____ on the other.
   a. AL 129-1
   b. AL 333
   c. AASHTO Soil Classification System
   d. Empire

16. _____ is a chemical element in the periodic table that has the symbol Pb and atomic number 82. A soft, heavy, toxic and malleable poor metal, _____ is bluish white when freshly cut but tarnishes to dull gray when exposed to air. _____ is used in building construction, _____-acid batteries, bullets and shot, and is part of solder, pewter, and fusible alloys.
   a. 1509 Istanbul earthquake
   b. 1703 Genroku earthquake
   c. 1700 Cascadia earthquake
   d. Lead

17. _____ is a medical condition caused by increased blood lead levels. The main sources of poisoning are from ingestion of lead contaminated soil and from ingestion of lead dust or chips from deteriorating lead-based paints. It can also be found in drinking water.
   a. Lead poisoning
   b. 1703 Genroku earthquake
   c. 1700 Cascadia earthquake
   d. 1509 Istanbul earthquake

18. _____ is a disease of uncontrolled cell growth in tissues of the lung. This growth may lead to metastasis, which is invasion of adjacent tissue and infiltration beyond the lungs. The vast majority of primary lung cancers are carcinomas of the lung, derived from epithelial cells.
   a. 1509 Istanbul earthquake
   b. 1700 Cascadia earthquake
   c. 1703 Genroku earthquake
   d. Lung cancer

19. _____ is a chemical element in the periodic table that has the symbol Rn and atomic number 86. A radioactive noble gas that is formed by the decay of radium, _____ is one of the heaviest gases and is considered to be a health hazard.
   a. 1703 Genroku earthquake
   b. 1700 Cascadia earthquake
   c. Radon
   d. 1509 Istanbul earthquake

20. The general effects of _____ to the human body are due to its radioactivity and consequent risk of radiation-induced cancer.
   a. 1700 Cascadia earthquake
   b. 1509 Istanbul earthquake
   c. 1703 Genroku earthquake
   d. Radon emissions

21. _____ is a parasitic disease caused by several species of flatworm. The acute form of it is sometimes known as snail fever and cutaneous is sometimes commonly called swimmer's itch.
   a. Schistosomiasis
   b. 1700 Cascadia earthquake
   c. 1703 Genroku earthquake
   d. 1509 Istanbul earthquake

Chapter 13. The Geologic Aspects of Environmental Health

22. The name _____ applies to most members of the molluscan class Gastropoda that have coiled shells. They are found in freshwater, marine, and terrestrial environments. Most are of herbivorous nature, though a few land species and many marine species may be omnivores or carnivores.
    a. 1509 Istanbul earthquake
    b. 1700 Cascadia earthquake
    c. 1703 Genroku earthquake
    d. Snail

23. Stomach or gastric cancer can develop in any part of the stomach and may spread throughout the stomach and to other organs; particularly the esophagus, lungs and the liver. _____ causes nearly one million deaths worldwide per year.

    _____ is the fourth most common cancer worldwide with 930,000 cases diagnosed in 2002.

    a. Stomach cancer
    b. 1509 Istanbul earthquake
    c. 1703 Genroku earthquake
    d. 1700 Cascadia earthquake

24. _____ is a class of diseases in which a group of cells display the traits of uncontrolled growth growth and division beyond the normal limits, invasion intrusion on and destruction of adjacent tissues, and sometimes metastasis spread to other locations in the body via lymph or blood. These three malignant properties of cancers differentiate them from benign tumors, which are self-limited, do not invade or metastasize. Most cancers form a tumor but some, like leukemia, do not.
    a. 1700 Cascadia earthquake
    b. 1509 Istanbul earthquake
    c. 1703 Genroku earthquake
    d. Cancer

25. _____ refers to the variation in the Earth's global climate or in regional climates over time. It describes changes in the variability or average state of the atmosphere over time scales ranging from decades to millions of years. These changes can be caused by processes internal to the Earth, external forces or, more recently, human activities.
    a. 1703 Genroku earthquake
    b. Climate change
    c. 1509 Istanbul earthquake
    d. 1700 Cascadia earthquake

26. An _____ is a type of atom that is defined by its atomic number; that is, by the number of protons in its nucleus.
    a. AL 129-1
    b. AL 333
    c. AASHTO Soil Classification System
    d. Element

27. _____ is the process of extracting a substance from a solid by dissolving it in a liquid.
    a. 1700 Cascadia earthquake
    b. 1703 Genroku earthquake
    c. Leaching
    d. 1509 Istanbul earthquake

28. The _____ of the chemical elements is a tabular method of displaying the chemical elements, first devized in 1869 by the Russian chemist Dmitri Mendeleev.
    a. 1509 Istanbul earthquake
    b. 1703 Genroku earthquake
    c. Periodic table
    d. 1700 Cascadia earthquake

29. In analytical chemistry, a _____ is an element in a sample that has an average concentration of less than 100 parts per million atoms, or less than 100 micrograms per gram.

Chapter 13. The Geologic Aspects of Environmental Health

In biochemistry, a _____ is a chemical element that is needed in minute quantities for the proper growth, development, and physiology of the organism. In biochemistry, a _____ is also referred to as a micronutrient.

   a. 1700 Cascadia earthquake
   b. 1703 Genroku earthquake
   c. 1509 Istanbul earthquake
   d. Trace element

30. _____ is the process of breaking down rocks, soils and their minerals through direct contact with the atmosphere. _____ occurs without movement. Two main classifications of _____ processes exist. Mechanical or physical _____ involves the breakdown of rocks and soils through direct contact with atmospheric conditions. The second classification, chemical _____, involves the direct effect of atmospheric chemicals in the breakdown of rocks, soils and minerals.
   a. 1509 Istanbul earthquake
   b. 1700 Cascadia earthquake
   c. Weathering
   d. 1703 Genroku earthquake

31. _____ is an ecological concept referring to the relative representation of a species in a particular ecosystem. It is usually measured as the mean number of individuals found per sample.
   a. AL 129-1
   b. AASHTO Soil Classification System
   c. AL 333
   d. Abundance

32. _____, also known as bioamplification, or biological magnification is the increase in concentration of a substance, such as the pesticide DDT, that occurs in a food chain as a consequence of: Food chain energetics, low rate of excretion/degradation of the substance.
   a. 1700 Cascadia earthquake
   b. 1703 Genroku earthquake
   c. 1509 Istanbul earthquake
   d. Biomagnification

33. _____ is the geological process whereby material is added to a landform. This is the process by which wind and water create a sediment deposit, through the laying down of granular material that has been eroded and transported from another geographical location.
   a. 1700 Cascadia earthquake
   b. 1509 Istanbul earthquake
   c. 1703 Genroku earthquake
   d. Deposition

34. _____ is a simple X-Y graph relating the magnitude of a stressor to the response of the receptor. The response is usually death, but other effects can be studied.
   a. 1700 Cascadia earthquake
   b. 1509 Istanbul earthquake
   c. Dose-response curve
   d. 1703 Genroku earthquake

35. An _____ in pharmacology is the amount of drug that produces a therapeutic response in 50% of the people taking it, sometimes also called _____-50. In radiation protection it is an estimate of the stochastic effect that a non-uniform radiation dose has on a human.

In pharmacology, _____ is the median dose that produces the desired effect of a drug.

a. Irradiance
b. AASHTO Soil Classification System
c. AL 129-1
d. Effective dose

36. _____ is a chemical element which has the symbol N and atomic number 7 in the periodic table. Elemental _____ is a colorless, odorless, tasteless and mostly inert diatomic gas at standard conditions, constituting 78.08% percent of Earth's atmosphere.
a. 1509 Istanbul earthquake
b. Nitrogen
c. 1703 Genroku earthquake
d. 1700 Cascadia earthquake

37. _____ is a chemical element in the periodic table that has the symbol Se and atomic number 34. It is a toxic nonmetal that is chemically related to sulfur and tellurium. It occurs in several different forms but one of these is a stable gray metallike form that conducts electricity better in the light than in the dark and is used in photocells.
a. 1509 Istanbul earthquake
b. 1700 Cascadia earthquake
c. Selenium
d. 1703 Genroku earthquake

38. A _____ is a bipedal primate belonging to the mammalian species Homo sapiens in the family Hominidae. Compared to other living organisms on Earth, a _____ has a highly developed brain capable of abstract reasoning, language, and introspection.
a. 1703 Genroku earthquake
b. 1509 Istanbul earthquake
c. Human
d. 1700 Cascadia earthquake

39. In biology a _____ is the collection of inter-breeding organisms of a particular species; in sociology, a collection of human beings. A _____ shares a particular characteristic of interest, most often that of living in a given geographic area. In taxonomy _____ is a low-level taxonomic rank.
a. 1700 Cascadia earthquake
b. Population
c. Metapopulation
d. 1509 Istanbul earthquake

40. _____ is the study of the adverse effects of chemicals on living organisms. It is the study of symptoms, mechanisms, treatments and detection of poisoning, especially the poisoning of people.
a. 1509 Istanbul earthquake
b. 1703 Genroku earthquake
c. Toxicology
d. 1700 Cascadia earthquake

41. A _____ is a poisonous substance produced by living cells or organisms.
a. 1509 Istanbul earthquake
b. 1703 Genroku earthquake
c. 1700 Cascadia earthquake
d. Toxin

42. _____ is the reduced form of fluorine. Both organic and inorganic compounds containing the element fluorine are considered fluorides. As a halogen, fluorine forms a monovalent ion. The range of fluorides is considerable as fluorine forms compounds with all elements except He, Ne, and Ar. Fluorides range from severe toxins such as sarin to life-saving pharmaceuticals such as efavirenz and from refractory materials such as calcium _____ to highly reactive sulfur tetrafluoride.
a. 1700 Cascadia earthquake
b. 1703 Genroku earthquake
c. 1509 Istanbul earthquake
d. Fluoride

Chapter 13. The Geologic Aspects of Environmental Health

43. _____ is the chemical element in the periodic table that has the symbol F and atomic number 9. Atomic _____ is univalent and is the most chemically reactive and electronegative of all the elements. In its pure form, it is a poisonous, pale, yellow-green gas. Like other halogens, molecular _____ is highly dangerous; it causes severe chemical burns on contact with skin.

   a. 1700 Cascadia earthquake
   b. 1703 Genroku earthquake
   c. 1509 Istanbul earthquake
   d. Fluorine

44. _____ is a chemical element in the periodic table that has the symbol I and atomic number 53. It is required as a trace element for most living organisms. Chemically, _____ is the least reactive of the halogens, and the most electropositive halogen. _____ is primarily used in medicine, photography and in dyes.

   a. AASHTO Soil Classification System
   b. AL 333
   c. AL 129-1
   d. Iodine

45. A _____ is an indication of the lethality of a given substance or type of radiation. Because resistance varies from one individual to another, the '_____' represents a dose (usually recorded as dose per kilogram of subject body weight) at which a given percentage of subjects will die.

   The most commonly-used lethality indicator is the _____$_{50}$ (or _____50), a dose at which 50% of subjects will die.

   a. 1509 Istanbul earthquake
   b. 1700 Cascadia earthquake
   c. 1703 Genroku earthquake
   d. Lethal dose

46. The _____ is one of the largest endocrine glands in the body. This gland is found in the neck inferior to (below) the _____ cartilage (also known as the Adam's apple in men) and at approximately the same level as the cricoid cartilage. The _____ controls how quickly the body burns energy, makes proteins, and how sensitive the body should be to other hormones.

   a. 1509 Istanbul earthquake
   b. 1700 Cascadia earthquake
   c. Thyroid
   d. 1703 Genroku earthquake

47. _____ is a condition of severely stunted physical and mental growth due to untreated congenital deficiency of thyroid hormones (hypothyroidism.)

   The term cretin describes a person so affected, but, like such words as spastic, idiot, lunatic, and retard, also is a word of abuse. Cretin became a medical term in the 18th century, from an Alpine French dialect prevalent in a region where persons with such a condition were especially common ; it saw wide medical use in the 19th and early 20th centuries, and then spread more widely in popular English as a markedly derogatory term for a person who behaves stupidly.

   a. Milutin Milanković
   b. Roald Amundsen
   c. George Santayana
   d. Cretinism

48. _____, officially the Democratic Socialist Republic of _____ is an island nation in South Asia, located about 31 kilometres off the southern coast of India. It is home to around twenty million people.

Chapter 13. The Geologic Aspects of Environmental Health

Because of its location in the path of major sea routes, _____ is a strategic naval link between West Asia and South East Asia, and has been a center of Buddhist religion and culture from ancient times.

a. 1509 Istanbul earthquake
b. Sri Lanka
c. 1703 Genroku earthquake
d. 1700 Cascadia earthquake

49. A _____ is a swelling in the neck due to an enlarged thyroid gland.
a. 1703 Genroku earthquake
b. 1700 Cascadia earthquake
c. 1509 Istanbul earthquake
d. Goitre

50. _____ is a chemical element in the periodic table that has the symbol Zn and atomic number 30. _____ is a moderately-reactive bluish-white metal that tarnishes in moist air and burns in air with a bright bluish-green flame, giving off plumes of _____ oxide.
a. 1700 Cascadia earthquake
b. 1509 Istanbul earthquake
c. 1703 Genroku earthquake
d. Zinc

51. _____ is the degree to which a substance is able to damage an exposed organism. _____ can refer to the effect on a whole organism, such as a human, bacterium, or plant, as well as the effect on a substructure of the organism, such as a cell or an organ such as the liver. By extension, the word may be metaphorically used to describe toxic effects on larger and more complex groups, such as the family unit or society at large.
a. 1509 Istanbul earthquake
b. Acute exposure
c. Toxicity
d. 1700 Cascadia earthquake

52. In medicine, a _____ is a disease that is long-lasting or recurrent. The term chronic describes the course of the disease, or its rate of onset and development. A chronic course is distinguished from a recurrent course; recurrent diseases relapse repeatedly, with periods of remission in between.
a. 1700 Cascadia earthquake
b. Chronic disease
c. 1509 Istanbul earthquake
d. 1703 Genroku earthquake

53. _____ is an umbrella term for a variety for different diseases affecting the heart. As of 2007, it is the leading cause of death in the United States, England, Canada and Wales, killing one person every 34 seconds in the United States alone.

Coronary artery disease is a disease of the artery caused by the accumulation of atheromatous plaques within the walls of the arteries that supply the myocardium.

a. 1703 Genroku earthquake
b. 1509 Istanbul earthquake
c. 1700 Cascadia earthquake
d. Heart disease

54. _____ (æ—¥æœ¬ Nihon or Nippon making it an archipelago. The largest islands are HonshÅ«, HokkaidÅ, KyÅ«shÅ« and Shikoku, together accounting for 97% of _____'s land area. Most of the islands are mountainous, many volcanic; for example, _____'s highest peak, Mount Fuji, is a volcano.
a. Kabul
b. Kenya
c. Java
d. Japan

55. _____ is the characteristic of a solid material expressing its resistance to permanent deformation.

a. 1700 Cascadia earthquake
c. 1509 Istanbul earthquake
b. 1703 Genroku earthquake
d. Hardness

56. _____ is the extraction of valuable minerals or other geological materials from the earth, usually from an ore body, vein, or seam. Any material that cannot be grown from agricultural processes, or created artificially in a laboratory or factory, is usually extracted from the earth by this method.
   a. 1700 Cascadia earthquake
   b. 1509 Istanbul earthquake
   c. 1703 Genroku earthquake
   d. Mining

57. _____ is a chronic inflammatory medical condition affecting the parenchymal tissue of the lungs. It occurs after long-term, heavy exposure to asbestos, e.g. in mining, and is therefore regarded as an occupational lung disease. Sufferers have severe dyspnea (shortness of breath) and are at an increased risk regarding several different types of lung cancer.
   a. AASHTO Soil Classification System
   b. Asbestosis
   c. AL 333
   d. AL 129-1

58. _____ are any of the several different forms of an element each having different atomic mass. _____ of an element have nuclei with the same number of protons but different numbers of neutrons.
   a. AL 129-1
   b. AASHTO Soil Classification System
   c. AL 333
   d. Isotopes

59. _____ refers to the phenomena of the physical world, and also to life in general. _____ is also generally distinguished from the supernatural. It ranges in scale from the subatomic to the galactic.
   a. Nature
   b. 1700 Cascadia earthquake
   c. 1703 Genroku earthquake
   d. 1509 Istanbul earthquake

60. _____ is the process in which an unstable atomic nucleus loses energy by emitting radiation in the form of particles or electromagnetic waves.
   a. 1509 Istanbul earthquake
   b. 1700 Cascadia earthquake
   c. 1703 Genroku earthquake
   d. Radioactive decay

61. _____ consist of two protons and two neutrons bound together into a particle identical to a helium nucleus. _____ are emitted by radioactive nuclei such as uranium or radium in a process known as alpha decay.
   a. Alpha particles
   b. AL 129-1
   c. AL 333
   d. AASHTO Soil Classification System

62. _____ are high-energy, high-speed electrons or positrons emitted by certain types of radioactive nuclei such as potassium-40.
   a. 1700 Cascadia earthquake
   b. 1509 Istanbul earthquake
   c. 1703 Genroku earthquake
   d. Beta particles

63. The _____ (symbol Ci) is a unit of radioactivity, defined as

   $1 \text{ Ci} = 3.7 \times 10^{10}$ decays per second or becquerels.

Chapter 13. The Geologic Aspects of Environmental Health 123

This is roughly the activity of 1 gramme of the radium isotope ^{226}Ra, a substance studied by the pioneers of radiology, Marie and Pierre _____. The _____ has since been replaced by an SI derived unit, the becquerel (Bq), which equates to one decay per second.

a. 1700 Cascadia earthquake
b. 1703 Genroku earthquake
c. 1509 Istanbul earthquake
d. Curie

64. _____ (November 7, 1867 - July 4, 1934) was a physicist and chemist of Polish upbringing and, subsequently, French citizenship. She was a pioneer in the field of radioactivity, the only person honored with Nobel Prizes in two different sciences, and the first female professor at the University of Paris.

She was born Maria SkÅ‚odowska in Warsaw, Vistula Country, Russian Empire, and lived there until she was 24.

a. Marie SkÅ‚odowska Curie
b. Pinochet
c. Milutin MilankoviÄ‡
d. Carl Schurz

65. _____ are forms of electromagnetic radiation or light emissions of a specific frequency produced from sub-atomic particle interaction, such as electron-positron annihilation and radioactive decay; most are generated from nuclear reactions occurring within the interstellar medium of space.

a. 1509 Istanbul earthquake
b. 1703 Genroku earthquake
c. Gamma Rays
d. 1700 Cascadia earthquake

66. The _____ of a quantity, subject to exponential decay, is the time required for the quantity to decay to half of its initial value. The concept originated in the study of radioactive decay, but applies to many other fields as well, including phenomena which are described by non-exponential decays.

a. 1509 Istanbul earthquake
b. 1700 Cascadia earthquake
c. 1703 Genroku earthquake
d. Half-life

67. Radionuclides are often referred to by chemists and physicists as radioactive isotopes or _____, and play an important part in the technologies that provide us with food, water and good health. However, they can also constitute real or perceived dangers.

Naturally occurring radionuclides fall into three categories: primordial radionuclides, secondary radionuclides and cosmogenic radionuclides.

a. 1700 Cascadia earthquake
b. 1703 Genroku earthquake
c. 1509 Istanbul earthquake
d. Radioisotopes

68. _____ are the fundamental building blocks of chemistry, and are conserved in chemical reactions.
a. Atoms
b. AASHTO Soil Classification System
c. AL 333
d. AL 129-1

69. _____ is the process of assigning a number to an attribute (or phenomenon) according to a rule or set of rules. The term can also be used to refer to the result obtained after performing the process.

Chapter 13. The Geologic Aspects of Environmental Health

The word _____ comes from the Greek 'metron', meaning limited proportion.

a. Measurement
b. 1703 Genroku earthquake
c. 1509 Istanbul earthquake
d. 1700 Cascadia earthquake

70. _____, as used in physics, is energy in the form of waves or moving subatomic particles emitted by an atom or other body as it changes from a higher energy state to a lower energy state. _____ can be classified as ionizing or non-ionizing _____, depending on its effect on atomic matter. The most common use of the word "_____" refers to ionizing _____. Ionizing _____ has enough energy to ionize atoms or molecules while non-ionizing _____ does not. Radioactive material is a physical material that emits ionizing _____.

a. Synthetic aperture radar
b. Radiation
c. Spectrum analysis
d. Rest energy

71. The _____ (symbol Bq) is the SI derived unit of radioactivity. 1 Bq is defined as the activity of a quantity of radioactive material in which one nucleus decays per second. It is therefore equivalent to s^{-1}.

a. 1700 Cascadia earthquake
b. 1509 Istanbul earthquake
c. 1703 Genroku earthquake
d. Becquerel

72. _____ is a concept that denotes the precise probability of specific eventualities. Technically, the notion of _____ is independent from the notion of value and, as such, eventualities may have both beneficial and adverse consequences. However, in general usage the convention is to focus only on potential negative impact to some characteristic of value that may arise from a future event.

a. 1703 Genroku earthquake
b. 1509 Istanbul earthquake
c. Risk
d. 1700 Cascadia earthquake

73. _____ is the science and study of the solid matter that constitute the Earth. Encompassing such things as rocks, soil, and gemstones, _____ studies the composition, structure, physical properties, history, and the processes that shape Earth's components.

a. 1700 Cascadia earthquake
b. 1509 Istanbul earthquake
c. Geology
d. 1703 Genroku earthquake

74. The _____ is a physiographic subprovince of the New England Uplands section of the New England province of the Appalachian Highlands. The prong consists of mountains comprised of crystalline metamorphic rock.

The _____ stretches from near Reading, Pennsylvania, through northern New Jersey and southern New York, reaching its northern terminus in Connecticut.

a. 1509 Istanbul earthquake
b. 1700 Cascadia earthquake
c. 1703 Genroku earthquake
d. Reading Prong

75. _____ is a branch of environmental science that focuses on the processes that take place at the interface between the environment containing the contaminant(s) of interest and the organism(s) being considered. These are the final steps in the path to release an environmental contaminant, through transport to its effect in a biological system. It tries to measure how much of a contaminant can be absorbed by an exposed target organism, in what form, at what rate and how much of the absorbed amount is actually available to produce a biological effect.

a. AASHTO Soil Classification System
b. AL 129-1
c. AL 333
d. Exposure assessment

76. _____ is a structured approach to managing uncertainty through, risk assessment, developing strategies to manage it. It is focused on risks stemming from physical or legal causes. Such as natural disasters or fires.
   a. 1700 Cascadia earthquake
   b. Risk management
   c. 1509 Istanbul earthquake
   d. 1703 Genroku earthquake

77. _____ is a qualitative or quantitative evaluation of the environmental and health risk resulting from exposure to a chemical agent. It combines exposure assessment results with toxicity assessment results to estimate risk.
   a. 1700 Cascadia earthquake
   b. 1703 Genroku earthquake
   c. Risk assessment
   d. 1509 Istanbul earthquake

Chapter 14. Mineral Resources and Environment

1. A _____ is a naturally occurring substance formed through geological processes that has a characteristic chemical composition, a highly ordered atomic structure and specific physical properties. A rock, by comparison, is an aggregate of minerals and need not have a specific chemical composition. Minerals range in composition from pure elements and simple salts to very complex silicates with thousands of known forms.
   a. 1509 Istanbul earthquake
   b. 1700 Cascadia earthquake
   c. 1703 Genroku earthquake
   d. Mineral

2. A _____ is a bipedal primate belonging to the mammalian species Homo sapiens in the family Hominidae. Compared to other living organisms on Earth, a _____ has a highly developed brain capable of abstract reasoning, language, and introspection.
   a. Human
   b. 1509 Istanbul earthquake
   c. 1703 Genroku earthquake
   d. 1700 Cascadia earthquake

3. _____ is the chemical element in the periodic table that has the symbol Al and atomic number 13. It is a silvery and ductile member of the poor metal group of chemical elements. _____ is found primarily as the ore bauxite and is remarkable for its resistance to corrosion (due to the phenomenon of passivation) and its light weight. _____ is used in many industries to make millions of different products and is very important to the world economy.
   a. AASHTO Soil Classification System
   b. AL 129-1
   c. AL 333
   d. Aluminum

4. The _____ is used to assess the economic feasibility of a mining operation: the cost of extracting a natural material from its ore is directly related to its concentration, and the cost of extraction must be less than the market value of the material being mined for the operation to be economically feasible
   a. 1700 Cascadia earthquake
   b. 1509 Istanbul earthquake
   c. 1703 Genroku earthquake
   d. Concentration factor of metal

5. _____ is a chemical element in the periodic table that has the symbol Au and atomic number 79. A soft, shiny, yellow, dense, malleable, ductile (trivalent and univalent) transition metal, _____ does not react with most chemicals but is attacked by chlorine, fluorine and aqua regia.
   a. 1700 Cascadia earthquake
   b. 1509 Istanbul earthquake
   c. 1703 Genroku earthquake
   d. Gold

6. _____ is a chemical element in the periodic table that has the symbol Hg and atomic number 80. A heavy, silvery, transition metal, _____ is one of five elements that are liquid at or near standard room temperature (the others are the metals caesium, francium, and gallium, and the nonmetal bromine).
   a. 1703 Genroku earthquake
   b. 1509 Istanbul earthquake
   c. 1700 Cascadia earthquake
   d. Mercury

7. An _____ is a volume of rock containing components or minerals in a mode of occurrence that renders it valuable for mining.
   a. AL 129-1
   b. AASHTO Soil Classification System
   c. AL 333
   d. Ore

8. _____ is the science and study of the solid matter that constitute the Earth. Encompassing such things as rocks, soil, and gemstones, _____ studies the composition, structure, physical properties, history, and the processes that shape Earth's components.

Chapter 14. Mineral Resources and Environment

a. Geology
b. 1703 Genroku earthquake
c. 1509 Istanbul earthquake
d. 1700 Cascadia earthquake

9. A biological process is a process of a living organism. _____ are made up of any number of chemical reactions or other events that results in a transformation.

Regulation of _____ occurs where any process is modulated in its frequency, rate or extent.

a. 1703 Genroku earthquake
b. 1700 Cascadia earthquake
c. 1509 Istanbul earthquake
d. Biological processes

10. A _____ is a solid in which the constituent atoms, molecules, or ions are packed in a regularly ordered, repeating pattern extending in all three spatial dimensions. Most metals encountered in everyday life are polycrystals. Crystals are often symmetrically intergrown to form _____ twins.

a. 1700 Cascadia earthquake
b. 1509 Istanbul earthquake
c. Crystal
d. 1703 Genroku earthquake

11. _____ are the hardest natural material known to man and the third-hardest known material. Its hardness and high dispersion of light make it useful for industrial applications and jewelry.

a. Francium
b. Canada
c. Metabolism
d. Diamonds

12. _____ rocks form when molten rock, magma, cools and solidifies, with or without crystallization, either below the surface as intrusive, plutonic rocks or on the surface as extrusive, volcanic, rocks.

a. Igneous
b. AL 129-1
c. AASHTO Soil Classification System
d. AL 333

13. _____ is a type of rock best known for sometimes containing diamonds. It is an ultrapotassic, ultramafic, igneous rock composed of olivine, phlogopite, pyroxene and garnet, with a variety of chemically anomalous trace minerals.

a. 1703 Genroku earthquake
b. Kimberlite
c. 1509 Istanbul earthquake
d. 1700 Cascadia earthquake

14. _____ can be defined as the solid state recrystallisation of pre-existing rocks due to changes in heat and/or pressure and/or introduction of fluids. There will be mineralogical, chemical and crystallographic changes. _____ produced with increasing pressure and temperature conditions is known as prograde _____. Conversely, decreasing temperatures and pressure characterize retrograde _____.

a. 1700 Cascadia earthquake
b. 1509 Istanbul earthquake
c. 1703 Genroku earthquake
d. Metamorphism

15. _____ rock is one of the three main rock groups. Rock formed from these covers 75% of the Earth's land area, and includes common types such as chalk, limestone, dolomite, sandstone, and shale.

a. Sedimentary basin
b. Clasts
c. Sedimentary depositional environment
d. Sedimentary

Chapter 14. Mineral Resources and Environment

16. _____ is the process of breaking down rocks, soils and their minerals through direct contact with the atmosphere. _____ occurs without movement. Two main classifications of _____ processes exist. Mechanical or physical _____ involves the breakdown of rocks and soils through direct contact with atmospheric conditions. The second classification, chemical _____, involves the direct effect of atmospheric chemicals in the breakdown of rocks, soils and minerals.
   a. 1703 Genroku earthquake
   b. 1700 Cascadia earthquake
   c. 1509 Istanbul earthquake
   d. Weathering

17. _____ occurs typically around intrusive igneous rocks as a result of the temperature increase caused by the intrusion of magma into cooler country rock. The area surrounding the intrusion (called aureoles) where the _____ effects are present is called the metamorphic aureole. Contact metamorphic rocks are usually known as hornfels.
   a. 1703 Genroku earthquake
   b. Contact metamorphism
   c. 1509 Istanbul earthquake
   d. 1700 Cascadia earthquake

18. _____ is a very coarse-grained igneous rock that has a grain size of 20 mm or more; such rocks are referred to as pegmatitic.
   a. 1703 Genroku earthquake
   b. Pegmatite
   c. 1700 Cascadia earthquake
   d. 1509 Istanbul earthquake

19. _____ is a theory of geology that has been developed to explain the observed evidence for large scale motions of the Earth's lithosphere. The theory encompassed and superseded the older theory of continental drift.
   a. Plate tectonics
   b. 1700 Cascadia earthquake
   c. 1509 Istanbul earthquake
   d. 1703 Genroku earthquake

20. _____ is a field of study within geology concerned generally with the structures within the crust of the Earth, or other planets, and particularly with the forces and movements that have operated in a region to create these structures.
   a. 1509 Istanbul earthquake
   b. Tectonics
   c. 1703 Genroku earthquake
   d. 1700 Cascadia earthquake

21. In geography and politics, a _____ is a political division of a geographical entity. Frequently, but not always, a _____ is considered a Sovereign territory and is associated with the notations of State, Nation and Government. Formal recognition as a state requires the fulfillment of the Constitutive theory of statehood.
   a. 1509 Istanbul earthquake
   b. Country
   c. 1703 Genroku earthquake
   d. 1700 Cascadia earthquake

22. In biology, a _____ is an organism that harbors a virus or parasite, or a mutual or commensal symbiont, typically providing nourishment and shelter. In botany, a _____ plant is one that supplies food resources and substrate for certain insects or other fauna. Examples of such interactions include a cell being _____ to a virus, a legume plant hosting helpful nitrogen-fixing bacteria, and animals as hosts to parasitic worms, e.g. nematodes.
   a. 1509 Istanbul earthquake
   b. Host
   c. 1700 Cascadia earthquake
   d. 1703 Genroku earthquake

23. In geology, _____ is a naturally occurring aggregate of minerals and/or mineraloids.

The Earth's outer solid layer, the lithosphere, is made of _____. In general rocks are of three types, namely, igneous, sedimentary, and metamorphic.

Chapter 14. Mineral Resources and Environment

a. 1509 Istanbul earthquake
c. 1703 Genroku earthquake
b. 1700 Cascadia earthquake
d. Rock

24. _____ is water saturated or nearly saturated with salt and is a common fluid used in the transport of heat from place to place. It is used because the addition of salt to water lowers the freezing temperature of the solution and a relatively great efficiency in the transport can be obtained for the low cost of the material.
a. Metalloid
c. Chemical waste
b. 1509 Istanbul earthquake
d. Brine

25. _____ refers to water-soluble, mineral sediments that result from the evaporation of bodies of surficial water.
a. AL 333
c. Evaporite
b. AASHTO Soil Classification System
d. AL 129-1

26. _____ is rock that is of a certain particle size range. In geology, _____ is any loose rock that is at least two millimeters in its largest dimension and no more than 75 millimeters.
a. Gravel
c. 1700 Cascadia earthquake
b. 1703 Genroku earthquake
d. 1509 Istanbul earthquake

27. A _____ is an accumulation of alluvium or eluvium containing valuable minerals which is formed by deposition of dense mineral phases in a trap site.
a. 1703 Genroku earthquake
c. Placer
b. 1700 Cascadia earthquake
d. 1509 Istanbul earthquake

28. According to the Oxford English Dictionary the correct spelling of the element is phosphorus. The word _____ is the adjectival form of the P^{3+} valency: so, just as sulfur forms sulfurous and sulfuric compounds, phosphorus forms _____ compounds and P^{5+} valency phosphoric compounds

Although twenty-three isotopes of phosphorus are known (all possibilities from ^{24}P up to ^{46}P), only ^{31}P, with spin 1/2, is stable and is therefore present at 100% abundance.

a. Phosphorous
c. 1703 Genroku earthquake
b. 1509 Istanbul earthquake
d. 1700 Cascadia earthquake

29. A _____ or place-value notation system is a numeral system in which each position is related to the next by a constant multiplier, a common ratio, called the base or radix of that numeral system. Each position may be represented by a unique symbol or by a limited set of symbols. The resultant value of each problem is the value of its symbol or symbols multiplied by a power of the base.
a. Amblypoda
c. Andrija Mohorovi ić
b. Ambulocetus
d. Positional notation

30. A _____ is formed when a thick bed of evaporite minerals found at depth intrudes vertically into surrounding rock strata, forming a diapir.
a. 1703 Genroku earthquake
c. Salt dome
b. 1700 Cascadia earthquake
d. 1509 Istanbul earthquake

Chapter 14. Mineral Resources and Environment

31. In geology, a _____ is a deformational feature consisting of symmetrically-dipping anticlines; their general outline on a geologic map is circular or oval.
   a. 1509 Istanbul earthquake
   b. 1700 Cascadia earthquake
   c. 1703 Genroku earthquake
   d. Dome

32. _____ is an aluminium ore. It consists largely of the Al minerals gibbsite, boehmite and diaspore, together with the iron oxides goethite and hematite, the clay mineral kaolinite and small amounts of anatase.
   a. 1700 Cascadia earthquake
   b. 1703 Genroku earthquake
   c. 1509 Istanbul earthquake
   d. Bauxite

33. The _____ is a region of central Florida, encompassing portions of present-day Hardee, Hillsborough, Manatee, and Polk counties, in which phosphate is mined for use in the production of agricultural fertilizer. Florida currently contains the largest known deposits of phosphate in the United States.

Large walking draglines, operating twenty-four hours a day in surface mines, excavate raw pebble phosphate mixed with clay and sand (known as matrix) using huge buckets which can hold more than forty cubic yards of earth.

   a. 1700 Cascadia earthquake
   b. 1703 Genroku earthquake
   c. 1509 Istanbul earthquake
   d. Bone Valley

34. _____ is the excrement (feces and urine) of seabirds, bats, and seals.

_____ manure is an effective fertilizer and gunpowder ingredient due to its high levels of phosphorus and nitrogen and also its lack of odor. Superphosphate made from _____ is used for aerial topdressing.

   a. Guano
   b. 1703 Genroku earthquake
   c. 1509 Istanbul earthquake
   d. 1700 Cascadia earthquake

35. _____ is a surface formation in hot and wet tropical areas which is enriched in iron and aluminium and develops by intensive and long lasting weathering of the underlying parent rock. Nearly all kinds of rocks can be deeply decomposed by the action of high rainfall and elevated temperatures. This gives rise to a residual concentration of more insoluble elements.
   a. 1703 Genroku earthquake
   b. Laterite
   c. 1700 Cascadia earthquake
   d. 1509 Istanbul earthquake

36. In geology, a _____ is a depression with predominant extent in one direction. The terms U-shaped and V-shaped are descriptive terms of geography to characterize the form of valleys. Most valleys belong to one of these two main types or a mixture of them, at least with respect of the cross section of the slopes or hillsides.
   a. 1509 Istanbul earthquake
   b. 1700 Cascadia earthquake
   c. 1703 Genroku earthquake
   d. Valley

37. A _____, is a fissure in a planet's surface from which geothermally heated water issues. Hydrothermal vents are commonly found near volcanically active places, tectonic plates that are moving apart, ocean basins, and hotspots.

Chapter 14. Mineral Resources and Environment

a. 1700 Cascadia earthquake
c. Hydrothermal vent

b. 1703 Genroku earthquake
d. 1509 Istanbul earthquake

38. _____ are a type of hydrothermal vent found on the ocean floor. The vents are formed in fields hundreds of meters wide when superheated water from below the Earth's crust comes through the ocean floor. It can also be known as a Sea Vent. The superheated water is rich in dissolved minerals from the crust, most notably sulfides, which crystallize to create a chimney-like structure around each vent. When the superheated water in the vent comes in contact with the cold ocean water, many minerals are precipitated, creating the distinctive black color.
 a. 1700 Cascadia earthquake
 c. 1703 Genroku earthquake

 b. 1509 Istanbul earthquake
 d. Black smokers

39. _____ is the biological conversion of 1-carbon molecules and nutrients into organic matter using the oxidation of inorganic molecules or methane as a source of energy, rather than sunlight, as in photosynthesis.
 a. 1700 Cascadia earthquake
 c. 1703 Genroku earthquake

 b. 1509 Istanbul earthquake
 d. Chemosynthesis

40. The term _____ refers to several types of chemical compounds containing sulfur in its lowest oxidation number of −2.
 a. Sulfide
 c. 1509 Istanbul earthquake

 b. 1703 Genroku earthquake
 d. 1700 Cascadia earthquake

41. _____ is a chemical element in the periodic table that has the symbol Mn and atomic number 25. It is found as the free element in nature (often in combination with iron), and in many minerals. The free element is a metal with important industrial metal alloy uses.
 a. 1700 Cascadia earthquake
 c. Manganese

 b. 1509 Istanbul earthquake
 d. 1703 Genroku earthquake

42. A _____ in petrology or mineralogy is an irregular rounded to spherical concretion. They are typically solid replacement bodies of chert or iron oxides formed during diagenesis of a sedimentary rock.
 a. 1703 Genroku earthquake
 c. 1700 Cascadia earthquake

 b. Nodule
 d. 1509 Istanbul earthquake

43. An _____ is a chemical compound containing an oxygen atom and other elements. Most of the earth's crust consists of them. They result when elements are oxidized by air.
 a. AL 333
 c. AASHTO Soil Classification System

 b. Oxide
 d. AL 129-1

44. The _____ is an open-pit mine extracting a large porphyry copper deposit southwest of Salt Lake City, Utah, USA, in the Oquirrh Mountains. It is owned by Rio Tinto plc through Kennecott Utah Copper Corporation which operates the mine, a concentrator and a smelter. The mine has been in production since 1906, and has resulted in the creation of a pit over 0.75 miles wide, and covering 1,900 acres.
 a. Bingham Mine
 c. 1703 Genroku earthquake

 b. 1700 Cascadia earthquake
 d. 1509 Istanbul earthquake

Chapter 14. Mineral Resources and Environment

45. A _____ is a deep valley between cliffs often carved from the landscape by a river. Most were formed by a process of long-time erosion from a plateau level. The cliffs form because harder rock strata that are resistant to erosion and weathering remain exposed on the valley walls.
   a. 1703 Genroku earthquake
   b. 1509 Istanbul earthquake
   c. 1700 Cascadia earthquake
   d. Canyon

46. _____ is a chemical element in the periodic table that has the symbol Cu and atomic number 29. It is a ductile metal with excellent electrical conductivity, and finds extensive use as a building material, as an electrical conductor, and as a component of various alloys.
   a. 1509 Istanbul earthquake
   b. 1703 Genroku earthquake
   c. Copper
   d. 1700 Cascadia earthquake

47. In geography, a _____ is a landscape form or region that receives very little precipitation. They are defined as areas that receive an average annual precipitation of less than 250 mm. A _____ where vegetation cover is exceedingly sparse correspond to the 'hyperarid' regions of the earth, where rainfall is exceedingly rare and infrequent.
   a. 1700 Cascadia earthquake
   b. Desert
   c. 1509 Istanbul earthquake
   d. 1703 Genroku earthquake

48. A _____ is a desert surface that is covered with closely packed, interlocking angular or rounded rock fragments of pebble and cobble size. It is thought that they are formed by the gradual removal of the sand, dust and other fine grained material by the wind and intermittent rain.
   a. 1700 Cascadia earthquake
   b. 1509 Istanbul earthquake
   c. 1703 Genroku earthquake
   d. Desert pavement

49. In geology, a _____ is the outermost layer of a planet, part of its lithosphere. They are generally composed of a less dense material than its deeper layers.Earths' is composed mainly of basalt and granite. It is cooler and more rigid than the deeper layers of the mantle and core.
   a. 1700 Cascadia earthquake
   b. 1509 Istanbul earthquake
   c. 1703 Genroku earthquake
   d. Crust

50. An _____ is an assessment of the likely influence a project may have on the environment. The purpose of the assessment is to ensure that decision-makers consider environmental impacts before deciding whether to proceed with new projects.
   a. Environmental impact
   b. AL 333
   c. AASHTO Soil Classification System
   d. AL 129-1

51. _____ is an industrial mining process to extract precious metals and copper compounds from ore.
   a. 1700 Cascadia earthquake
   b. 1703 Genroku earthquake
   c. Heap leaching
   d. 1509 Istanbul earthquake

52. _____ is the process of extracting a substance from a solid by dissolving it in a liquid.
   a. 1509 Istanbul earthquake
   b. 1703 Genroku earthquake
   c. Leaching
   d. 1700 Cascadia earthquake

Chapter 14. Mineral Resources and Environment 133

53. _____ is the introduction of substances or energy into the environment, resulting in deleterious effects of such a nature as to endanger human health, harm living resources and ecosystems, and impair or interfere with amenities and other legitimate uses of the environment.
   a. 1509 Istanbul earthquake
   b. 1703 Genroku earthquake
   c. Pollution
   d. 1700 Cascadia earthquake

54. An _____ is traditionally considered any chemical compound that, when dissolved in water, gives a solution with a hydrogen ion activity greater than in pure water, i.e. a pH less than 7.0. That approximates the modern definition of Johannes Nicolaus Brønsted and Martin Lowry, who independently defined an _____ as a compound which donates a hydrogen ion to another compound. Common examples include acetic _____ and sulfuric _____. _____/base systems are different from redox reactions in that there is no change in oxidation state.
   a. AASHTO Soil Classification System
   b. Acid
   c. AL 333
   d. AL 129-1

55. _____ refers to the outflow of acidic water from abandoned metal mines. However, other areas where the earth has been disturbed may also contribute _____ to the environment
   a. AL 333
   b. AL 129-1
   c. AASHTO Soil Classification System
   d. Acid mine drainage

56. _____ is a layer of gases surrounding the planet Earth and retained by the Earth's gravity, protecting life on Earth by absorbing ultraviolet solar radiation and reducing temperature extremes between day and night.
   a. AL 333
   b. Earths atmosphere
   c. AASHTO Soil Classification System
   d. AL 129-1

57. A _____ describes one of a number of pieces of legislation relating to the reduction of smog and air pollution in general. The use of governments to enforce clean air standards has contributed to an improvement in human health and longer life spans.
   a. 1700 Cascadia earthquake
   b. 1509 Istanbul earthquake
   c. 1703 Genroku earthquake
   d. Clean Air Act

58. _____ refers to a characteristic of living organisms. It always refers to the interaction of organisms with other organisms and to their collective co-existence, irrespective of whether they are aware of it or not, and irrespective of whether the interaction is voluntary or involuntary.

In the absence of agreement about its meaning, the term '_____' is used in many different senses, referring among other things to:

- attitudes, orientations or behaviours which take the interests, intentions or needs of other people into account;
- common characteristics of people or descriptions of collectivities;
- relations between people generally, or particular associations among people;
- interactions between people;
- membership of a group of people or inclusion or belonging to a community of people;
- co-operation or co-operative characteristics between people;
- relations of dependence;
- the public sector or the need for governance for the good of all, contrasted with the private sector;
- in existentialist and postmodernist thought, relationships between the Self and the Other;
- interactive systems in communities of people, animal or insect populations, or any living organisms.

In one broad meaning, '_____' refers only to society as 'a system of common life', but in another sense it contrasts specifically with 'individual' and individualist theories of society. This is reflected for instance in the different perspectives of liberalism and socialism on society and public affairs.

   a. 1700 Cascadia earthquake
   c. 1703 Genroku earthquake
   b. 1509 Istanbul earthquake
   d. Social

59. In business and government policy, _____ refers to how the organization's actions affect the surrounding community.
   a. 1509 Istanbul earthquake
   c. Social impact
   b. 1703 Genroku earthquake
   d. 1700 Cascadia earthquake

60. _____ is the natural or artificial removal of surface and sub-surface water from a given area. Many agricultural soils need _____ to improve production or to manage water supplies.
   a. 1700 Cascadia earthquake
   c. Drainage
   b. 1703 Genroku earthquake
   d. 1509 Istanbul earthquake

61. _____ is the extraction of valuable minerals or other geological materials from the earth, usually from an ore body, vein, or seam. Any material that cannot be grown from agricultural processes, or created artificially in a laboratory or factory, is usually extracted from the earth by this method.
   a. 1509 Istanbul earthquake
   c. 1703 Genroku earthquake
   b. 1700 Cascadia earthquake
   d. Mining

62. _____ is the extraction of specific metals from their ores through the use of bacteria.
   a. 1700 Cascadia earthquake
   c. 1509 Istanbul earthquake
   b. Bioleaching
   d. 1703 Genroku earthquake

63. _____ is technology based on biology, especially when used in agriculture, food science, and medicine.

Chapter 14. Mineral Resources and Environment

a. 1700 Cascadia earthquake
c. 1703 Genroku earthquake
b. 1509 Istanbul earthquake
d. Biotechnology

64. The _____ is a deep underground gold mine located near Lead, South Dakota. Until it closed in 2002 it was the largest, oldest, and deepest mine in the Western Hemisphere.
   a. 1509 Istanbul earthquake
   c. 1703 Genroku earthquake
   b. Homestake Mine
   d. 1700 Cascadia earthquake

65. _____ is the reprocessing of materials into new products. It prevents useful material resources being wasted, reduces the consumption of raw materials and reduces energy usage, and hence greenhouse gas emissions, compared to virgin production.
   a. Recycling
   c. 1703 Genroku earthquake
   b. 1509 Istanbul earthquake
   d. 1700 Cascadia earthquake

66. _____ is a term used to describe recyclable materials left over from every manner of product consumption, such as parts of vehicles, building supplies, and surplus materials. Often confused with waste, _____ in fact has monetary value. In 2007 the United States' exported over 10 billion dollars worth of _____ steel.
   a. 1509 Istanbul earthquake
   c. Scrap
   b. 1703 Genroku earthquake
   d. 1700 Cascadia earthquake

Chapter 15. Energy and Environment

1. In physics, _____ is a scalar physical quantity that describes the amount of work that can be performed by a force. _____ is an attribute of objects and systems that is subject to a conservation law. Several different forms of _____ exist to explain all known natural phenomena.
   a. Energy
   b. AASHTO Soil Classification System
   c. AL 333
   d. AL 129-1

2. _____ describes market relations between prospective sellers and buyers of a good. The model predicts that in a competitive market, price will function to equalize the quantity demanded by consumers and the quantity supplied by producers, resulting in an economic equilibrium of price and quantity.
   a. 1703 Genroku earthquake
   b. 1509 Istanbul earthquake
   c. 1700 Cascadia earthquake
   d. Demand and supply

3. Fossils are the mineralized or otherwise preserved remains or traces of animals, plants, and other organisms. The totality of fossils, both discovered and undiscovered, and their placement in fossiliferous rock formations and sedimentary layers is known as the _____ record.
   a. 1700 Cascadia earthquake
   b. 1509 Istanbul earthquake
   c. 1703 Genroku earthquake
   d. Fossil

4. _____ are hydrocarbons, primarily coal and petroleum, formed from the fossilized remains of dead plants and animals by exposure to heat and pressure in the Earth's crust over hundreds of millions of years. The burning of _____ by humans is the largest source of emissions of carbon dioxide, which is one of the greenhouse gases that enhances radiative forcing and contributes to global warming.
   a. 1700 Cascadia earthquake
   b. Fossil fuels
   c. 1509 Istanbul earthquake
   d. 1703 Genroku earthquake

5. _____ are the SI unit of energy.
   a. 1509 Istanbul earthquake
   b. 1703 Genroku earthquake
   c. 1700 Cascadia earthquake
   d. Joules

6. _____ is a fossil fuel formed in swamp ecosystems where plant remains were saved by water and mud from oxidization and biodegradation. It is a sedimentary rock, but the harder forms, such as anthracite _____, can be regarded as metamorphic rocks because of later exposure to elevated temperature and pressure. It is composed primarily of carbon along with assorted other elements, including sulfur.
   a. Coal
   b. 1703 Genroku earthquake
   c. 1509 Istanbul earthquake
   d. 1700 Cascadia earthquake

7. _____ is the science and study of the solid matter that constitute the Earth. Encompassing such things as rocks, soil, and gemstones, _____ studies the composition, structure, physical properties, history, and the processes that shape Earth's components.
   a. 1700 Cascadia earthquake
   b. 1703 Genroku earthquake
   c. Geology
   d. 1509 Istanbul earthquake

8. _____ is the chemical element in the periodic table that has the symbol S and atomic number 16. It is an abundant, tasteless, odorless, multivalent non-metal. _____, in its native form, is a yellow crystaline solid. In nature, it can be found as the pure element or as sulfide and sulfate minerals.

Chapter 15. Energy and Environment

a. 1700 Cascadia earthquake
b. 1509 Istanbul earthquake
c. 1703 Genroku earthquake
d. Sulfur

9. _____ is a quantity expressing the two-dimensional size of a defined part of a surface, typically a region bounded by a closed curve. The term surface _____ refers to the total _____ of the exposed surface of a 3-dimensional solid, such as the sum of the areas of the exposed sides of a polyhedron. _____ is an important invariant in the differential geometry of surfaces.
   a. AL 333
   b. AL 129-1
   c. AASHTO Soil Classification System
   d. Area

10. _____ is commonly practiced where a coal seam outcrops a hilly terrain. It removes the overburden above the coal seam and then creates a bench arounf the hill.
   a. 1700 Cascadia earthquake
   b. 1703 Genroku earthquake
   c. Contour strip mining
   d. 1509 Istanbul earthquake

11. _____ is the practice of mining a seam of mineral by first removing a long strip of overlying soil and rock.
   a. 1703 Genroku earthquake
   b. 1509 Istanbul earthquake
   c. Strip mining
   d. 1700 Cascadia earthquake

12. _____ is the extraction of valuable minerals or other geological materials from the earth, usually from an ore body, vein, or seam. Any material that cannot be grown from agricultural processes, or created artificially in a laboratory or factory, is usually extracted from the earth by this method.
   a. Mining
   b. 1509 Istanbul earthquake
   c. 1703 Genroku earthquake
   d. 1700 Cascadia earthquake

13. An _____ is an assessment of the likely influence a project may have on the environment. The purpose of the assessment is to ensure that decision-makers consider environmental impacts before deciding whether to proceed with new projects.
   a. AL 129-1
   b. AASHTO Soil Classification System
   c. AL 333
   d. Environmental impact

14. _____, is the unbranched alkane with four carbon atoms. It is highly flammable, colorless, easily liquefied gases. The name _____ was derived by back-formation from the name of butyric acid. _____ gas is sold bottled as a fuel for cooking and camping. It is also used as a petrol component, as a feedstock for the production of base petrochemicals in steam cracking, as fuel for cigarette lighters and as a propellant in aerosol sprays.
   a. 1700 Cascadia earthquake
   b. Butane
   c. 1703 Genroku earthquake
   d. 1509 Istanbul earthquake

15. _____ is a chemical element in the periodic table that has the symbol H and atomic number 1. At standard temperature and pressure it is a colorless, odorless, nonmetallic, univalent, tasteless, highly flammable diatomic gas.
   a. 1700 Cascadia earthquake
   b. 1703 Genroku earthquake
   c. 1509 Istanbul earthquake
   d. Hydrogen

16. _____ is a gaseous fossil fuel consisting primarily of methane but including significant quantities of ethane, butane, propane, carbon dioxide, nitrogen, helium and hydrogen sulfide.

Chapter 15. Energy and Environment

    a. 1703 Genroku earthquake
    b. 1700 Cascadia earthquake
    c. 1509 Istanbul earthquake
    d. Natural gas

17. _____ is a three-carbon alkane, normally a gas, but compressible to a transportable liquid. It is derived from other petroleum products during oil or natural gas processing. It is commonly used as a fuel for engines, barbecues, and home heating systems.
    a. 1700 Cascadia earthquake
    b. 1509 Istanbul earthquake
    c. 1703 Genroku earthquake
    d. Propane

18. Most often, a _____ refers to an artificial lake, used to store water for various uses. Reservoirs are created first by building a sturdy dam, usually out of cement, earth, rock, or a mixture. Once the dam is completed, a stream is allowed to flow behind it and eventually fill it to capacity.
    a. 1700 Cascadia earthquake
    b. 1509 Istanbul earthquake
    c. 1703 Genroku earthquake
    d. Reservoir

19. For morphological image processing operations, see Erosion (morphology)For use of in dermatopathology, see Erosion (dermatopathology) Severe _____ in a wheat field near Washington State University, USA.

Erosion is the removal of solids (sediment, soil, rock and other particles) in the natural environment. It usually occurs due to transport by wind, water, or ice; by down-slope creep of soil and other material under the force of gravity; or by living organisms, such as burrowing animals, in the case of bioerosion.

Erosion is distinguished from weathering, which is the process of chemical or physical breakdown of the minerals in the rocks, although the two processes may occur concurrently.

    a. 1700 Cascadia earthquake
    b. 1703 Genroku earthquake
    c. 1509 Istanbul earthquake
    d. Soil erosion

20. _____ is a combination of clay, sand, water, and bitumen. On average bitumen contains 83.2% carbon, 10.4% hydrogen, 4.8% sulphur, 0.94% oxygen, and 0.36% nitrogen.
    a. 1700 Cascadia earthquake
    b. 1509 Istanbul earthquake
    c. Tar sand
    d. 1703 Genroku earthquake

21. _____ is displacement of solids by the agents of ocean currents, wind, water, or ice by downward or down-slope movement in response to gravity or by living organisms.
    a. Erosion
    b. AL 333
    c. AL 129-1
    d. AASHTO Soil Classification System

22. In organic chemistry, a _____ is an organic compound consisting entirely of hydrogen and carbon. With relation to chemical terminology, aromatic hydrocarbons or arenes, alkanes, alkenes and alkyne-based compounds composed entirely of carbon or hydrogen are referred to as "Pure" hydrocarbons, whereas other hydrocarbons with bonded compounds or impurities of sulphur or nitrogen, are referred to as "impure", and remain somewhat erroneously referred to as hydrocarbons.
    a. 1700 Cascadia earthquake
    b. Hydrocarbon
    c. 1703 Genroku earthquake
    d. 1509 Istanbul earthquake

23. _____ refers to directed, regular, or systematic movement of a group of objects, organisms, or people.

a. 1509 Istanbul earthquake
c. 1703 Genroku earthquake
b. Migration
d. 1700 Cascadia earthquake

24. In geology, _____ is a naturally occurring aggregate of minerals and/or mineraloids.

The Earth's outer solid layer, the lithosphere, is made of _____. In general rocks are of three types, namely, igneous, sedimentary, and metamorphic.

a. 1509 Istanbul earthquake
c. 1703 Genroku earthquake
b. 1700 Cascadia earthquake
d. Rock

25. A _____ is a massive, luminous ball of plasma. Stars group together to form galaxies, and they dominate the visible universe. The nearest _____ to Earth is the Sun, which is the source of most of the energy on Earth, including daylight. Other stars are visible in the night sky, when they are not outshone by the Sun. A _____ shines because nuclear fusion in its core releases energy which traverses the _____'s interior and then radiates into outer space.

a. 1703 Genroku earthquake
c. 1700 Cascadia earthquake
b. 1509 Istanbul earthquake
d. Star

26. In thermodynamics, the _____ of a substance is the temperature and pressure at which three phases (for example, gas, liquid, and solid) of that substance coexist in thermodynamic equilibrium. For example, the _____ of mercury occurs at a temperature of −38.8344 °C and a pressure of 0.2 mPa.

In addition to the _____ between solid, liquid, and gas, there can be triple points involving more than one solid phase, for substances with multiple polymorphs.

a. Triple point
c. 1509 Istanbul earthquake
b. 1703 Genroku earthquake
d. 1700 Cascadia earthquake

27. Faults are planar rock fractures, which show evidence of relative movement. Large faults within the Earth's crust are the result of shear motion and active _____ zones are the causal locations of most earthquakes. Earthquakes are caused by energy release during rapid slippage along faults.

a. 1509 Istanbul earthquake
c. 1703 Genroku earthquake
b. 1700 Cascadia earthquake
d. Fault

28. _____, a branch of geology, studies rock layers and layering. It is primarily used in the study of sedimentary and layered volcanic rocks. _____ includes two related subfields: lithologic or lithostratigraphy and biologic _____ or biostratigraphy.

a. 1700 Cascadia earthquake
c. 1703 Genroku earthquake
b. 1509 Istanbul earthquake
d. Stratigraphy

29. An _____ is a buried erosion surface separating two rock masses or strata of different ages, indicating that sediment deposition was not continuous. In general, the older layer was exposed to erosion for an interval of time before deposition of the younger, but the term is used to describe any break in the sedimentary geologic record.

a. AL 129-1
c. AL 333
b. AASHTO Soil Classification System
d. Unconformity

Chapter 15. Energy and Environment

30. _____ is a naturally occurring liquid found in formations in the Earth consisting of a complex mixture of hydrocarbons of various lengths.
    a. 1509 Istanbul earthquake
    b. 1703 Genroku earthquake
    c. 1700 Cascadia earthquake
    d. Petroleum

31. The _____ is a tributary of the Colorado River, 730 mi long, in the western United States. The _____ Basin covers parts of Wyoming, Utah, and Colorado. The river begins in the Wind River Mountains of Wyoming, and flows through Utah for much of its course, draining the northeastern portion of the state while looping for 40 mi into western Colorado.
    a. Lake Louise
    b. Green River
    c. Niigata
    d. Craters of the Moon

32. The _____ is an Eocene geologic formation that records the sedimentation in a series of intermontane lakes. The sedimentary layers were formed in a large area of interconnecting lakes.
    a. 1703 Genroku earthquake
    b. 1509 Istanbul earthquake
    c. 1700 Cascadia earthquake
    d. Green River Formation

33. _____ is a general term applied to a fine-grained sedimentary rock containing significant traces of kerogen that have not been buried for sufficient time to produce conventional fossil fuels. When heated to a sufficiently high temperature a vapor is driven off which can be distilled to yield a petroleum.
    a. AL 333
    b. Oil shale
    c. AASHTO Soil Classification System
    d. AL 129-1

34. _____ is a fine-grained sedimentary rock whose original constituents were clays or muds. It is characterized by thin laminae breaking with an irregular curving fracture, often splintery and usually parallel to the often-indistinguishable bedding plane.
    a. Shale
    b. 1703 Genroku earthquake
    c. 1509 Istanbul earthquake
    d. 1700 Cascadia earthquake

35. An _____ is traditionally considered any chemical compound that, when dissolved in water, gives a solution with a hydrogen ion activity greater than in pure water, i.e. a pH less than 7.0. That approximates the modern definition of Johannes Nicolaus Brønsted and Martin Lowry, who independently defined an _____ as a compound which donates a hydrogen ion to another compound. Common examples include acetic _____ and sulfuric _____. _____/base systems are different from redox reactions in that there is no change in oxidation state.
    a. AASHTO Soil Classification System
    b. AL 129-1
    c. AL 333
    d. Acid

36. The term _____ is commonly used to mean the deposition of acidic components in rain, snow, dew, or dry particles. _____ occurs when sulfur dioxide and nitrogen oxides are emitted into the atmosphere, undergo chemical transformations and are absorbed by water droplets in clouds. The droplets then fall to earth as rain, snow, mist, dry dust, hail, or sleet. This increases the acidity of the soil, and affects the chemical balance of lakes and streams.
    a. Acid precipitation
    b. AL 333
    c. AASHTO Soil Classification System
    d. AL 129-1

37. A _____ is a body of water, not part of the ocean, that is larger and deeper than a pond.

Chapter 15. Energy and Environment

   a. 1509 Istanbul earthquake
   b. Lake
   c. 1703 Genroku earthquake
   d. 1700 Cascadia earthquake

38. _____ is a general term for the plant life of a region; it refers to the ground cover provided by plants, and is, by far, the most abundant biotic element of the biosphere. Primeval redwood forests, coastal mangrove stands, sphagnum bogs, desert soil crusts, roadside weed patches, wheat fields, cultivated gardens and lawns; are all encompassed by the term _____.
   a. 1700 Cascadia earthquake
   b. Vegetation
   c. 1509 Istanbul earthquake
   d. 1703 Genroku earthquake

39. An _____ is a natural unit consisting of all plants, animals and micro organisms in an area functioning together with all the non living physical factors of the environment.
   a. AASHTO Soil Classification System
   b. AL 333
   c. AL 129-1
   d. Ecosystem

40. A _____ is a bipedal primate belonging to the mammalian species Homo sapiens in the family Hominidae. Compared to other living organisms on Earth, a _____ has a highly developed brain capable of abstract reasoning, language, and introspection.
   a. 1700 Cascadia earthquake
   b. 1509 Istanbul earthquake
   c. 1703 Genroku earthquake
   d. Human

41. A _____ is a sequence of reactions where a reactive product or by-product causes additional reactions to take place.
   a. Chain reaction
   b. 1703 Genroku earthquake
   c. 1509 Istanbul earthquake
   d. 1700 Cascadia earthquake

42. _____ is energy released from the atomic nucleus.
   a. 1509 Istanbul earthquake
   b. 1703 Genroku earthquake
   c. 1700 Cascadia earthquake
   d. Nuclear energy

43. _____ is a white/black metallic chemical element in the actinide series of the periodic table that has the symbol U and atomic number 92. When refined, _____ is a silvery white, weakly radioactive metal, which is slightly softer than steel. It is malleable, ductile, and slightly paramagnetic.
   a. AASHTO Soil Classification System
   b. AL 129-1
   c. AL 333
   d. Uranium

44. _____ is a sample of uranium in which the percent composition of uranium-235 has been increased through the process of isotope separation
   a. AL 129-1
   b. AL 333
   c. AASHTO Soil Classification System
   d. Enriched uranium

45. A _____ is a type of nuclear reactor developed by the Idaho National Laboratory and General Electric in the mid-1950s. In the present, General Electric specializes in the design and construction of this type of reactor. The _____ is characterized by two-phase fluid flow (water and steam) in the upper part of the reactor core.

Chapter 15. Energy and Environment

a. 1700 Cascadia earthquake
b. 1509 Istanbul earthquake
c. Boiling water reactor
d. 1703 Genroku earthquake

46. A _____, in its most common usage, is a steel or reinforced concrete structure enclosing a nuclear reactor. It is designed to, in any emergency, contain the escape of radiation to a maximum pressure in the range of 60 to 200 psi (410 to 1400 kPa.) The containment is the final barrier to radioactive release (part of a nuclear reactor's Defence in depth strategy), the first being the fuel ceramic itself, the second being the metal fuel cladding tubes, the third being the reactor vessel and coolant system.
a. 1703 Genroku earthquake
b. 1700 Cascadia earthquake
c. 1509 Istanbul earthquake
d. Containment building

47. A _____ is a rod made of chemical elements capable of absorbing many neutrons without fissioning themselves. They are used in nuclear reactors to control the rate of fission of uranium and plutonium. Chemical elements with a sufficiently high capture cross section for neutrons include silver, indium and cadmium.
a. 1703 Genroku earthquake
b. 1509 Istanbul earthquake
c. 1700 Cascadia earthquake
d. Control rod

48. A _____ is a fluid which flows through a device in order to prevent its overheating, transferring the heat produced by the device to other devices that utilize or dissipate it. An ideal _____ has high thermal capacity, low viscosity, is low-cost, and is chemically inert, neither causing nor promoting corrosion of the cooling system.
a. 1703 Genroku earthquake
b. 1700 Cascadia earthquake
c. 1509 Istanbul earthquake
d. Coolant

49. The _____ is the portion of the electromagnetic spectrum that is visible to the human eye.
a. Visible spectrum
b. 1703 Genroku earthquake
c. 1509 Istanbul earthquake
d. 1700 Cascadia earthquake

50. A _____ is a themal nuclear reactor that uses ordinary water. It uses uranium 235 as a fuel, enriched to approximately 3 percent. Although this is its major fuel, the uranium 238 atoms also contribute to the fission process by converting to plutonium 239 — about one-half of which is consumed in the reactor.
a. 1703 Genroku earthquake
b. 1509 Istanbul earthquake
c. 1700 Cascadia earthquake
d. Light-water reactor

51. _____ (_____s) are generation II nuclear power reactors that use ordinary water under high pressure (superheated water) as coolant to remove heat generated by nuclear chain reaction from nuclear fuel, and as the moderator to thermalise the neutron flux so that it interacts with the nuclear fuel to maintain the chain reaction. The primary coolant loop is kept under high pressure to prevent the water from reaching film boiling, hence the name. _____s are the most common type of power producing nuclear reactor, and are widely used in power stations, ships and submarines all over the world.
a. 1509 Istanbul earthquake
b. 1703 Genroku earthquake
c. Pressurized water reactor
d. 1700 Cascadia earthquake

52. In a nuclear power plant, the _____ is a pressure vessel containing the coolant and reactor core.

Not all power reactors have a _____. Power reactors are generally classified by the type of coolant rather than the by the configuration of the _____ used to contain the coolant.

Chapter 15. Energy and Environment 143

  a. 1703 Genroku earthquake
  c. 1700 Cascadia earthquake
  b. 1509 Istanbul earthquake
  d. Reactor vessel

53. A _____ is a person who practices the vocation of mating carefully selected specimens of the same breed to reproduce specific, consistently replicable qualities and characteristics.
  a. 1509 Istanbul earthquake
  c. 1703 Genroku earthquake
  b. 1700 Cascadia earthquake
  d. Breeder

54. _____ are nuclear reactors that consumes fissile and fertile material at the same time as they creates new fissile material.
  a. Breeder reactors
  c. 1703 Genroku earthquake
  b. 1509 Istanbul earthquake
  d. 1700 Cascadia earthquake

55. _____ is an abandoned city in northern Ukraine, in the Kiev Oblast near the border with Belarus. The city was evacuated in 1986 due to the disaster at the _____ Nuclear Power Plant, which is located 14.5 kilometers north-northwest.
  a. 1703 Genroku earthquake
  c. 1700 Cascadia earthquake
  b. 1509 Istanbul earthquake
  d. Chernobyl

56. The _____ was a nuclear reactor accident in the Chernobyl Nuclear Power Plant in the Soviet Union. It was the worst nuclear power plant disaster ever and the only level 7 instance on the International Nuclear Event Scale. It resulted in a severe release of radioactivity into the environment following a massive power excursion which destroyed the reactor.
  a. 1700 Cascadia earthquake
  c. Chernobyl disaster
  b. 1509 Istanbul earthquake
  d. 1703 Genroku earthquake

57. _____ is a concept that denotes the precise probability of specific eventualities. Technically, the notion of _____ is independent from the notion of value and, as such, eventualities may have both beneficial and adverse consequences. However, in general usage the convention is to focus only on potential negative impact to some characteristic of value that may arise from a future event.
  a. 1509 Istanbul earthquake
  c. 1703 Genroku earthquake
  b. 1700 Cascadia earthquake
  d. Risk

58. In geology, _____ refers to heat sources within the planet. The planet's internal heat was originally generated during its accretion, due to gravitational binding energy, and since then additional heat has continued to be generated by the radioactive decay of elements such as uranium, thorium, and potassium.
  a. 1509 Istanbul earthquake
  c. 1703 Genroku earthquake
  b. 1700 Cascadia earthquake
  d. Geothermal

59. An _____ is any piece of land that is completely surrounded by water, above high tide. There are two main types of islands: continental islands and oceanic islands. There are also artificial islands. A grouping of geographically and/or geologically related islands is called an archipelago.
  a. AL 129-1
  c. AL 333
  b. AASHTO Soil Classification System
  d. Island

Chapter 15. Energy and Environment

60. _____ in the most general terms refers to the movement of currents within fluids. _____ is one of the major modes of Heat and mass transfer. In fluids, convective heat and mass transfer take place through both diffusion and by advection, in which matter or heat is transported by the larger-scale motion of currents in the fluid.
   a. 1509 Istanbul earthquake
   b. 1703 Genroku earthquake
   c. Convection
   d. 1700 Cascadia earthquake

61. _____ rocks form when molten rock, magma, cools and solidifies, with or without crystallization, either below the surface as intrusive, plutonic rocks or on the surface as extrusive, volcanic, rocks.
   a. AL 129-1
   b. Igneous
   c. AASHTO Soil Classification System
   d. AL 333

62. _____ is the use of geothermal heat to generate electricity.
   a. 1700 Cascadia earthquake
   b. 1509 Istanbul earthquake
   c. 1703 Genroku earthquake
   d. Geothermal power

63. _____ is water located beneath the ground surface in soil pore spaces and in the fractures of geologic formations. _____ is recharged from, and eventually flows to, the surface naturally; natural discharge often occurs at springs and seeps, streams and can often form oases or wetlands.
   a. 1700 Cascadia earthquake
   b. 1509 Istanbul earthquake
   c. 1703 Genroku earthquake
   d. Groundwater

64. A natural resource qualifies as a _____ resource if it is replenished by natural processes at a rate comparable or faster than its rate of consumption by humans or other users. Resources such as solar radiation, tides, and winds are perpetual resources that are in no danger of being used in excess of their long-term availability.
   a. 1509 Istanbul earthquake
   b. 1700 Cascadia earthquake
   c. 1703 Genroku earthquake
   d. Renewable

65. _____ is Solar Radiation emitted from our sun. It has been used in many traditional technologies for centuries, and has come into widespread use where other power supplies are absent, such as in remote locations and in space.
   a. 1700 Cascadia earthquake
   b. 1509 Istanbul earthquake
   c. Solar power
   d. 1703 Genroku earthquake

66. _____ technologies are employed to convert solar energy into usable heat, cause air-movement for ventilation or cooling, or store heat for future use. _____ uses electrical or mechanical equipment, such as pumps and fans, to increase the usable heat in a system. Solar energy collection and utilization systems that do not use external energy, like a solar chimney, are classified as passive solar technologies.
   a. AL 333
   b. AASHTO Soil Classification System
   c. AL 129-1
   d. Active solar

67. _____ technologies convert sunlight into usable heat, cause air-movement for ventilation or cooling, or store heat for future use, without the assistance of other energy sources. Technologies that use a significant amount of conventional energy to power pumps or fans are classified as active solar technologies.
   a. 1700 Cascadia earthquake
   b. 1703 Genroku earthquake
   c. 1509 Istanbul earthquake
   d. Passive solar

Chapter 15. Energy and Environment

68. _____, or PV for short, is a solar power technology that uses solar cells or solar photovoltaic arrays to convert light from the sun directly into electricity.
   a. Photovoltaics
   b. 1703 Genroku earthquake
   c. 1700 Cascadia earthquake
   d. 1509 Istanbul earthquake

69. A _____ is a device that converts light energy into electrical energy.
   a. Photovoltaic cell
   b. 1509 Istanbul earthquake
   c. 1700 Cascadia earthquake
   d. 1703 Genroku earthquake

70. _____ utilizes the temperature difference that exists between deep and shallow waters — within 20° of the equator in the tropics — to run a heat engine. Because the oceans are continually heated by the sun and cover nearly 70% of the Earth's surface, this temperature difference contains a vast amount of solar energy which could potentially be trapped for human use. If this extraction could be done profitably on a large scale, it could be a solution to some of the human population's energy problems.
   a. AL 129-1
   b. AL 333
   c. AASHTO Soil Classification System
   d. Ocean thermal energy conversion

71. A _____ column is a column of rizing air in the lower altitudes of the Earth's atmosphere. Thermals are created by the uneven heating of the Earth's surface from solar radiation, and are an example of convection. The Sun warms the ground, which in turn warms the air directly above it.
   a. Thermal
   b. 1703 Genroku earthquake
   c. 1509 Istanbul earthquake
   d. 1700 Cascadia earthquake

72. In thermal physics, _____ is the energy portion of a system that increases with its temperature. In thermodynamics, _____ is the internal energy present in a system in a state of thermodynamic equilibrium by virtue of its temperature.
   a. Supersaturation
   b. Superconductivity
   c. Thermal energy
   d. Velocity

73. Hydroelectricity is electricity generated by hydropower. It is the most widely used form of renewable energy. Once a _____ complex is constructed, the project produces no direct waste, and has a considerably different output level of the greenhouse gas carbon dioxide than fossil fuel powered energy plants.
   a. Kabul
   b. Hydroelectric
   c. Japan
   d. Latin America

74. _____ is electricity produced by hydropower. _____ now supplies about 715,000 MWe or 19% of world electricity. It is also the world's leading form of renewable energy, accounting for over 63% of the total in 2005.
   a. Hydroelectricity
   b. 1703 Genroku earthquake
   c. 1509 Istanbul earthquake
   d. 1700 Cascadia earthquake

75. _____ is the capture of the energy of moving water for some useful purpose.
   a. 1509 Istanbul earthquake
   b. 1700 Cascadia earthquake
   c. Water power
   d. 1703 Genroku earthquake

76. A _____ is a barrier across flowing water that obstructs, directs or slows down the flow, often creating a reservoir, lake or impoundment.

Chapter 15. Energy and Environment

a. 1703 Genroku earthquake
b. 1509 Istanbul earthquake
c. 1700 Cascadia earthquake
d. Dam

77. A _____ is a deep valley between cliffs often carved from the landscape by a river. Most were formed by a process of long-time erosion from a plateau level. The cliffs form because harder rock strata that are resistant to erosion and weathering remain exposed on the valley walls.
a. 1700 Cascadia earthquake
b. 1703 Genroku earthquake
c. 1509 Istanbul earthquake
d. Canyon

78. The _____ is a hydroelectric river dam that spans the Yangtze River in Sandouping, Yichang, Hubei, China. It is the largest hydro-electric power station in the world. Except for a planned ship lift, all the original plan of the project was completed on Oct.
a. 1700 Cascadia earthquake
b. Three Gorges Dam
c. Hydroelectricity
d. 1509 Istanbul earthquake

79. _____ is energy derived by exploiting the rise and fall in sea levels due to the tides.
a. 1509 Istanbul earthquake
b. 1703 Genroku earthquake
c. 1700 Cascadia earthquake
d. Tidal power

80. _____ is the flow of air. More generally, it is the flow of the gases which compose an atmosphere; since _____ is not only an Earth based phenomenon.
a. 1700 Cascadia earthquake
b. 1509 Istanbul earthquake
c. 1703 Genroku earthquake
d. Wind

81. _____ is the conversion of wind into more useful forms, usually electricity, using wind turbines.
a. 1509 Istanbul earthquake
b. 1700 Cascadia earthquake
c. 1703 Genroku earthquake
d. Wind power

82. _____, in the energy production industry, refers to living and recently dead biological material which can be used as fuel or for industrial production. In ecology, _____ refers to the accumulation of life that is possibly living matter.
a. 1700 Cascadia earthquake
b. 1703 Genroku earthquake
c. 1509 Istanbul earthquake
d. Biomass

83. _____ is the use of a heat engine or a power station to simultaneously generate both electricity and useful heat.
a. 1703 Genroku earthquake
b. 1509 Istanbul earthquake
c. 1700 Cascadia earthquake
d. Cogeneration

84. The _____ is a diverse scientific, social, and political movement for addressing the concerns of environmentalism. The _____ is represented by a range of organizations, from the large to grassroots. Due to its large membership, varying and strong beliefs, and occasionally speculative nature, the _____ is not always united in its goals.
a. Andrija Mohorović iÄ‡
b. Environmental movement
c. Amblypoda
d. Ambulocetus

Chapter 15. Energy and Environment

85. In physics, the _____ states that the total amount of energy in an isolated system remains constant, although it may change forms, e.g. friction turns kinetic energy into thermal energy. In thermodynamics, the first law of thermodynamics is a statement of the _____ for thermodynamic systems, and is the more encompassing version of the _____.
   a. 1700 Cascadia earthquake
   b. 1703 Genroku earthquake
   c. 1509 Istanbul earthquake
   d. Conservation of energy

86. _____ is the manner a given entity has decided to address issues of energy development including energy production, distribution and consumption. The attributes of _____ may include legislation, international treaties, incentives to investment, guidelines for energy conservation, taxation and other public policy techniques.
   a. AL 129-1
   b. AL 333
   c. AASHTO Soil Classification System
   d. Energy policy

87. _____ is Chairman and Chief Scientist of the Rocky Mountain Institute, a MacArthur Fellowship recipient (1993), and author and co-author of many books on renewable energy and energy efficiency.

Lovins has worked professionally as an environmentalist and an advocate for a 'soft energy path' for the United States and other nations. He has promoted energy-use and energy-production concepts based on conservation, efficiency, the use of renewable sources of energy, and on generation of energy at or near the site where the energy is actually used.

   a. Amory Bloch Lovins
   b. Amblypoda
   c. Aung San Suu Kyi
   d. Ambulocetus

88. A _____ is an electrochemical energy conversion device. It produces electricity from external supplies of fuel and oxidant.
   a. Fuel cell
   b. 1700 Cascadia earthquake
   c. 1703 Genroku earthquake
   d. 1509 Istanbul earthquake

89. _____ is the term used to encompass a multitude of environmental and ecological changes that have been noticed, measured and studied on Earth. It encompasses the study of climate change, species extinction, land use change, changes in the carbon cycle and hydrologic cycle.
   a. 1700 Cascadia earthquake
   b. 1703 Genroku earthquake
   c. 1509 Istanbul earthquake
   d. Global change

Chapter 16. Global Change and Earth System Science

1. A _____ is flat or nearly flat land adjacent to a stream or river that experiences occasional or periodic flooding. It includes the floodway, which consists of the stream channel and adjacent areas that carry flood flows, and the flood fringe, which are areas covered by the flood, but which do not experience a strong current.
   a. Floodplain
   b. 1703 Genroku earthquake
   c. 1509 Istanbul earthquake
   d. 1700 Cascadia earthquake

2. _____ is the science and study of the solid matter that constitute the Earth. Encompassing such things as rocks, soil, and gemstones, _____ studies the composition, structure, physical properties, history, and the processes that shape Earth's components.
   a. 1700 Cascadia earthquake
   b. 1509 Istanbul earthquake
   c. 1703 Genroku earthquake
   d. Geology

3. The _____ in stratigraphy, Chronostratigraphy, paleontology and other natural sciences refers to the entirety of the layers of rock strata -- depositions laid down in volcanism or by weathering detritus (clays, sands etc.) including all its fossil content and the information it yields about the history of the Earth: its past climate, geography, geology and the evolution of life on its surface. According to the Law of Superposition (first proposed in the mid-seventeenth century by the Danish naturalist Nicolas Steno) sedimentary and volcanic rocklayers are deposited on top of each other.
   a. 1700 Cascadia earthquake
   b. 1703 Genroku earthquake
   c. 1509 Istanbul earthquake
   d. Geologic record

4. Glacier ice is the largest reservoir of fresh water on Earth, and second only to oceans as the largest reservoir of total water. Glaciers cover vast areas of polar regions, are found in mountain ranges of every continent, and are restricted to the highest mountains in the tropics. The processes and landforms caused by glaciers and related to them are referred to as _____.
   a. Global warming controversy
   b. General circulation model
   c. 1509 Istanbul earthquake
   d. Glacial

5. _____ occurs when snow falls on a glacier, is compressed, and becomes part of a glacier that winds its way toward a body of water.
   a. 1703 Genroku earthquake
   b. 1700 Cascadia earthquake
   c. Blue ice
   d. 1509 Istanbul earthquake

6. _____ is an accumulate in the abyssal plain of the deep ocean, far away from terrestrial sources that provide terrigenous sediments; the latter are primarily limited to the continental shelf, and deposited by rivers.
   a. 1700 Cascadia earthquake
   b. 1509 Istanbul earthquake
   c. 1703 Genroku earthquake
   d. Pelagic sediment

7. _____ is the term used to encompass a multitude of environmental and ecological changes that have been noticed, measured and studied on Earth. It encompasses the study of climate change, species extinction, land use change, changes in the carbon cycle and hydrologic cycle.
   a. 1703 Genroku earthquake
   b. 1700 Cascadia earthquake
   c. 1509 Istanbul earthquake
   d. Global change

8. _____ is any particulate matter that can be transported by fluid flow and which eventually is deposited as a layer of solid particles on the bed or bottom of a body of water or other liquid.

Chapter 16. Global Change and Earth System Science   149

a. 1509 Istanbul earthquake
b. 1700 Cascadia earthquake
c. Sediment
d. 1703 Genroku earthquake

9. _____ is the method of scientific dating based on the analysis of tree-ring growth patterns. Growth rings, also referred to as tree rings or annular rings, can be seen in a horizontal cross section cut through the trunk of a tree. Visible rings result from the change in growth speed through the seasons of the year, thus one ring usually marks the passage of one year in the life of the tree.

a. 1703 Genroku earthquake
b. 1509 Istanbul earthquake
c. 1700 Cascadia earthquake
d. Dendrochronology

10. _____ are a class of computer-driven models for weather forecasting, understanding climate and projecting climate change.

a. 1703 Genroku earthquake
b. Global circulation Models
c. 1509 Istanbul earthquake
d. 1700 Cascadia earthquake

11. A _____ uses mathematical language to describe a system. Mathematical models are used not only in the natural sciences and engineering disciplines (such as physics, biology, earth science, meteorology, and electrical engineering) but also in the social sciences (such as economics, psychology, sociology and political science); physicists, engineers, computer scientists, and economists use mathematical models most extensively.

Eykhoff (1974) defined a _____ as 'a representation of the essential aspects of an existing system (or a system to be constructed) which presents knowledge of that system in usable form'.

a. 1509 Istanbul earthquake
b. Mathematical model
c. 1703 Genroku earthquake
d. 1700 Cascadia earthquake

12. In computer science, _____ computing (RTC) is the study of hardware and software systems that are subject to a '_____ constraint'--i.e., operational deadlines from event to system response. By contrast, a non-_____ system is one for which there is no deadline, even if fast response or high performance is desired or preferred. The needs of _____ software are often addressed in the context of _____ operating systems, and synchronous programming languages, which provide frameworks on which to build _____ application software.

a. Real-time
b. 1509 Istanbul earthquake
c. 1700 Cascadia earthquake
d. 1703 Genroku earthquake

13. An _____ is a layer of gases that may surround a material body of sufficient mass, by the gravity of the body, and are retained for a longer duration if gravity is high and the _____'s temperature is low. Some planets consist mainly of various gases, and therefore have very deep atmospheres

The term stellar _____ describes the outer region of a star, and typically includes the portion starting from the opaque photosphere outwards.

a. AASHTO Soil Classification System
b. Atmosphere
c. AL 333
d. AL 129-1

14. _____ is a chemical element in the periodic table that has the symbol C and atomic number 6. An abundant nonmetallic, tetravalent element, _____ has several allotropic forms.

Chapter 16. Global Change and Earth System Science

    a. 1703 Genroku earthquake
    b. 1509 Istanbul earthquake
    c. 1700 Cascadia earthquake
    d. Carbon

15. _____ is a chemical compound, normally in a gaseous state, and is composed of one carbon and two oxygen atoms. It is often referred to by its formula CO2. It is present in the Earth's atmosphere at a concentration of approximately .000383 by volume and is an important greenhouse gas due to its ability to absorb many infrared wavelengths of sunlight, and due to the length of time it stays in the atmosphere.
    a. Carbon dioxide
    b. 1703 Genroku earthquake
    c. 1509 Istanbul earthquake
    d. 1700 Cascadia earthquake

16. In physics, _____ is a scalar physical quantity that describes the amount of work that can be performed by a force. _____ is an attribute of objects and systems that is subject to a conservation law. Several different forms of _____ exist to explain all known natural phenomena.
    a. Energy
    b. AASHTO Soil Classification System
    c. AL 333
    d. AL 129-1

17. The Earth can be considered as a physical system with an _____ that includes all gains of incoming energy and all losses of outgoing energy.
    a. AL 129-1
    b. AL 333
    c. Energy budget
    d. AASHTO Soil Classification System

18. _____ is a layer of gases surrounding the planet Earth and retained by the Earth's gravity, protecting life on Earth by absorbing ultraviolet solar radiation and reducing temperature extremes between day and night.
    a. AL 129-1
    b. AL 333
    c. AASHTO Soil Classification System
    d. Earths atmosphere

19. The _____ is the range of all possible electromagnetic radiation. The _____ of an object is the frequency range of electromagnetic radiation with wavelengths from thousands of kilometres down to fractions of the size of an atom.
    a. AL 333
    b. AL 129-1
    c. Electromagnetic spectrum
    d. AASHTO Soil Classification System

20. _____, as used in physics, is energy in the form of waves or moving subatomic particles emitted by an atom or other body as it changes from a higher energy state to a lower energy state. _____ can be classified as ionizing or non-ionizing _____, depending on its effect on atomic matter. The most common use of the word "_____" refers to ionizing _____. Ionizing _____ has enough energy to ionize atoms or molecules while non-ionizing _____ does not. Radioactive material is a physical material that emits ionizing _____.
    a. Synthetic aperture radar
    b. Radiation
    c. Spectrum analysis
    d. Rest energy

21. _____ is radiant energy emitted by the sun from a nuclear fusion reaction that creates electromagnetic energy. The spectrum of _____ is close to that of a black body with a temperature of about 5800 K. About half of the radiation is in the visible short-wave part of the electromagnetic spectrum. The other half is mostly in the near-infrared part, with some in the ultraviolet part of the spectrum.
    a. 1700 Cascadia earthquake
    b. 1703 Genroku earthquake
    c. Solar radiation
    d. 1509 Istanbul earthquake

Chapter 16. Global Change and Earth System Science

22. _____ light is electromagnetic radiation with a wavelength shorter than that of visible light, but longer than soft X-rays. The color violet has the shortest wavelength in the visible spectrum. UV light has a shorter wavelength than that of violet light.
   a. AASHTO Soil Classification System
   b. AL 129-1
   c. AL 333
   d. Ultraviolet

23. A _____ is a condition or value that is not limited to a specific set of values but can vary infinitely within a continuum. The word saw its first scientific use within the field of optics to describe the rainbow of colors in visible light when separated using a prism; it has since been applied by analogy to many fields.
   a. 1700 Cascadia earthquake
   b. 1509 Istanbul earthquake
   c. Spectrum
   d. 1703 Genroku earthquake

24. In photometry and heat transfer, _____ is the fraction of incident radiation reflected by a surface. In general it must be treated as a directional property that is a function of the reflected direction, the incident direction, and the incident wavelength. However it is also commonly averaged over the reflected hemisphere to give the hemispherical spectral _____:

$$\rho(\lambda) = \frac{G_{refl}(\lambda)}{G_{incid}(\lambda)}$$

where $G_{refl}(\lambda)$ and $G_{incid}(\lambda)$ are the reflected and incident spectral (per wavelength) intensity, respectively.

   a. 1700 Cascadia earthquake
   b. 1509 Istanbul earthquake
   c. 1703 Genroku earthquake
   d. Reflectivity

25. _____ is a physical property of a system that underlies the common notions of hot and cold; something that is hotter has the greater _____. _____ is one of the principal parameters of thermodynamics.
   a. 1700 Cascadia earthquake
   b. 1703 Genroku earthquake
   c. 1509 Istanbul earthquake
   d. Temperature

26. A _____ column is a column of rizing air in the lower altitudes of the Earth's atmosphere. Thermals are created by the uneven heating of the Earth's surface from solar radiation, and are an example of convection. The Sun warms the ground, which in turn warms the air directly above it.
   a. 1509 Istanbul earthquake
   b. 1700 Cascadia earthquake
   c. 1703 Genroku earthquake
   d. Thermal

27. In thermal physics, _____ is the energy portion of a system that increases with its temperature. In thermodynamics, _____ is the internal energy present in a system in a state of thermodynamic equilibrium by virtue of its temperature.
   a. Supersaturation
   b. Superconductivity
   c. Velocity
   d. Thermal energy

28. The _____ of an object is the extent to which it reflects light, defined as the ratio of reflected to incident electromagnetic radiation. It is a unitless measure indicative of a surface's or body's diffuse reflectivity.

a. AASHTO Soil Classification System
b. AL 333
c. AL 129-1
d. Albedo

29. A _____ is a building where plants are cultivated.
a. 1700 Cascadia earthquake
b. 1703 Genroku earthquake
c. Greenhouse
d. 1509 Istanbul earthquake

30. The _____, discovered by Joseph Fourier in 1829 and first investigated quantitatively by Svante Arrhenius in 1896, is the process in which the emission of infrared radiation by the atmosphere warms a planet's surface.
a. 1703 Genroku earthquake
b. Greenhouse effect
c. 1509 Istanbul earthquake
d. 1700 Cascadia earthquake

31. _____ is present in a low concentration on earth. It is essential to photosynthesis in plants and other photoautotrophs, and is also a prominent greenhouse gas.
a. Atmospheric carbon dioxide
b. AL 129-1
c. AL 333
d. AASHTO Soil Classification System

32. _____ is the increase in the average temperature of the Earth's near-surface air and oceans in recent decades and its projected continuation. An increase in global temperatures can in turn cause other changes, including sea level rise, and changes in the amount and pattern of precipitation resulting in floods and drought. There may also be changes in the frequency and intensity of extreme weather events.
a. 1700 Cascadia earthquake
b. 1703 Genroku earthquake
c. 1509 Istanbul earthquake
d. Global warming

33. _____ are components of the atmosphere that contribute to the greenhouse effect. Some _____ occur naturally in the atmosphere, while others result from human activities such as burning of fossil fuels such as coal.
a. 1700 Cascadia earthquake
b. 1703 Genroku earthquake
c. 1509 Istanbul earthquake
d. Greenhouse gases

34. _____ are compounds containing chlorine, fluorine and carbon only, that is they contain no hydrogen. They were formerly used widely in industry, for example as refrigerants, propellants, and cleaning solvents. Their use has been regularly prohibited by the Montreal Protocol, because of effects on the ozone layer.
a. 1700 Cascadia earthquake
b. Chlorofluorocarbons CFCs
c. 1703 Genroku earthquake
d. 1509 Istanbul earthquake

35. _____ is a chemical compound with the molecular formula CH_4. It is the simplest alkane, and the principal component of natural gas. Burning one molecule of _____ in the presence of oxygen releases one molecule. _____'s relative abundance and clean burning process makes it a very attractive fuel.
a. Methane
b. 1703 Genroku earthquake
c. 1509 Istanbul earthquake
d. 1700 Cascadia earthquake

36. An _____ is a period of long-term reduction in the temperature of Earth's climate, resulting in an expansion of the continental ice sheets, polar ice sheets and mountain glaciers .
a. AL 129-1
b. AL 333
c. Ice Age
d. AASHTO Soil Classification System

Chapter 16. Global Change and Earth System Science

37. The _____ was a period of cooling occurring after a warmer era known as the Medieval climate optimum. It is generally agreed that there were three minima, beginning about 1650, about 1770, and 1850, each separated by slight warming intervals.
   a. 1700 Cascadia earthquake
   b. 1509 Istanbul earthquake
   c. 1703 Genroku earthquake
   d. Little Ice Age

38. _____ is used in motor racing as an oxidizer to increase the power output of engines. It is major greenhouse gas. It's persistence in the atmosphere, when considered over a 100 year period, per unit of weight, has 310 times more impact on global warming. _____ is emitted by bacteria in soils and oceans, and thus has been a part of Earth's atmosphere for aeons.
   a. 1700 Cascadia earthquake
   b. Nitrous oxide
   c. 1703 Genroku earthquake
   d. 1509 Istanbul earthquake

39. _____ in its broadest sense includes everything that is used to determine or demonstrate the truth of an assertion. Giving or procuring _____ is the process of using those things that are either a) presumed to be true, or b) were themselves proven via _____, to demonstrate an assertion's truth. _____ is the currency by which one fulfills the burden of proof.
   a. AL 129-1
   b. AASHTO Soil Classification System
   c. AL 333
   d. Evidence

40. An _____ is a chemical compound containing an oxygen atom and other elements. Most of the earth's crust consists of them. They result when elements are oxidized by air.
   a. Oxide
   b. AL 333
   c. AASHTO Soil Classification System
   d. AL 129-1

41. _____ are tiny particles of solid or liquid suspended in a gas. They range in size from less than 10 nanometres to more than 100 micrometres in diameter.
   a. 1509 Istanbul earthquake
   b. 1703 Genroku earthquake
   c. 1700 Cascadia earthquake
   d. Particulates

42. _____ is the average and variations of weather over long periods of time. _____ zones can be defined using parameters such as temperature and rainfall.
   a. Climate
   b. 1703 Genroku earthquake
   c. 1509 Istanbul earthquake
   d. 1700 Cascadia earthquake

43. A _____ refers to natural cyclic variations in the earth's surface temperature, as indicated by temperature proxies found in glacier ice, sea bed sediment, tree ring studies or otherwise.

One difficulty in detecting climate cycles is that the earth's climate has been changing in non-cyclic ways over most scales of time. For instance, we are now in a period of anthropogenic global warming.

   a. Climate cycle
   b. 1703 Genroku earthquake
   c. 1700 Cascadia earthquake
   d. 1509 Istanbul earthquake

44. _____ cycles are the collective effect of changes in the Earth's movements upon its climate.

Chapter 16. Global Change and Earth System Science

a. 1700 Cascadia earthquake
c. 1509 Istanbul earthquake
b. 1703 Genroku earthquake
d. Milankovitch

45. _____ are the collective effect of changes in the Earth's movements upon its climate, named after Serbian civil engineer and mathematician Milutin Milankoviæ.

a. 1509 Istanbul earthquake
c. Milankovitch cycles
b. 1703 Genroku earthquake
d. 1700 Cascadia earthquake

46. The thermohaline circulation is sometimes called the _____, the great ocean conveyor, or the global conveyor belt. On occasion, it is used to refer to the meridional overturning circulation The term MOC, however, is more accurate and well defined, as it is difficult to separate the part of the circulation which is actually driven by temperature and salinity alone as opposed to other factors such as the wind.

a. AASHTO Soil Classification System
c. AL 333
b. AL 129-1
d. Ocean conveyor belt

47. _____ is a global coupled ocean-atmosphere phenomenon. The Pacific ocean signatures, are important temperature fluctuations in surface waters of the tropical Eastern Pacific Ocean.

a. AL 129-1
c. AL 333
b. AASHTO Soil Classification System
d. El Nino

48. _____ is an active stratovolcano in Skamania County, Washington, in the Pacific Northwest region of the United States. It is located 96 miles northeast of Portland, Oregon.

a. 1509 Istanbul earthquake
c. 1703 Genroku earthquake
b. 1700 Cascadia earthquake
d. Mount St. Helens

49. The Persian _____ or _____ was a United Nations-authorized military conflict between Iraq and a coalition force from 34 nations commissioned with expelling Iraqi forces from Kuwait after Iraq's occupation and annexation of Kuwait in August of 1990. Though there were nearly three dozen member states of the coalition, the overwhelming majority of the military forces participating were from the United States and the United Kingdom.

The invasion of Kuwait by Iraqi troops was met with immediate economic sanctions against Iraq by some members of the UN Security Council, and with immediate preparation for war by the United States of America and the United Kingdom.

a. 1703 Genroku earthquake
c. 1700 Cascadia earthquake
b. 1509 Istanbul earthquake
d. Gulf War

50. _____ is an active stratovolcano located on the island of Luzon in the Philippines, at the intersection of the borders of the provinces of Zambales, Tarlac, and Pampanga.

a. 1703 Genroku earthquake
c. 1700 Cascadia earthquake
b. 1509 Istanbul earthquake
d. Mount Pinatubo

51. The _____ in the Southwest Asian region, is an extension of the Gulf of Oman located between Iran and the Arabian Peninsula. The _____ was the focus of the Iraq-Iran War that lasted from 1980 to 1988, with each side attacking the other's oil tankers.

Chapter 16. Global Change and Earth System Science   155

a. 1509 Istanbul earthquake
b. Persian Gulf
c. 1703 Genroku earthquake
d. 1700 Cascadia earthquake

52. _____ is the introduction of substances or energy into the environment, resulting in deleterious effects of such a nature as to endanger human health, harm living resources and ecosystems, and impair or interfere with amenities and other legitimate uses of the environment.
a. 1509 Istanbul earthquake
b. 1703 Genroku earthquake
c. 1700 Cascadia earthquake
d. Pollution

53. Mean _____ is the average height of the sea, with reference to a suitable reference surface.
a. 1700 Cascadia earthquake
b. 1703 Genroku earthquake
c. 1509 Istanbul earthquake
d. Sea level

54. _____ is an increase in sea level. Multiple complex factors may influence such changes.
a. 1703 Genroku earthquake
b. 1700 Cascadia earthquake
c. 1509 Istanbul earthquake
d. Sea level rise

55. _____ refers to the variation in the Earth's global climate or in regional climates over time. It describes changes in the variability or average state of the atmosphere over time scales ranging from decades to millions of years. These changes can be caused by processes internal to the Earth, external forces or, more recently, human activities.
a. 1703 Genroku earthquake
b. 1700 Cascadia earthquake
c. 1509 Istanbul earthquake
d. Climate Change

56. The _____ is an international environmental treaty produced at the United Nations Conference on Environment and Development, informally known as the Earth Summit, held in Rio de Janeiro in 1992. The treaty aimed at reducing emissions of greenhouse gas in order to combat global warming.
a. 1700 Cascadia earthquake
b. 1703 Genroku earthquake
c. 1509 Istanbul earthquake
d. Framework Convention on Climate Change

57. _____ (ä°¬éƒ½ KyÅ to

The new city, Heian-kyÅ , became the seat of Japan's imperial court in 794, beginning the Heian period of Japanese history. In Japanese, the city has been called Kyo , Miyako or Kyo no Miyako . In the 11th century, the city was renamed _____ .

a. Kyoto
b. Kampala
c. Lao
d. Katanga Province

58. _____ is a triatomic molecule, consisting of three oxygen atoms. It is an allotrope of oxygen that is much less stable than the diatomic species O2. Ground-level _____ is an air pollutant with harmful effects on the respiratory systems of animals. On the other hand, _____ in the upper atmosphere protects living organisms by preventing damaging ultraviolet light from reaching the Earth's surface.
a. AL 333
b. AASHTO Soil Classification System
c. AL 129-1
d. Ozone

59. _____ describes two distinct, but related observations: a slow, steady decline of about 4 percent per decade in the total amount of ozone in Earth's stratosphere since around 1980; and a much larger, but seasonal, decrease in stratospheric ozone over Earth's polar regions during the same period.
   a. AASHTO Soil Classification System
   b. Ozone depletion
   c. AL 333
   d. AL 129-1

60. _____ is a malignant growth on the skin which can have many causes. _____ generally develops in the epidermis, so a tumor is usually clearly visible.
   a. 1703 Genroku earthquake
   b. 1700 Cascadia earthquake
   c. 1509 Istanbul earthquake
   d. Skin cancer

61. _____ is a class of diseases in which a group of cells display the traits of uncontrolled growth growth and division beyond the normal limits, invasion intrusion on and destruction of adjacent tissues, and sometimes metastasis spread to other locations in the body via lymph or blood. These three malignant properties of cancers differentiate them from benign tumors, which are self-limited, do not invade or metastasize. Most cancers form a tumor but some, like leukemia, do not.
   a. 1703 Genroku earthquake
   b. 1509 Istanbul earthquake
   c. 1700 Cascadia earthquake
   d. Cancer

Chapter 17. Air Pollution

1. _____ is a chemical, physical, or biological agent that modifies the natural characteristics of the atmosphere. The atmosphere is a complex, dynamic natural gaseous system that is essential to support life on planet Earth. Stratospheric ozone depletion due to _____ has long been recognized as a threat to human health as well as to the Earth's ecosystems. Worldwide _____ is responsible for large numbers of deaths and cases of respiratory disease.
    a. Air pollution
    b. AL 333
    c. AASHTO Soil Classification System
    d. AL 129-1

2. _____ is the introduction of substances or energy into the environment, resulting in deleterious effects of such a nature as to endanger human health, harm living resources and ecosystems, and impair or interfere with amenities and other legitimate uses of the environment.
    a. 1509 Istanbul earthquake
    b. 1703 Genroku earthquake
    c. 1700 Cascadia earthquake
    d. Pollution

3. _____ refers to a major group of organisms. In general they are multicellular, responsive to their environment, and feed by consuming other organisms or parts of them. Their body plan becomes fixed as they develop, usually early on in their development as embryos, although some undergo a process of metamorphosis later on.
    a. Animal
    b. AL 129-1
    c. AL 333
    d. AASHTO Soil Classification System

4. _____ is a kind of air pollution; the word "_____" is a portmanteau of smoke and fog. Classic _____ results from large amounts of coal burning in an area and is caused by a mixture of smoke and sulphur dioxide.
    a. 1700 Cascadia earthquake
    b. 1703 Genroku earthquake
    c. 1509 Istanbul earthquake
    d. Smog

5. In geology, a _____ is a depression with predominant extent in one direction. The terms U-shaped and V-shaped are descriptive terms of geography to characterize the form of valleys. Most valleys belong to one of these two main types or a mixture of them, at least with respect of the cross section of the slopes or hillsides.
    a. Valley
    b. 1509 Istanbul earthquake
    c. 1703 Genroku earthquake
    d. 1700 Cascadia earthquake

6. _____ is a layer of gases surrounding the planet Earth and retained by the Earth's gravity, protecting life on Earth by absorbing ultraviolet solar radiation and reducing temperature extremes between day and night.
    a. AL 333
    b. Earths atmosphere
    c. AASHTO Soil Classification System
    d. AL 129-1

7. _____ is the capital and largest urban area of both England and the United Kingdom. An important settlement for two millennia, _____'s history goes back to its founding by the Romans. Since its foundation, _____ has been part of many movements and phenomena throughout history, including the English Renaissance, the Industrial Revolution, and the Gothic Revival.
    a. 1700 Cascadia earthquake
    b. Barcelona
    c. London
    d. 1509 Istanbul earthquake

8. _____ is a quantity expressing the two-dimensional size of a defined part of a surface, typically a region bounded by a closed curve. The term surface _____ refers to the total _____ of the exposed surface of a 3-dimensional solid, such as the sum of the areas of the exposed sides of a polyhedron. _____ is an important invariant in the differential geometry of surfaces.

Chapter 17. Air Pollution

   a. AASHTO Soil Classification System
   b. Area
   c. AL 129-1
   d. AL 333

9. _____ is a chemical element which has the symbol N and atomic number 7 in the periodic table. Elemental _____ is a colorless, odorless, tasteless and mostly inert diatomic gas at standard conditions, constituting 78.08% percent of Earth's atmosphere.
   a. Nitrogen
   b. 1509 Istanbul earthquake
   c. 1703 Genroku earthquake
   d. 1700 Cascadia earthquake

10. _____$_x$ is a generic term for mono-_____ (_____ and _____$_2$.) These oxides are produced during combustion, especially combustion at high temperatures.

At ambient temperatures, the oxygen and nitrogen gases in air will not react with each other.

   a. 1700 Cascadia earthquake
   b. 1703 Genroku earthquake
   c. Nitrogen oxides
   d. 1509 Istanbul earthquake

11. _____ is a triatomic molecule, consisting of three oxygen atoms. It is an allotrope of oxygen that is much less stable than the diatomic species O2. Ground-level _____ is an air pollutant with harmful effects on the respiratory systems of animals. On the other hand, _____ in the upper atmosphere protects living organisms by preventing damaging ultraviolet light from reaching the Earth's surface.
   a. AASHTO Soil Classification System
   b. AL 129-1
   c. AL 333
   d. Ozone

12. _____ is the chemical element in the periodic table that has the symbol S and atomic number 16. It is an abundant, tasteless, odorless, multivalent non-metal. _____, in its native form, is a yellow crystaline solid. In nature, it can be found as the pure element or as sulfide and sulfate minerals.
   a. 1700 Cascadia earthquake
   b. 1509 Istanbul earthquake
   c. 1703 Genroku earthquake
   d. Sulfur

13. _____ is a chemical compound with the formula SO2. This important gas is the main product from the combustion of sulfur compounds and is of significant environmental concern. Sulphur dioxide is produced by volcanoes and in various industrial processes.
   a. 1700 Cascadia earthquake
   b. Sulfur dioxide
   c. 1509 Istanbul earthquake
   d. 1703 Genroku earthquake

14. An _____ is a chemical compound containing an oxygen atom and other elements. Most of the earth's crust consists of them. They result when elements are oxidized by air.
   a. AL 129-1
   b. AL 333
   c. AASHTO Soil Classification System
   d. Oxide

15. Pollution is the introduction of contaminants into an environment that causes instability, disorder, harm or discomfort to the physical systems or living organisms. Pollution can take the form of chemical substances, or energy, such as noise, heat, or light energy. _____, the elements of pollution, can be foreign substances or energies, or naturally occurring; when naturally occurring, they are considered contaminants when they exceed natural levels.

a. 1700 Cascadia earthquake
b. 1703 Genroku earthquake
c. 1509 Istanbul earthquake
d. Pollutants

16. _____ is a chemical element in the periodic table that has the symbol C and atomic number 6. An abundant nonmetallic, tetravalent element, _____ has several allotropic forms.
   a. 1703 Genroku earthquake
   b. 1700 Cascadia earthquake
   c. 1509 Istanbul earthquake
   d. Carbon

17. _____, with the chemical formula CO, is a colorless, odorless, and tasteless gas. It is the product of the incomplete combustion of carbon-containing compounds, notably in internal-combustion engines. It has significant fuel value, burning in air with a characteristic blue flame, producing carbon dioxide.
   a. 1509 Istanbul earthquake
   b. 1703 Genroku earthquake
   c. Carbon monoxide
   d. 1700 Cascadia earthquake

18. In organic chemistry, a _____ is an organic compound consisting entirely of hydrogen and carbon. With relation to chemical terminology, aromatic hydrocarbons or arenes, alkanes, alkenes and alkyne-based compounds composed entirely of carbon or hydrogen are referred to as "Pure" hydrocarbons, whereas other hydrocarbons with bonded compounds or impurities of sulphur or nitrogen, are referred to as "impure", and remain somewhat erroneously referred to as hydrocarbons.
   a. Hydrocarbon
   b. 1509 Istanbul earthquake
   c. 1703 Genroku earthquake
   d. 1700 Cascadia earthquake

19. _____, a sub-discipline of chemistry, is the study of the interactions between atoms, small molecules, and light.
   a. 1703 Genroku earthquake
   b. 1509 Istanbul earthquake
   c. Photochemistry
   d. 1700 Cascadia earthquake

20. Volatile Organic Compounds (_____) are organic chemical compounds that have high enough vapor pressures under normal conditions to significantly vaporize and enter the atmosphere. A wide range of carbon-based molecules, such as aldehydes, ketones, and other light hydrocarbons are _____. The term often is used in a legal or regulatory context and in such cases the precise definition is a matter of law.
   a. VOCs
   b. 1509 Istanbul earthquake
   c. 1700 Cascadia earthquake
   d. 1703 Genroku earthquake

21. _____ are organic chemical compounds that have high enough vapour pressures under normal conditions to significantly vaporize and enter the atmosphere.
   a. 1509 Istanbul earthquake
   b. 1700 Cascadia earthquake
   c. 1703 Genroku earthquake
   d. Volatile organic compounds

22. A _____ is a chemical substance of two or more different chemically bonded chemical elements, with a fixed ratio determining the composition. The ratio of each element is usually expressed by chemical formula.
   a. 1703 Genroku earthquake
   b. 1700 Cascadia earthquake
   c. 1509 Istanbul earthquake
   d. Chemical compound

23. _____ farming is a form of agriculture that excludes the use of synthetic fertilizers and pesticides, plant growth regulators, livestock feed additives, and genetically modified organisms.

a. AL 129-1
b. AL 333
c. AASHTO Soil Classification System
d. Organic

24. An _____ is any member of a large class of chemical compounds whose molecules contain carbon.
   a. AL 333
   b. Organic compound
   c. AASHTO Soil Classification System
   d. AL 129-1

25. _____ are chemical compounds that readily transfer oxygen atoms or substances that gain electrons in a redox chemical reaction.
   a. AL 333
   b. AASHTO Soil Classification System
   c. Oxidants
   d. AL 129-1

26. _____ is a chemical element in the periodic table that has the symbol H and atomic number 1. At standard temperature and pressure it is a colorless, odorless, nonmetallic, univalent, tasteless, highly flammable diatomic gas.
   a. 1700 Cascadia earthquake
   b. 1509 Istanbul earthquake
   c. 1703 Genroku earthquake
   d. Hydrogen

27. _____ is a chemical compound with the formula HF. Together with hydrofluoric acid, it is the principal industrial source of fluorine and hence the precursor to many important compounds including pharmaceuticals and polymers. HF is widely used in the petrochemical industry and a component of many superacids.
   a. 1509 Istanbul earthquake
   b. 1703 Genroku earthquake
   c. 1700 Cascadia earthquake
   d. Hydrogen fluoride

28. _____ is the chemical compound with the formula H2S. This colorless, toxic and flammable gas is responsible for the foul odor of rotten eggs and flatulence. It often results from the bacterial break down of organic matter in the absence of oxygen, such as in swamps and sewers. It also occurs in volcanic gases, natural gas and some well waters.
   a. 1509 Istanbul earthquake
   b. 1700 Cascadia earthquake
   c. 1703 Genroku earthquake
   d. Hydrogen sulfide

29. _____ was discovered in 1888 as an ester of isocyanic acid. As a highly toxic and irritating material, it is hazardous to human health.
   a. 1509 Istanbul earthquake
   b. 1700 Cascadia earthquake
   c. 1703 Genroku earthquake
   d. Methyl isocyanate

30. _____ is the reduced form of fluorine. Both organic and inorganic compounds containing the element fluorine are considered fluorides. As a halogen, fluorine forms a monovalent ion. The range of fluorides is considerable as fluorine forms compounds with all elements except He, Ne, and Ar. Fluorides range from severe toxins such as sarin to life-saving pharmaceuticals such as efavirenz and from refractory materials such as calcium _____ to highly reactive sulfur tetrafluoride.
   a. 1703 Genroku earthquake
   b. 1509 Istanbul earthquake
   c. 1700 Cascadia earthquake
   d. Fluoride

31. The term _____ refers to several types of chemical compounds containing sulfur in its lowest oxidation number of −2.

Chapter 17. Air Pollution

a. 1509 Istanbul earthquake
c. 1703 Genroku earthquake
b. 1700 Cascadia earthquake
d. Sulfide

32. _____ describes any of a group of minerals that can be fibrous, many of which are metamorphic and are hydrous magnesium silicates.
   a. AL 129-1
   c. AASHTO Soil Classification System
   b. Asbestos
   d. AL 333

33. In meteorology, an _____ is a deviation from the normal change of a property with altitude. It almost always refers to temperature, i.e., an increase in temperature with height, or to the layer within which such an increase occurs.
   a. AL 129-1
   c. AASHTO Soil Classification System
   b. AL 333
   d. Atmospheric inversion

34. _____, also known as bioamplification, or biological magnification is the increase in concentration of a substance, such as the pesticide DDT, that occurs in a food chain as a consequence of: Food chain energetics, low rate of excretion/degradation of the substance.
   a. Biomagnification
   c. 1509 Istanbul earthquake
   b. 1703 Genroku earthquake
   d. 1700 Cascadia earthquake

35. _____ is a chemical element in the periodic table that has the symbol Cd and atomic number 48. A relatively rare, soft, bluish-white, toxic transition metal, _____ occurs with zinc ores and is used largely in batteries.
   a. Cadmium
   c. 1703 Genroku earthquake
   b. 1509 Istanbul earthquake
   d. 1700 Cascadia earthquake

36. In meteorology, an _____ is a deviation from the normal change of an atmospheric property with altitude. It almost always refers to temperature.
   a. AASHTO Soil Classification System
   c. AL 129-1
   b. AL 333
   d. Inversion

37. The _____ in thermodynamics and cryogenics is the critical temperature below which a non-ideal gas (all gases in reality) that is expanded at constant enthalpy will experience a temperature decrease, and above which will experience a temperature increase. This temperature change is known as the Joule-Thomson effect, and is exploited in the liquefaction of gases.

The Joule-Thomson effect cannot be described in the theory of ideal gases, in which interactions between particles are ignored.

   a. Inversion temperature
   c. AASHTO Soil Classification System
   b. AL 333
   d. AL 129-1

38. _____ is a chemical element in the periodic table that has the symbol Pb and atomic number 82. A soft, heavy, toxic and malleable poor metal, _____ is bluish white when freshly cut but tarnishes to dull gray when exposed to air.
_____ is used in building construction, _____-acid batteries, bullets and shot, and is part of solder, pewter, and fusible alloys.

Chapter 17. Air Pollution

    a. 1509 Istanbul earthquake
    b. 1700 Cascadia earthquake
    c. 1703 Genroku earthquake
    d. Lead

39. _____ is a physical property of a system that underlies the common notions of hot and cold; something that is hotter has the greater _____. _____ is one of the principal parameters of thermodynamics.
    a. 1700 Cascadia earthquake
    b. Temperature
    c. 1509 Istanbul earthquake
    d. 1703 Genroku earthquake

40. _____, is an increase in temperature with height, or to the layer within which such an increase occurs.
    a. 1509 Istanbul earthquake
    b. Temperature inversion
    c. 1703 Genroku earthquake
    d. 1700 Cascadia earthquake

41. A _____ is a local atmospheric zone where the climate differs from the surrounding area. The term may refer to areas as small as a few square feet or as large as many square miles. A _____ can exist, for example, near bodies of water which may cool the local atmosphere, or in heavily urban areas where brick, concrete, and asphalt absorb the sun's energy, heat up, and reradiate that heat to the ambient air: the resulting urban heat island is a kind of _____.
    a. 1509 Istanbul earthquake
    b. 1703 Genroku earthquake
    c. Microclimate
    d. 1700 Cascadia earthquake

42. An _____ is a metropolitan area which is significantly warmer than its surroundings. As population centres grow in size from village to town to city, they tend to have a corresponding increase in average temperature, which is more often welcome in winter months than in summertime.
    a. AL 129-1
    b. AL 333
    c. AASHTO Soil Classification System
    d. Urban heat island

43. Smog is a kind of air pollution; the word 'smog' is a portmanteau of smoke and fog. Classic smog results from large amounts of coal burning in an area caused by a mixture of smoke and sulfur dioxide. Modern smog does not usually come from coal but from vehicular and industrial emissions that are acted on in the atmosphere by sunlight to form secondary pollutants that also combine with the primary emissions to form _____.
    a. 1700 Cascadia earthquake
    b. Flue gas stack
    c. 1509 Istanbul earthquake
    d. Photochemical smog

44. In geology, a _____ is a deformational feature consisting of symmetrically-dipping anticlines; their general outline on a geologic map is circular or oval.
    a. 1509 Istanbul earthquake
    b. Dome
    c. 1700 Cascadia earthquake
    d. 1703 Genroku earthquake

45. _____ refers to chemical or biological contaminants in indoor air. Indoor Air Quality may be compromised by microbial contaminants, chemicals, any mass or energy stressor that can induce health effects.
    a. AL 129-1
    b. AASHTO Soil Classification System
    c. AL 333
    d. Indoor air pollution

46. A _____ or medical condition is an abnormal condition of an organism that impairs bodily functions and can be deadly. It is also defined as a way of the body harming itself in an abnormal way, associated with specific symptoms and signs.

Chapter 17. Air Pollution

In human beings,'_____' is often used more broadly to refer to any condition that causes extreme pain, dysfunction, distress, social problems, and/or death to the person afflicted, or similar problems for those in contact with the person.

   a. 1700 Cascadia earthquake
   b. Black lung disease
   c. 1509 Istanbul earthquake
   d. Disease

47. An _____ or motor car is a wheeled motor vehicle for transporting passengers, which also carries its own engine or motor. Most definitions of the term specify that automobiles are designed to run primarily on roads, to have seating for one to eight people, to typically have four wheels, and to be constructed principally for the transport of people rather than goods. However, the term '_____' is far from precise, because there are many types of vehicles that do similar tasks.
   a. Feebate
   b. Automobile
   c. AASHTO Soil Classification System
   d. AL 129-1

48. A _____ is a device used to reduce the toxicity of emissions from an internal combustion engine.
   a. Catalytic converter
   b. 1700 Cascadia earthquake
   c. 1509 Istanbul earthquake
   d. 1703 Genroku earthquake

49. _____ are tiny particles of solid or liquid suspended in a gas. They range in size from less than 10 nanometres to more than 100 micrometres in diameter.
   a. 1700 Cascadia earthquake
   b. 1703 Genroku earthquake
   c. 1509 Istanbul earthquake
   d. Particulates

50. _____ is a combustion technology used in power plants. _____ plants are more flexible than conventional plants in that they can be fired on coal and biomass, among other fuels. Fluidized beds suspend solid fuels on upward-blowing jets of air during the combustion process.
   a. 1509 Istanbul earthquake
   b. 1703 Genroku earthquake
   c. 1700 Cascadia earthquake
   d. Fluidized bed combustion

51. A _____ describes one of a number of pieces of legislation relating to the reduction of smog and air pollution in general. The use of governments to enforce clean air standards has contributed to an improvement in human health and longer life spans.
   a. 1703 Genroku earthquake
   b. Clean Air Act
   c. 1509 Istanbul earthquake
   d. 1700 Cascadia earthquake

52. _____ is the current state-of-the art technology used for removing sulfur dioxide from the exhaust flue gases in power plants that burn coal or oil to produce steam for the steam turbines that drive their electricity generators.
   a. 1700 Cascadia earthquake
   b. Photochemical smog
   c. 1509 Istanbul earthquake
   d. Flue gas desulfurization

Chapter 18. Landscape Evaluation and Land Use

1. A _____ comprises the visible features of an area of land, including physical elements such as landforms, living elements of flora and fauna, abstract elements such as lighting and weather conditions, and human elements, for instance human activity or the built environment.
   - a. 1703 Genroku earthquake
   - b. Landscape
   - c. 1509 Istanbul earthquake
   - d. 1700 Cascadia earthquake

2. _____ involves the study of the interaction of humans with the geologic environment including the biosphere, the lithosphere, the hydrosphere, and to some extent the atmosphere.
   - a. Isostasy
   - b. Ubehebe Crater
   - c. Engineering geology
   - d. Environmental geology

3. _____ is the science and study of the solid matter that constitute the Earth. Encompassing such things as rocks, soil, and gemstones, _____ studies the composition, structure, physical properties, history, and the processes that shape Earth's components.
   - a. 1700 Cascadia earthquake
   - b. Geology
   - c. 1509 Istanbul earthquake
   - d. 1703 Genroku earthquake

4. A _____ is a visual representation of an area--a symbolic depiction highlighting relationships between elements of that space such as objects, regions, and themes.

   Many maps are static two-dimensional, geometrically accurate representations of three-dimensional space, while others are dynamic or interactive, even three-dimensional. Although most commonly used to depict geography, maps may represent any space, real or imagined, without regard to context or scale; e.g. Brain mapping, DNA mapping, and extraterrestrial mapping.
   - a. Cartography
   - b. 1700 Cascadia earthquake
   - c. 1509 Istanbul earthquake
   - d. Map

5. A _____ is flat or nearly flat land adjacent to a stream or river that experiences occasional or periodic flooding. It includes the floodway, which consists of the stream channel and adjacent areas that carry flood flows, and the flood fringe, which are areas covered by the flood, but which do not experience a strong current.
   - a. 1700 Cascadia earthquake
   - b. 1703 Genroku earthquake
   - c. 1509 Istanbul earthquake
   - d. Floodplain

6. _____ captures, stores, analyzes, manages, and presents data that refers to or is linked to location.

   In the strictest sense, the term describes any information system that integrates, stores, edits, analyzes, shares, and displays geographic information. In a more generic sense, _____ applications are tools that allow users to create interactive queries (user created searches), analyze spatial information, edit data, maps, and present the results of all these operations.
   - a. 1700 Cascadia earthquake
   - b. 1703 Genroku earthquake
   - c. 1509 Istanbul earthquake
   - d. GIS

7. A _____ is a system for capturing, storing, analyzing and managing data and associated attributes which are spatially referenced to the earth. In the strictest sense, it is a computer system capable of integrating, storing, editing, analyzing, sharing, and displaying geographically-referenced information.

Chapter 18. Landscape Evaluation and Land Use 165

   a. 1700 Cascadia earthquake
   b. Geographic Information System
   c. 1509 Istanbul earthquake
   d. 1703 Genroku earthquake

8. A _____ is a linear ridge composed of steeply tilted hard and soft strata of rock that protrude out of the surrounding strata. The softer rock erodes quicker than the capping harder rock above. In some cases the two strata that compose a _____ are different types of sedimentary rock that have differing weathering rates.
   a. 1703 Genroku earthquake
   b. 1509 Istanbul earthquake
   c. 1700 Cascadia earthquake
   d. Hogback

9. A _____ is a landform that extends above the surrounding terrain in a limited area. A _____ is generally steeper than a hill, but there is no universally accepted standard definition for the height of a _____ or a hill although a _____ usually has an identifiable summit.
   a. 1703 Genroku earthquake
   b. Mountain
   c. 1509 Istanbul earthquake
   d. 1700 Cascadia earthquake

10. The _____ on the geologic timescale had been intended to cover the world's recent period of repeated glaciations. The _____ follows the Pliocene and is followed by the Holocene. The _____ is the third epoch of the Neogene period or 6th epoch of the Cenozoic era. The end of the _____ corresponds with the end of the Paleolithic age used in archaeology. The _____ is divided into the Early _____, Middle _____ and Late _____, and numerous faunal stages.
   a. Pleistocene
   b. 1700 Cascadia earthquake
   c. 1703 Genroku earthquake
   d. 1509 Istanbul earthquake

11. _____ is a chemical element in the periodic table that has the symbol Rn and atomic number 86. A radioactive noble gas that is formed by the decay of radium, _____ is one of the heaviest gases and is considered to be a health hazard.
   a. 1509 Istanbul earthquake
   b. 1703 Genroku earthquake
   c. 1700 Cascadia earthquake
   d. Radon

12. The general effects of _____ to the human body are due to its radioactivity and consequent risk of radiation-induced cancer.
   a. 1509 Istanbul earthquake
   b. Radon emissions
   c. 1703 Genroku earthquake
   d. 1700 Cascadia earthquake

13. A _____ is an area with a high density of trees, historically, a wooded area set aside for hunting. These plant communities cover large areas of the globe and function as animal habitats, hydrologic flow modulators, and soil conservers, constituting one of the most important aspects of the Earth's biosphere.
   a. 1703 Genroku earthquake
   b. Forest
   c. 1509 Istanbul earthquake
   d. 1700 Cascadia earthquake

14. _____ is the term given to land colonised or sown with plant communities dominated by grasses and herbaceous plants. They are very varied; they can be found in most terrestrial climates.
   a. 1700 Cascadia earthquake
   b. 1703 Genroku earthquake
   c. 1509 Istanbul earthquake
   d. Grassland

Chapter 18. Landscape Evaluation and Land Use

15. _____ is the process of breaking a complex topic or substance into smaller parts to gain a better understanding of it. The technique has been applied in the study of mathematics and logic since before Aristotle, though _____ as a formal concept is a relatively recent development.

As a formal concept, the method has variously been ascribed by Ibn al-Haytham, Descartes (Discourse on the Method), Galileo, and Isaac Newton, as a practical method of physical discovery.

   a. AL 129-1
   b. AASHTO Soil Classification System
   c. AL 333
   d. Analysis

16. _____ may refer to either the private sector or the public sector. In the public sector it generally refers to a government's use and creation of the laws, regulations, and other policy mechanisms concerning environmental issues and sustainability. In the private sector it usually refers to the compliance with those tools, or the independent development of self-regulation and rule-making that may go beyond what is required by governments.
   a. AASHTO Soil Classification System
   b. AL 333
   c. AL 129-1
   d. Environmental Policy

17. An _____ is an assessment of the likely influence a project may have on the environment. The purpose of the assessment is to ensure that decision-makers consider environmental impacts before deciding whether to proceed with new projects.
   a. Environmental impact
   b. AL 333
   c. AASHTO Soil Classification System
   d. AL 129-1

18. An _____ is an assessment of the likely influence a project may have on the environment. It is the process of identifying, predicting, evaluating and mitigating the biophysical, social, and other relevant effects of development proposals prior to major decisions being taken and commitments made, to ensure that decision-makers consider environmental impacts before deciding whether to proceed with new projects.
   a. AL 333
   b. AL 129-1
   c. AASHTO Soil Classification System
   d. Environmental Impact Report

19. According to the National Environmental Policy Act whenever the US Federal Government takes a "major Federal action significantly affecting the quality of the human environment" it must first consider the environmental impact in a document called an _____.
   a. AL 129-1
   b. AL 333
   c. AASHTO Soil Classification System
   d. Environmental impact statement

20. The _____ (_____) is a United States environmental law that was signed into law on January 1, 1970 by U.S. President Richard Nixon. The law established a U.S. national policy promoting the enhancement of the environment and also established the President's Council on Environmental Quality (CEQ.) But _____'s most significant effect was to set up procedural requirements for all federal government agencies to prepare Environmental Assessments (EAs) and Environmental Impact Statements (EISs.)
   a. Water Quality Act
   b. NEPA
   c. Mediation
   d. Fish and Wildlife Coordination Act

Chapter 18. Landscape Evaluation and Land Use

21. The _____ is a United States environmental law that was signed into law on January 1, 1970 by U.S. President Richard Nixon. The law applies only to federal agencies and the programs they fund. Essentially it requires that, prior to taking any "major" or "significant" action, the agency must consider the environmental impacts of that action.
    a. 1700 Cascadia earthquake
    b. 1703 Genroku earthquake
    c. 1509 Istanbul earthquake
    d. National Environmental Policy Act

22. One of the basic reasons for _____ is to keep variables in different parts of the program distinct from one another. Since there are only a small number of short variable names, and programmers share habits about the naming of variables (e.g., i for an array index), in any program of moderate size the same variable name will be used in multiple different scopes. The question of how to match various variable occurrences to the appropriate binding sites is generally answered in one of two ways: static _____ and dynamic _____.
    a. Scoping
    b. 1509 Istanbul earthquake
    c. 1703 Genroku earthquake
    d. 1700 Cascadia earthquake

23. _____ is a state on the West Coast of the United States, along the Pacific Ocean. It is bordered by Oregon to the north, Nevada to the east, Arizona to the southeast, and to the south the Mexican state of Baja _____. _____ is the most populous U.S. state.
    a. 1703 Genroku earthquake
    b. 1509 Istanbul earthquake
    c. California
    d. 1700 Cascadia earthquake

24. The _____ is a California law passed shortly after the Federal Government passed the National Environmental Policy Act. _____ does not directly regulate land uses, but instead requires development projects submit documentation of their potential environmental impact.
    a. 1703 Genroku earthquake
    b. 1700 Cascadia earthquake
    c. California Environmental Quality Act
    d. 1509 Istanbul earthquake

25. A _____ is a political association with effective sovereignty over a geographic area and representing a population. These may be nation states, sub-national states or multinational states. A _____ usually includes the set of institutions that claim the authority to make the rules that govern the exercise of coercive violence for the people of the society in that territory, though its status as a _____ often depends in part on being recognized by a number of other states as having internal and external sovereignty over it.
    a. 1700 Cascadia earthquake
    b. State
    c. 1509 Istanbul earthquake
    d. Extraterritoriality

26. At times when larger waves attack the beach berm, some of the beach material is redistributed offshore to become a _____ possibly visible at low tide.
    a. 1700 Cascadia earthquake
    b. 1509 Istanbul earthquake
    c. 1703 Genroku earthquake
    d. Longshore bar

27. _____ preserves the portion of the Outer Banks of North Carolina from Bodie Island to Ocracoke Island, stretching over 70 miles (110 km.) Included within this section of barrier islands along N.C. Route 12, but outside the National Seashore boundaries, are Pea Island National Wildlife Refuge and several private communities, such as Rodanthe, Buxton, and Ocracoke.

Once dubbed the 'Graveyard of the Atlantic' for its treacherous currents, shoals, and storms, Cape Hatteras has a wealth of history relating to shipwrecks, lighthouses, and the US Lifesaving Service.

Chapter 18. Landscape Evaluation and Land Use

    a. 1509 Istanbul earthquake
    b. 1703 Genroku earthquake
    c. Cape Hatteras National Seashore
    d. 1700 Cascadia earthquake

28. An _____ is any piece of land that is completely surrounded by water, above high tide. There are two main types of islands: continental islands and oceanic islands. There are also artificial islands. A grouping of geographically and/or geologically related islands is called an archipelago.
    a. AASHTO Soil Classification System
    b. Island
    c. AL 129-1
    d. AL 333

29. The _____ are a 100-mile long string of narrow barrier islands off the coast of North Carolina on the East Coast of the United States. They cover approximately the northern half of North Carolina's coastline, separating the Albemarle Sound and Pamlico Sound from the Atlantic Ocean.
    a. AL 129-1
    b. AL 333
    c. AASHTO Soil Classification System
    d. Outer Banks

30. _____ is the artificial application of water to the soil usually for assisting in growing crops. In crop production it is mainly used to replace missing rainfall in periods of drought, but also to protect plants against frost.
    a. AL 333
    b. AL 129-1
    c. AASHTO Soil Classification System
    d. Irrigation

31. _____ refers to the area of the Central Valley of California that lies south of the Sacramento-San Joaquin Delta in Stockton. Although most of the valley is rural, it does contain major urban cities such as Stockton, Fresno, Modesto, Bakersfield, and Merced.
    a. San Joaquin Valley
    b. 1509 Istanbul earthquake
    c. 1703 Genroku earthquake
    d. 1700 Cascadia earthquake

32. In geology, a _____ is a depression with predominant extent in one direction. The terms U-shaped and V-shaped are descriptive terms of geography to characterize the form of valleys. Most valleys belong to one of these two main types or a mixture of them, at least with respect of the cross section of the slopes or hillsides.
    a. 1700 Cascadia earthquake
    b. 1509 Istanbul earthquake
    c. 1703 Genroku earthquake
    d. Valley

33. _____ is water located beneath the ground surface in soil pore spaces and in the fractures of geologic formations. _____ is recharged from, and eventually flows to, the surface naturally; natural discharge often occurs at springs and seeps, streams and can often form oases or wetlands.
    a. 1700 Cascadia earthquake
    b. 1703 Genroku earthquake
    c. Groundwater
    d. 1509 Istanbul earthquake

34. The _____ is part of the current San Luis National Wildlife Refuge. The site gained national attention during the later half of the 20th century due to selenium toxicity and rapid die off of migratory waterfowl, fish, insects, plants and algae within the _____.
    a. 1700 Cascadia earthquake
    b. 1509 Istanbul earthquake
    c. Kesterson Reservoir
    d. 1703 Genroku earthquake

Chapter 18. Landscape Evaluation and Land Use

35. Most often, a _____ refers to an artificial lake, used to store water for various uses. Reservoirs are created first by building a sturdy dam, usually out of cement, earth, rock, or a mixture. Once the dam is completed, a stream is allowed to flow behind it and eventually fill it to capacity.
   a. 1703 Genroku earthquake
   b. 1700 Cascadia earthquake
   c. 1509 Istanbul earthquake
   d. Reservoir

36. _____, also known as bioamplification, or biological magnification is the increase in concentration of a substance, such as the pesticide DDT, that occurs in a food chain as a consequence of: Food chain energetics, low rate of excretion/degradation of the substance.
   a. 1509 Istanbul earthquake
   b. 1700 Cascadia earthquake
   c. 1703 Genroku earthquake
   d. Biomagnification

37. _____ is the human modification of natural environment or wilderness into built environment such as fields, pastures, and settlements. The major effect of _____ on land cover since 1750 has been deforestation of temperate regions. More recent significant effects of _____ include urban sprawl, soil erosion, soil degradation, salinization, and desertification.
   a. 1700 Cascadia earthquake
   b. Land use
   c. 1509 Istanbul earthquake
   d. 1703 Genroku earthquake

38. The _____ is a diverse scientific, social, and political movement for addressing the concerns of environmentalism. The _____ is represented by a range of organizations, from the large to grassroots. Due to its large membership, varying and strong beliefs, and occasionally speculative nature, the _____ is not always united in its goals.
   a. Ambulocetus
   b. Amblypoda
   c. Andrija Mohorovičić
   d. Environmental movement

39. In the terminology of political geography and historiography a national _____ is an administrative political subdivision of a country established by the cognizant government authority holding sovereign power for the territory.

Departments are roughly equivalent to a state, province or county, and may exist either with or without a subnational representative assembly and executive head depending upon the countries constitutional structure.

Â· Benin Â· Bolivia Â· Burkina Faso Â· Cameroon Â· Colombia Â· Côte d'Ivoire Â· El Salvador Â· France Â· Gabon Â· Guatemala Â· Haiti Â· Honduras Â· Nicaragua Â· Niger Â· Peru Â· Paraguay Â· Senegal Â· Uruguay

- Category:Departments of the Duchy of Warsaw
- Category:Administrative divisions

   a. 1509 Istanbul earthquake
   b. 1700 Cascadia earthquake
   c. Department
   d. 1703 Genroku earthquake

40. The _____ is a group of floral display gardens in Brentwood Bay, British Columbia, Canada, near Victoria on Vancouver Island which claims to receive more than a million visitors each year. The Ross Fountain

Robert Pim Butchart (1856-1943) began manufacturing Portland cement in 1888 near his birthplace of Owen Sound, Ontario, Canada. He and his wife Jennie Butchart (1866-1950) came to the west coast of Canada because of rich limestone deposits necessary for cement production.

a. 1703 Genroku earthquake
b. Butchart Gardens
c. 1509 Istanbul earthquake
d. 1700 Cascadia earthquake

41. _____ can be defined as the process of managing the use and development (in both urban and suburban settings) of land resources in a sustainable way. Land resources are used for a variety of purposes which interact and may compete with one another; therefore, it is desirable to plan and manage all uses in an integrated manner.

- Environmental management scheme
- Land Allocation Decision Support System
- Land Analysis Lab (LAL)
- Subdivision (land)
- Sustainable agriculture
- Urban planning

a. 1509 Istanbul earthquake
b. 1700 Cascadia earthquake
c. 1703 Genroku earthquake
d. Land management

42. _____ is a body of law, which is a system of complex and interlocking statutes, common law, treaties, conventions, regulations and policies which seek to protect the natural environment which may be affected, impacted or endangered by human activities.
a. AL 333
b. Environmental law
c. AL 129-1
d. AASHTO Soil Classification System

43. _____, a form of alternative dispute resolution (ADR) or 'appropriate dispute resolution', aims to assist two (or more) disputants in reaching an agreement. The parties themselves determine the conditions of any settlements reached-- rather than accepting something imposed by a third party. The disputes may involve (as parties) states, organizations, communities, individuals or other representatives with a vested interest in the outcome.
a. Water Quality Act
b. Fish and Wildlife Coordination Act
c. NEPA
d. Mediation

44. _____ is the term used for a branch of public policy which encompasses various disciplines which seek to order and regulate the use of land in an efficient and ethical way.
a. Land use planning
b. 1700 Cascadia earthquake
c. 1703 Genroku earthquake
d. 1509 Istanbul earthquake

45. _____ is a chemical element in the periodic table that has the symbol Cu and atomic number 29. It is a ductile metal with excellent electrical conductivity, and finds extensive use as a building material, as an electrical conductor, and as a component of various alloys.

Chapter 18. Landscape Evaluation and Land Use   171

    a. 1509 Istanbul earthquake
    b. Copper
    c. 1703 Genroku earthquake
    d. 1700 Cascadia earthquake

46. _____ was one of the most powerful hurricanes on record in the Atlantic basin, with maximum sustained winds of 180 mph (285 km/h.) The storm was the thirteenth tropical storm, ninth hurricane, and third major hurricane of the 1998 Atlantic hurricane season. At the time, _____ was the strongest Atlantic hurricane observed in the month of October, though it has since been surpassed by Hurricane Wilma of the 2005 season.
    a. Helium
    b. Hippocrates
    c. Francium
    d. Hurricane Mitch

47. _____ is a chemical element with the symbol Fe and atomic number 26. _____ is a lustrous, silvery soft metal. _____ and nickel are notable for being the final elements produced by stellar nucleosynthesis, and thus are the heaviest elements which do not require a supernova or similarly cataclysmic event for formation.
    a. AL 129-1
    b. AL 333
    c. AASHTO Soil Classification System
    d. Iron

48. A _____ is any disturbed state of an astronomical body's atmosphere, especially affecting its surface, and strongly implying severe weather. It may be marked by strong wind, thunder and lightning, heavy precipitation, such as ice, or wind transporting some substance through the atmosphere.
    a. 1700 Cascadia earthquake
    b. Storm
    c. 1509 Istanbul earthquake
    d. 1703 Genroku earthquake

49. Fossils are the mineralized or otherwise preserved remains or traces of animals, plants, and other organisms. The totality of fossils, both discovered and undiscovered, and their placement in fossiliferous rock formations and sedimentary layers is known as the _____ record.
    a. 1700 Cascadia earthquake
    b. 1703 Genroku earthquake
    c. 1509 Istanbul earthquake
    d. Fossil

50. The _____ is a division of the White House that coordinates federal environmental efforts in the United States and works closely with agencies and other White House offices in the development of environmental and energy policies and initiatives.
    a. 1700 Cascadia earthquake
    b. 1509 Istanbul earthquake
    c. 1703 Genroku earthquake
    d. Council on Environmental Quality

Chapter 1

1. d	2. d	3. b	4. d	5. d	6. d	7. b	8. a	9. d	10. d
11. a	12. d	13. d	14. a	15. c	16. d	17. d	18. d	19. b	20. b
21. d	22. d	23. d	24. d	25. d	26. d	27. d	28. d	29. b	30. d
31. b	32. a	33. d	34. c	35. d	36. d	37. d	38. d	39. d	40. d
41. a	42. d	43. c	44. a	45. a	46. d	47. c	48. d	49. d	50. d
51. b	52. d	53. a	54. d	55. c	56. d	57. d	58. b	59. b	60. a
61. d	62. c	63. d	64. c	65. d	66. c	67. d	68. d	69. d	70. d
71. c	72. d	73. d	74. a	75. a	76. d	77. d	78. d	79. b	80. c
81. c	82. d	83. a	84. b	85. d	86. d	87. d	88. c	89. b	90. c
91. b	92. a	93. b							

Chapter 2

1. d	2. d	3. c	4. a	5. d	6. d	7. d	8. d	9. d	10. b
11. d	12. d	13. c	14. a	15. d	16. d	17. d	18. d	19. a	20. b
21. c	22. c	23. a	24. d	25. a	26. d	27. d	28. d	29. c	30. b
31. d	32. d	33. a	34. b	35. d	36. d	37. d	38. c	39. c	40. d
41. b	42. d	43. d	44. d	45. c	46. d	47. b	48. d	49. d	50. d
51. d	52. b	53. d	54. b	55. b	56. d	57. b	58. a	59. d	60. c
61. d	62. d	63. d	64. a	65. a	66. c	67. b	68. d	69. d	70. d
71. d	72. b	73. a	74. d	75. a	76. c	77. d	78. a	79. c	80. d
81. c	82. c	83. a	84. d	85. a	86. b	87. c	88. d	89. a	90. c
91. a	92. c	93. a	94. b	95. b	96. c	97. c	98. c	99. d	100. d
101. c	102. a	103. a	104. d	105. c	106. d	107. b	108. c	109. a	110. a
111. d	112. d	113. b	114. d	115. d	116. d	117. d	118. d	119. d	120. d
121. b	122. d	123. b	124. a	125. a	126. d	127. d	128. d		

Chapter 3

1. a	2. a	3. a	4. b	5. c	6. a	7. a	8. d	9. d	10. b
11. b	12. b	13. a	14. c	15. d	16. d	17. d	18. d	19. d	20. d
21. a	22. b	23. d	24. d	25. c	26. a	27. d	28. d	29. d	30. d
31. a	32. d	33. b	34. c	35. a	36. d	37. d	38. d	39. d	40. d
41. d	42. d	43. d	44. a	45. b	46. a	47. a	48. a	49. a	50. c
51. d	52. d	53. d	54. a	55. d	56. c	57. a	58. d	59. d	60. c
61. a	62. d	63. b	64. a	65. d	66. b	67. d			

Chapter 4

1. d	2. d	3. d	4. b	5. a	6. d	7. b	8. d	9. d	10. a
11. b	12. d	13. c	14. c	15. b	16. d	17. b	18. a	19. d	20. a
21. c	22. d	23. d	24. a	25. b	26. d	27. d	28. a	29. d	30. c

ANSWER KEY

Chapter 5

1. b	2. a	3. a	4. d	5. c	6. c	7. c	8. d	9. c	10. d
11. a	12. a	13. d	14. a	15. d	16. d	17. c	18. d	19. b	20. d
21. c	22. d	23. a	24. d	25. d	26. d	27. c	28. c	29. d	30. c
31. b	32. d	33. d	34. d	35. d	36. d	37. b	38. a	39. d	40. d
41. b	42. a	43. c	44. b						

Chapter 6

1. d	2. d	3. d	4. b	5. a	6. d	7. a	8. b	9. c	10. c
11. b	12. d	13. a	14. d	15. d	16. b	17. d	18. d	19. a	20. b
21. a	22. c	23. a	24. d	25. d	26. a	27. a	28. d	29. a	30. a
31. c	32. d	33. d	34. d	35. a	36. d	37. d	38. a	39. d	40. d
41. d	42. d	43. c	44. a						

Chapter 7

1. d	2. d	3. b	4. d	5. c	6. d	7. b	8. a	9. a	10. b
11. b	12. a	13. d	14. b	15. c	16. d	17. d	18. b	19. d	20. d
21. d	22. b	23. a	24. b	25. b	26. d	27. a	28. d	29. d	30. d
31. d	32. d	33. c	34. c	35. d	36. d	37. c	38. d	39. c	40. b
41. b	42. d	43. d	44. b	45. b	46. d	47. d	48. c	49. d	50. a
51. d	52. c	53. c	54. b	55. d	56. c	57. d	58. a	59. a	60. b
61. c	62. d	63. d	64. a	65. d					

Chapter 8

1. d	2. b	3. d	4. d	5. a	6. d	7. c	8. d	9. c	10. c
11. d	12. d	13. d	14. d	15. a	16. b	17. a	18. d	19. b	20. d
21. b	22. d	23. b	24. b	25. d	26. d	27. d	28. d	29. d	30. d
31. d	32. c	33. d	34. d	35. d	36. d	37. d	38. d	39. c	40. b
41. b	42. d	43. d	44. d	45. a	46. d	47. d	48. d	49. d	50. c
51. a	52. b	53. d	54. d	55. d	56. d	57. d	58. b	59. d	60. d
61. d									

Chapter 9

1. a	2. c	3. d	4. d	5. c	6. a	7. a	8. d	9. d	10. d
11. d	12. d	13. d	14. d	15. d	16. d	17. d	18. c	19. d	20. d
21. d	22. a	23. d	24. d	25. d	26. d	27. c	28. b	29. d	30. d
31. c	32. d	33. a	34. d	35. d	36. d	37. c	38. d	39. c	40. d
41. d	42. d	43. b	44. d	45. d	46. a	47. d	48. b	49. b	50. a
51. a	52. d	53. d	54. d	55. b	56. c	57. c			

Chapter 10

1. d	2. c	3. b	4. d	5. a	6. c	7. d	8. d	9. a	10. b
11. d	12. d	13. d	14. b	15. b	16. d	17. d	18. a	19. a	20. a
21. b	22. c	23. d	24. c	25. a	26. c	27. d	28. d	29. d	30. d
31. c	32. b	33. a	34. c	35. d	36. d	37. d	38. a	39. d	40. a
41. d	42. d	43. a	44. d	45. a	46. a	47. b	48. a	49. b	50. c
51. b	52. c	53. d	54. d	55. d	56. d	57. c	58. a	59. d	60. c

Chapter 11

1. a	2. d	3. d	4. b	5. c	6. d	7. c	8. d	9. d	10. d
11. d	12. a	13. d	14. c	15. d	16. a	17. a	18. d	19. b	20. c
21. c	22. b	23. b	24. c	25. d	26. d	27. c	28. c	29. d	30. c
31. b	32. a	33. d	34. c	35. d	36. d	37. d	38. a	39. b	40. a
41. a	42. c	43. b	44. a	45. b	46. b	47. c	48. c	49. c	50. a
51. d	52. b	53. c	54. d	55. a	56. d	57. c	58. c	59. c	60. c
61. d	62. d	63. d	64. c	65. d	66. b	67. c	68. c	69. d	70. c
71. d	72. d	73. d	74. d	75. a	76. a	77. b	78. d	79. d	80. a
81. c	82. d								

Chapter 12

1. d	2. c	3. d	4. d	5. d	6. b	7. d	8. d	9. d	10. d
11. c	12. d	13. d	14. a	15. d	16. d	17. c	18. b	19. b	20. c
21. d	22. d	23. a	24. d	25. d	26. d	27. c	28. d	29. a	30. d
31. a	32. d	33. c	34. d	35. a	36. d	37. b	38. d	39. a	40. b
41. d	42. d	43. b							

Chapter 13

1. b	2. c	3. d	4. d	5. b	6. b	7. d	8. a	9. d	10. b
11. c	12. d	13. d	14. d	15. d	16. d	17. a	18. d	19. c	20. d
21. a	22. d	23. a	24. d	25. b	26. d	27. c	28. c	29. d	30. c
31. d	32. d	33. d	34. c	35. d	36. b	37. c	38. c	39. b	40. c
41. d	42. d	43. d	44. d	45. d	46. c	47. d	48. b	49. d	50. d
51. c	52. b	53. d	54. d	55. d	56. d	57. b	58. d	59. a	60. d
61. a	62. d	63. d	64. a	65. c	66. d	67. d	68. a	69. a	70. b
71. d	72. c	73. c	74. d	75. d	76. b	77. c			

Chapter 14

1. d	2. a	3. d	4. d	5. d	6. d	7. d	8. a	9. d	10. c
11. d	12. a	13. b	14. d	15. d	16. d	17. b	18. b	19. a	20. b
21. b	22. b	23. d	24. d	25. c	26. a	27. c	28. a	29. d	30. c
31. d	32. d	33. d	34. a	35. b	36. d	37. c	38. d	39. d	40. a
41. c	42. b	43. b	44. a	45. d	46. c	47. b	48. d	49. d	50. a
51. c	52. c	53. c	54. b	55. d	56. b	57. d	58. d	59. c	60. c
61. d	62. b	63. d	64. b	65. a	66. c				

ANSWER KEY

Chapter 15

1. a	2. d	3. d	4. b	5. d	6. a	7. c	8. d	9. d	10. c
11. c	12. a	13. d	14. b	15. d	16. d	17. d	18. d	19. d	20. c
21. a	22. b	23. b	24. d	25. d	26. a	27. d	28. d	29. d	30. d
31. b	32. d	33. b	34. a	35. d	36. a	37. b	38. b	39. d	40. d
41. a	42. d	43. d	44. d	45. c	46. d	47. d	48. d	49. a	50. d
51. c	52. d	53. d	54. a	55. d	56. c	57. d	58. d	59. d	60. c
61. b	62. d	63. d	64. d	65. c	66. d	67. d	68. a	69. a	70. d
71. a	72. c	73. b	74. a	75. c	76. d	77. d	78. b	79. d	80. d
81. d	82. d	83. d	84. b	85. d	86. d	87. a	88. a	89. d	

Chapter 16

1. a	2. d	3. d	4. d	5. c	6. d	7. d	8. c	9. d	10. b
11. b	12. a	13. b	14. d	15. a	16. a	17. c	18. d	19. c	20. b
21. c	22. d	23. c	24. d	25. d	26. d	27. d	28. d	29. c	30. b
31. a	32. d	33. d	34. b	35. a	36. c	37. d	38. b	39. d	40. a
41. d	42. a	43. a	44. d	45. c	46. d	47. d	48. d	49. d	50. d
51. b	52. d	53. d	54. d	55. d	56. d	57. a	58. d	59. b	60. d
61. d									

Chapter 17

1. a	2. d	3. a	4. d	5. a	6. b	7. c	8. b	9. a	10. c
11. d	12. d	13. b	14. d	15. d	16. d	17. c	18. a	19. c	20. a
21. d	22. d	23. d	24. b	25. c	26. d	27. d	28. d	29. d	30. d
31. d	32. b	33. d	34. a	35. a	36. d	37. a	38. d	39. b	40. b
41. c	42. d	43. d	44. b	45. d	46. d	47. b	48. a	49. d	50. d
51. b	52. d								

Chapter 18

1. b	2. d	3. b	4. d	5. d	6. d	7. b	8. d	9. b	10. a
11. d	12. b	13. b	14. d	15. d	16. d	17. a	18. d	19. d	20. b
21. d	22. a	23. c	24. c	25. b	26. d	27. c	28. b	29. d	30. d
31. a	32. d	33. c	34. c	35. d	36. d	37. b	38. d	39. c	40. b
41. d	42. b	43. d	44. a	45. b	46. d	47. d	48. b	49. d	50. d